The
EVERYTHING.
Horse Care Book

Dear Reader,

I came to horses in my early twenties, relatively late in life compared to most professionals. As my experience grew one thing became clear: most horse professionals have different ways of doing things. The never-ending supply of advice from non-professionals can also be confusing. Remember, everyone is an expert when they're talking about someone else's horse. The truly knowledgeable people in the business are rarely the ones imposing their advice.

There are more and more astonishingly knowledgeable horse people out there, who combine rapidly progressing scientific advances with their own wide experience to institute revolutions in the theory and practice of horse care and training. More than ever, this ethic is coming up against the traditional biases, rigidity, and ignorances to which the horse business is bound. My aim in this book is to represent a balance between the tried and true methods of caring for horses and the new science and methods of horse care.

I hope that my various experiences in the horse business have allowed me to present the information in this book in an unbiased, clear, and open way, which will guide you to a happy, safe, healthy, and open-minded relationship with your horse.

Christopher DeFilippis

The EVERYTHING® Series

Editorial

Publishing Director	Gary M. Krebs
Associate Managing Editor	Laura M. Daly
Associate Copy Chief	Brett Palana-Shanahan
Acquisitions Editor	Kate Burgo
Development Editor	Jessica LaPointe
Associate Production Editor	Casey Ebert

Production

Director of Manufacturing	Susan Beale
Associate Director of Production	Michelle Roy Kelly
Cover Design	Paul Beatrice Erick DaCosta Matt LeBlanc
Design and Layout	Colleen Cunningham Holly Curtis Sorae Lee
Series Cover Artist	Barry Littmann
Interior Illustrations	Kathie Kelleher Barry Littmann

THE
EVERYTHING®
HORSE CARE
BOOK

A complete guide to the
well-being of your horse

Christopher DeFilippis

Adams Media
Avon, Massachusetts

This book is dedicated to Claudia Barron, the best horsewoman I know, and a one-of-a-kind human being, whose help in the writing of this book, with my horses over the years, and love and support has been invaluable to me.

An Everything® Series Book.
Everything® and everything.com® are registered trademarks of F+W Publications, Inc.

Published by Adams Media, an F+W Publications Company
57 Littlefield Street, Avon, MA 02322 U.S.A.
www.adamsmedia.com

ISBN: 1-59337-530-1

Printed in the United States of America.

J   I   H   G   F   E   D   C   B   A

Library of Congress Cataloging-in-Publication Data
DeFilippis, Christopher.
The everything horse care book : a complete guide to the
well-being of your horse / Christopher DeFilippis.
p. cm.
Includes index.
ISBN 1-59337-530-1
1. Horses. I. Title.

SF285.3.D44 2006
636.1--dc22

2005034599

This book is available at quantity discounts for bulk purchases.
For information, please call 1-800-872-5627.

Contents

Acknowledgments

Thanks to my friends and clients, who have been loyal, supportive, and dedicated to me and my farm, especially Pat Borgen, who has stuck with me from the beginning; Eve Marks, who helped and encouraged me to get back to writing; Alexa Coyne, who believes in me; and Philip Gotswald. I would have lost heart for the horse business if not for you all. To my agent, June Clark, and editor, Kate Burgo, thanks for helping and putting up with me through this process. I am also grateful to those colleagues of mine who have demonstrated to me how to be in the horse business, or, more crucially, how not to be. Thanks to my vet, Dr. Christine Koch, Betsy Merit of Bare Foot Performance, my farrier, Bob Ellis, and Tim Murphy of Arroway Chevrolet for providing me with information for this book. And an inexpressible thank you to my seeing soul dog Hailey, who has been through it all with me, and my horse, Valentine. Their giant hearts and gentility will inspire my endeavors forever. It is these two animals who have trained me in this life to be a human.

Top Ten Ways
That Horses Can Change Your Life

1. Caring for horses will give you a sense of discipline. They need you 24/7, on a regular schedule.

2. Getting involved in the world of horses will make you lots of friends. There is a camaraderie among horse people.

3. Caring for or riding horses can keep you physically fit.

4. Owning horses is mentally stimulating. You will learn something every day, either about them or about yourself.

5. Having horses is a good way to get to know your neighbors and fellow horse people in the area. There is an ethic of helping out among horse people.

6. Horses are intellectually stimulating. Whether you are an artist, a scientist, a mathematician, or just someone with an active imagination, understanding the horse is an endless pursuit.

7. Horses are a ubiquitous subject. Knowledge of horses is a commodity that you can take with you anywhere in the world, whether for work or pleasure.

8. Whether you are a kid who gets into trouble or an adult who watches too much television, being responsible for horses will get you outside and working in all kinds of weather and on yourself.

9. Horses offer an endless array of social and competitive activities that will build your sense of accomplishment, confidence, and prowess in life.

10. A well-kept and happy horse will be a loving friend and companion.

Introduction

▶WHEN PEOPLE ASK ME HOW I GOT INTO HORSES, my simple answer is that it was something that I just kept falling into, having been raised in northern Westchester County, New York, which is a very horsy area of the country. Wherever I traveled or lived after that, I could always find work with horses, albeit often for low wages and in dangerous conditions. Three things happened during my experiences with horses, however, that eventually focused me toward a career and dedication of my heart, mind, spirit, and imagination to my work with them.

The first and most transformative was a night I spent in a pasture under a makeshift tent of hay bales and canvas with a downed and dying 2,000-pound Clydesdale horse. A kerosene heater kept him warm enough to live through the night. My purpose was to shove hay bales under his shoulder to help him when he would lift his head in his sporadic attempts to stand up. It was one of many inanely dangerous situations my boss had put me in that year I spent in New Mexico, and to which I obliged in my best subservient cowboy manner. But I cursed the situation most of the night, as the horse's attempts to get up threatened to collapse the precarious structure on top of us and, more importantly, on top of the heater. As the night progressed and his efforts waned, I found myself of a different mind toward this dying animal. By morning, I understood something of a bond between horse and man—a debt of care and compassion that we owe to our domestic animals that must never be denied.

I was paid meagerly to break a horse that had been sent to pasture a few years earlier to breed and raise her foal. This mare didn't want me on her back, period, and after a few warnings, threw herself up and backward, landing on top of me. The message was clear, and the lesson invaluable. Know what you're doing when dealing with an animal that is capable of killing you. Sometimes, horses have only a thin veneer of domestication. Even a well-trained horse can revert to wild instinct in which our partnership of domestication is forfeited to millions of years of her genetic evolution as a self-sufficient prey animal.

That same spring I took an interest in a fine young Arabian horse. He was a nonworking member of the herd on a ranch where I was employed. I later found out that he was in fact a very fancy blood horse, being kept as a favor to his owner who wanted this horse herd raised on the ranch. An anomaly among rough ranch quarter horses, appaloosas, and paints, he was about thirty horses down at the very bottom of the pecking order. With my special attention, some groundwork, and confidence building exercises, he quickly climbed the ranks. He became so full of himself that he would make precocious attempts at the feed of the dominant horses, who luckily didn't take him too seriously. He was a horse that wanted to go to work for me, and within a few weeks, became my lead horse for trekking tours. One night, after a full day's work that never tired him but only seemed to inflate his new pride and confidence of purpose, I took him for a mile-long gallop into the open range. I have never since ridden a finer or faster horse or had quite the sensation of flying as I experienced in his gait. I walked him back home in the final light of the day, a calm, proud, satisfied, and trusting animal. Rarely have I met a horse with such heart and spirit.

Anyone who rides or cares for horses has had experiences that have fostered in them a love, dedication, and respect for them. After all the knowledge and expertise you can attain in the world of horses—the victories, unpleasantness, accidents, and egomaniacal, confidence destroying horse people you might encounter—it is these simple, sympathetic bonds of partnership and learning from horses that is what it is all about.

The format of the Everything® series has given me the opportunity to present the basic tenets of horse care, as well as a license to put out on the table a lot of random experiential information that will help you to effectively and efficiently manage your farm and horses, and guide you on your way to a healthy relationship with your horse. Your experience with horses can be everything you imagine. Have fun.

Chapter 1

Understanding the Nature of the Horse

Though horses are greatly various in type, personality, and temperament, they are all consistent in their instincts and senses. By putting together what has been learned about horses from scientists and professional trainers with your own observations, you will begin to understand how and why horses act and react in certain ways to people as well as to other horses. As science catches up with the experience and imagination of the horse, there is much you can learn about his nature, so you can move toward a better, safer, and more productive partnership.

Instincts and Mentality

The human relationship to the horse in domesticity is relatively new. To understand the horse, you must appreciate the natural instincts and behaviors that have led him through 75 million years of evolution. The horse is first and foremost a herd animal. When trying to understand his behaviors, actions, and reactions in almost all situations, you must consider his herd instinct and dynamics, and realize that these are centered around one dominant horse. By understanding and observing horses alone and together, you will come to a safer and more profound relationship with the horse.

Herd Instinct

The structure of a herd is hierarchical, meaning that there's a pecking order of subordinate horses, leading up to one alpha stallion and one lead mare, who together give the herd a sense of order, harmony, and safety. In the wild, this order is not static; rather, a horse's status might change within the herd. This can happen as they age, and young males challenge the alpha stallion for the harem, choose to leave the herd, or are driven out. Rogue stallions trying to start their own harem will steal mares and fillies, disrupting temporarily the order of a herd.

Even in small groups of domestic horses, you can observe this kind of behavior at work and learn from it. Variations in your domestic herd will be somewhat artificial, since you will choose which horses to put in a group. This, and the probable absence of stallions on your farm, will create a hierarchy that is more static but nevertheless dynamically the same as in a wild herd.

A horse's gentle nature and inclination to submit to a dominant force makes it possible for her to exist not only in a pecking ordered society, but also in domestication. The bonds of friendship, loyalty, and safety that are innately instilled in a pecking order society are all transferable to you in a domestic situation. These bonds made the horse capable of domestication in the first place and makes it possible to train them.

As his caretaker, trainer, or rider, your horse looks to you as his alpha horse, and so he must have trust and confidence in you. You can encourage this by making him feel secure. You must assume the role of lead horse for a safe and productive relationship. Your horse might continue to test you throughout your relationship, just as he might an alpha horse. And like an alpha horse, you must be deliberate, assertive, and undoubting in your actions. For example, in the simplest exercises of leading, grooming, or mounting your horse, you must insist that he is obedient, pays attention, and follows your rules. He should not be permitted to push you around, use you as a rubbing post, or walk away without a command or signal.

Flight Instinct

A horse's great gift in the wild is and has always been his speed. The corresponding instinct is to flee when he feels threatened. In domesticity, this remains a powerful, and often primary, response that can be trouble for both of you on the ground and under saddle. A runaway horse can be unpredictable and dangerous to both you and himself.

QUESTION?

When were the first horses domesticated?
It is believed that the first horses were domesticated in Asia about 4,000 years ago. The Mongolian wild horse, or the Przewalski horse, is the closest relative to this first domesticated horse. Before that, horses were hunted for food by humans and animals.

But as your horse gets used to his surroundings and daily routine, he should become more discerning about what is actually dangerous to him and what is not. Through patience, and consistent handling, your relationship with your horse will deepen and a bond of trust and confidence will form between the two of you. This flight instinct should be reduced to a harmless spook or startle once in a while, or be completely eradicated. However, it is important to remember that what seems safe to you might not seem safe to your horse. Many of the things you ask of him, such as trailering or standing for a bath, are situations he would never face in nature where his natural instincts of self-preservation have evolved over millions of years. Horses do these things because we ask them to. So before asking your horse to do anything, make sure it is indeed safe. With every positive experience, your horse will learn to trust and defer to your good judgment. If his flight instinct is triggered, he will often have no regard for your safety or even for his own.

Temperament

The terms hot blood, warm blood, and cold blood are used to describe a type of horse according to his origin and temperament. The terms have nothing to do with the temperature of a type of horse's blood; however, the terms do often correspond to the climates the horses evolved in or were adapted for.

Hot Blood

A hot-blooded horse is one whose ancestry can be traced back to the Arabian, Barb, Turk, or thoroughbred. This heritage disposes a horse toward speed, endurance, and a spirited, competitive nature. Hot bloods were developed in southern regions of the world and tend to be thin skinned, light coated, tall, and slight in build. They are considered by most experts to be the most intelligent of the three distinctions, the most athletic, versatile, and perhaps the most trainable. However, these horses tend to be hot-tempered and physically more delicate than other types of horses. For these reasons, among others, they are not easy keepers.

Some thoroughbred experts say that there is no reason to own any other kind of horse, no matter what your riding discipline. This is an exaggeration, but nonetheless a powerful testament to the respect and dedication the thoroughbred has acquired in its 250 years of existence.

The thoroughbred was originally developed in eighteenth-century England, exclusively for racing, from the three original hot bloods mentioned above. To the western world, they best embody what you think of when a horse is referred to as hot-blooded. More than any other horse, the thoroughbred has been used to develop and improve breeds throughout the world.

Cold Blood

Cold-blooded horses evolved in the northern regions of the world and are thought to be the oldest kind of horse. They are heavy boned, slower moving, thicker skinned and coated, and generally equipped to handle harsher climates. Horses in this category include many of the pony breeds, such as Halflingers, Connemara, and Icelandics, as well as what is more commonly thought of as the draft horse.

FACT

A horse is measured from the top of his withers to the ground. The standard measurement for a horse is "hands." A hand is equivalent to four inches. The first riding horses were thought to be about 12 hands high. Today's horse stands at least 14.3 hands. Any horse smaller than this is considered a pony.

Among the most popular draft horses are Clydesdales, Percherons, and Shires. Draft horses were probably first used as war mounts, and later were adapted because of their easygoing nature, endurance, and power for agriculture. They can measure over 20 hands and can weigh in excess of 2,000 pounds, yet have a slower metabolism than do hot bloods. More often than not, their modern use is as carriage horses, since they are built for pulling and are less competitive among each other, and so work well as a team.

Warm Blood

Warm-blooded horses are a cross between cold-blooded, typically draft horses, and hot-blooded, typically light, thoroughbred horses. They were bred to embody the favorable aesthetic and utilitarian characteristics of both. An ideal warm blood has the ruggedness, size, and calm temperament of a draft horse, while maintaining the presence, intelligence, heart, and athletic ability of a thoroughbred. The modern warm blood has been increasingly bred to develop finer thoroughbred tendencies, thus producing the most commonly used horses for dressage and show jumping throughout the world.

In America, Ireland, and Canada, these horses are usually referred to as sport horses or draft crosses, and they make excellent field mounts. However, more often than not, they lack the refinement, presence, and careful breeding of the European breeds, like Dutch, Swedish, French, and the many German breeds, including Holsteiner, Hanovarian, Oldenburg, and Trekkenier, for which the term "warm blood" is truly reserved.

Horse Sense

A horse has the largest eye of any land mammal. The lateral placement of his eyes is consistent with that of most prey animals high in the food chain and is particularly suited to an animal that spends most of its time grazing and that must be constantly on the lookout for predators.

The first known horses had much shorter noses. The modern horse's elongated nose might have evolved so that while grazing he has a higher field of vision and therefore is more likely to spot predators.

Vision

A horse sees with monocular vision, which means that each eye can work independently to relay separate messages to her brain. She also sees binocularly, wherein both eyes might focus together on the same object.

Monocular sight affords a horse a panoramic view of her world. She has three blind spots. The first is a couple of inches directly in front of her face. The second is directly behind her. The third is directly under her. Excluding these blind spots, her field of vision is nearly 360 degrees (as shown in **Figure 1.1**).

Figure 1.1:
The Horse's
Field of Vision

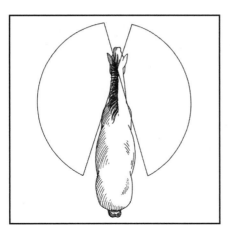

Binocular sight allows for a modicum of depth perception, or "stereo-scopic" vision. This ability is very poor in horses. Her faculty of binocular vision expands to about 65 degrees directly in front of her. In order to increase this advantage, she need only to turn her head toward whatever she is looking at.

FACT

A horse possesses two external eyelids and one inner eyelid. The eyelids together help keep her eye safe from debris or foreign objects that are ever present in her environment and keep the eye lubricated.

A horse's ability to focus on objects that are close up is generally poor. However, a horse possesses a high degree of acuity, which is the ability to distinguish the details of objects at a distance. Their acuity is about one-third worse than a human's, and about one-third better than a dog's.

Horses have excellent night vision due to an abundance of rods, which are the cells of the retina that are sensitive to dim light, in the eye. Night vision is increased by the tapetum, a group of cells behind the retina, which reflects light back to it. An excess of rods comes at a cost of cones, the cells that allow an eye to see color. The jury is still out on whether or not horses can see in color. Some researchers suggest that horses might be able to see shades of yellow, green, blue, and red.

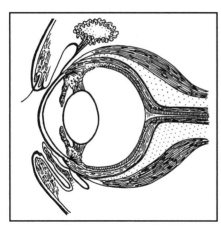

Figure 1.2: The Horse's Eye

Horses have trouble adjusting to sudden changes of light conditions because of a lack of cones, the cells that capture bright light and color. This should always be considered when leading a horse from low light to bright, or vice versa.

Hearing

A horse's hearing is exceptional. The outside ear is mostly cartilage, with the ability to move independently and in all directions, controlled by sixteen different muscles. Along with its wide, funnel shaped opening, the ear, like a horse's vision, is designed to pick up sound from a 360 radius. A horse's ears are uniquely sensitive to a wide range of both low- and high-frequency sounds and can discern between near or faraway sounds.

Smell

A horse's keen sense of smell is her best aid to memory. It helps her in the wild to detect predators, and remember where the best grasses grow and where water can be found. A domestic horse uses smell to determine if his grain, hay, grass, and water are fresh and not poisonous. They are particularly attracted to sweet smells and tastes, such as apples, carrots, bananas, candy, and even beer.

FACT

The flehmen response is when a horse curls his upper lip in reaction to an odd smell or taste, or even a mare in season. It is thought to heighten his sense of smell.

Touch

Touch is said to be a horse's most acute sense. He gathers information with his lips, skin and hair, and his nose, which is mostly cartilage and soft tissue. Their bodies are so sensitive that they can feel a fly anywhere on them, isolate the muscle, and twitch to dispel the fly.

Touch is of great importance to a horse socially as well. They are herd animals. As such, they need the contact with other horses that comes with daily rituals of grooming, nudging, or horse play for their happiness, sense of security, and general well-being. If you cannot provide your horse with the company of another horse, then a farm animal, such as a goat or pig, will often suffice. Your human contact and affection is important too, but probably not constant enough for sufficient companionship. The horse's practice of mutual grooming, nudging, and general horsing around demonstrates their need for the intimacy of touch.

Vocalizations

Besides communicating by touch, horses have a vocal language that communicates a wide range of needs, desires, and emotions to their herd mates and to you as well.

- **The Snort.** The snort signifies curiosity, fear, or a cross between the two. It also acts as an intimidation to a possible predator or challenger.
- **The Squeal.** The squeal is a warning or sign of defensiveness, telling another horse to beware. Two horses getting to know each other will squeal.
- **The Nicker.** The nicker is a low-pitched sound meant as a greeting or beckoning to other horses or humans in close proximity.

- **The Neigh or Whinny.** This is the loudest of the horse's vocalizations. It is often used as a location call from horses that are out of visual range from each other.

How and when your horse uses these vocalizations will often point to strong characteristics of her personality. If you pay attention to what your horse is telling you, your mutual bond will deepen.

A Sixth Sense?

What you attribute to a horse's uncanny abilities to read your mind, anticipate your actions, or just know things that seem outside of the realm of sensory perception is mostly due to the horse's extremely acute senses that work together to form intuition. When a horse seems to know that a rider is nervous, or a handler inexperienced, it is more likely that he smells sudden perspiration, feels the vibration of tense muscles, recognizes improper actions and responses, or all of the above.

How a Horse Thinks

A horse's powers of cognition are dependent upon their senses. Horses have excellent memories. They remember a person, place, or thing by smell, taste, voice recognition, and sight recognition, as well as more subtle, and personal, methods of touch. They are not good problem solvers, but rather creatures of habit. For this reason, training methods of positive and negative reinforcement seem to work best when practiced with consistency.

What you might think of as clever problem solving can usually be attributed rather to his penchant to make associations, since a particular action will yield a favorable consequence. A horse, for instance, that can consistently negotiate the latch on his stall and escape is practicing a function not of problem solving, but of his ability to learn, teamed with a good memory and habituation.

Body Language

Just as horses communicate through their body posturing, so is your body language around him a silent conversation. Quiet, gradual, and deliberate motions are best when working around or with a horse. On the other hand, horses have various ways of indicating their moods, some of which can be interpreted as a threat or warning. In other words, there doesn't have to be actual physical aggression, but a message is conveyed which most times will suffice to warn you.

An extended foreleg or foot stomp, or a lifted hind end, is a muted strike, or kick, respectively. A head swing, accompanied by an open mouth, is a threat to bite. Likewise, a horse that has folded his ears back has done so to protect those vulnerable parts of his body in preparation for battle. Others will understand his intention and keep away. However, when his ears are cocked in a direction other than folded back, it can mean quite the opposite: curiosity or interest. Tail swishing or a wrinkled nose are signs that a horse is irritated, while a dropped lower lip means that he is relaxed. Lip smacking, however, is an exhibition of submission by young horses to dominant horses.

The effects of body language are worth experimenting with, as these games can be fun and fascinating. For instance, you might feign disinterest in a hard to catch horse by nonchalantly looking off elsewhere. This might spur his curiosity and get him to come to you.

It is important for your safety and your horse's comfort that you recognize these signs and symbols, because they are meant to signify discomfort or warn of possible aggression, which might or might not be sincere. This doesn't mean that you should necessarily defer to his warning. You are the lead horse and should reiterate this to him if your horse warns you to stay away. You might do this with a stern voice command or bodily gesture, such as a bold stance or forward action, telling your horse to stand down.

Just as a dog will raise his hackles in order to appear bigger for a confrontation, a horse might raise his carriage, protrude his chest, and stick his tail out horizontally in order to intimidate. If we pose in our version of this pre-conflict stance, with chest expanded and arms out, this signals offensive behavior and might be met with the same from your horse, or you may frighten him. Neither one of these effects is productive. However, if done deliberately as a training technique to prove dominance over a young horse in the manner of an alpha horse, it can be effective.

Chapter 2

How to Buy a Horse

There is much to consider when you start your search for a horse to call your own. You will have to choose between a mare and a gelding and decide what type of horse will suit you best depending on your chosen riding discipline. How much money you are prepared to spend will also be a big factor. Most importantly, you must know what qualities to look for in a horse and what to avoid, or you'll need to bring someone along with you who does.

The Difference Between Mares and Geldings

Like almost any aspect of the horse business, you will hear differing opinions on whether or not a gelding is a better riding horse than a mare. These opinions are by no means absolute truths but rather generalizations. There is both truth and bias in what professionals will say, so keep an open mind while shopping for a horse.

A saying that might come in handy in your choice of whether to buy a mare or a gelding is that geldings are more like dogs, and mares are more like cats. That is to say, a mare might seem to have a little more going on mentally, and so might be more complicated, which might suit you—or not. Like all generalizations, this one has its place, but is, by no means, a hard and fast rule. Any horse should always be considered for its individual merits before its sex.

Mares

From the spring through the fall, mares have an estrus cycle once every month, which can make them unpredictable and moody for about a week during this time. If your pleasure horse has difficult estrus periods, you can simply keep a calendar of her cycles and consider not asking too much of her during these times, or at least be extra vigilant when you are riding her. If you are buying a potential show horse, this can be more of a problem, especially in the spring when her cycle begins again. Her ovaries, which are located just behind where you would place a saddle and sit on her, are acutely sensitive.

Veterinarian-prescribed medications can help to alleviate discomfort or pain associated with estrus. However, estrus temperaments vary from horse to horse. Some even say that because of her extra sensitivity a mare can be more responsive than a gelding.

Horses with Sex

Another commonly held belief is that a horse with "sex," which would also include a stallion, can have more "heart," or "personality." That is to say, a mare or a stallion might enjoy performing for you and competing against other horses more than a gelding.

However, owning a stallion can be extremely dangerous for the amateur horse caretaker and rider. When a mare comes in season, whether it is next door or miles away, there is little that will prevent him from getting to her. He might hurt you, himself, or other horses trying. Stallions are kept intact almost exclusively for breeding purposes, and so with few exceptions there is no reason to own one. This, of course, varies from breed to breed and from horse to horse.

FACT

Some stallions of certain breeds tend to have very calm temperaments. "Cutting" such a horse might ruin his vitality and personality.

Geldings

Geldings are generally considered to be more even-tempered, and so easier to train, ride, and care for. Most of the horses you will see at other farms and for sale will be geldings, and there is a good reason for this. Geldings will cause less trouble among each other during turnout, while a mare will cause competition and in-fighting among geldings. A gelding might be stronger than a mare of similar breeding and size, especially if he is gelded late and given the chance to develop a stallion's musculature. Some say that geldings are more dedicated to you, less distractible, more reliable mounts, and more affectionate than mares. As you will learn on your search, such generalizations are useful, but not always applicable.

What Type of Horse Will Suit You Best?

Your horse will more than likely be a big investment of time, energy, and money. If you find the right horse, your investment will prove more than worth it. With patience, realistic expectations, and sound judgment, the right match is out there for you. There will be many pitfalls along the way to buying a horse, so have a clear idea of what you want, do your homework, and be careful. Trust your intuition and be alert for a horse that feels right to you. He might not always be the flashiest one in the sale barn.

If you don't yet know what discipline of riding you want to do, it is best to ride different kinds of horses, in different settings and disciplines, before you buy. If you still can't decide what kind of riding you want to do, and you choose to buy, then consider a horse that is multi-suited for all-around riding, with an easy-going disposition, and that won't mind changing jobs. A quarter horse might fit the bill.

What Conformation Faults Matter

Very few horses have perfect conformation, so unless you are prepared to spend a lot of money, and you are looking for a horse for serious competition, it is best to forgive some conformation faults that might not affect the horse for the job you intend him to do. However, different riding disciplines stress different points on a horse's body and might require a horse to be correctly conformed in these areas. Conformation faults and their possible effects will be discussed in Chapter 12, Horse Faults.

Her New Job

Whatever horse you decide to purchase, she will have to adjust to her new job of being your horse. Eventing requires a high level of agility, stamina, versatility, and heart. Almost exclusively at the higher levels of competition, these horses are thoroughbreds or mostly thoroughbred. A thoroughbred that makes a successful physical and mental transition from the track often proves an excellent pleasure horse. However, because of its hot temperament, a thoroughbred tends to be better suited to a more experienced rider. They enjoy popularity as hunter-jumpers and dressage horses as well, but at the higher levels of these competitions, the "warm bloods" dominate.

Types of Horses to Consider

The type of horse you buy should be primarily determined by what you intend to use the horse for. Each breed of horse has its virtues, as well as its limitations, and is generally disposed in conformation, size, and temperament toward certain kinds of work. Forcing a horse to perform a job he is not suited for will be a waste of time, money, and energy, and might be dangerous to you and your horse.

FACT

Two famous thoroughbred racehorses are known to have reached exceptional years. Pocahontas lived to be thirty-three years old while Parrot lived to thirty-six. Both of these horses lived to an age equivalent to a ninety-five-year-old human.

Thoroughbred

The thoroughbred is possibly the most versatile horse. An excellently bred thoroughbred can often be purchased very affordably from racetrack auctions and adoption organizations. Only a handful of them ever make it to serious racing competition, which is almost exclusively what they are bred for. They are often started young on the track and might have consequently sustained leg injuries requiring long lay up periods. Bringing such a horse back to health can be an invaluable bonding experience. Since their first and only training is often purely to race, they must be retrained, or "let down," gradually, which can take up to a year. In this time, the horse should be allowed to relax from the high stress demands of the racetrack. With a little luck, patience, and hard work, her mind and muscle will change to accommodate her new job. A seasoned horseman will be able to tell what discipline she has the brain and body for.

Warm Blood

The warm blood's magnificent presence, together with their size, agility, trainability, temperament, strength, and high initial expense, make them the predominant horse for high-level show hunting, jumping, and dressage competition. Their powerful rear ends and typically strong hocks give them great "carrying capacity" and suspension for an eminently elegant gait, fluid movement, and "scope" over jumps. Their willingness and easy-going nature also means that they can make excellent driving horses. Warm bloods are preferred over draft horses for any form of competitive or combined driving because of their superior agility and elegant movement.

Drafts are mainly used for driving, specifically coaching, although some of the "lighter" breeds, like the Percheron, are favorites of fox hunters for their ruggedness and power. Some of the draft breeds include the Shire of England, the Friesian of France, and the Clydesdale—originally from Scotland but more common now to Canada and the United States. The Clydesdale's size and uniformity make them an impressive team of drivers, known worldwide in their role as the "Budweiser" horses.

Sport Horse

The sport horse, or "cross bred," is becoming a popular choice of field horse for the pleasure rider, fox hunter, and eventer. Cross breds are a mix of a "light" (hot-blooded horse) with a "heavy" (cold-blooded horse) or a warm-blooded horse. Careful breeding can yield a horse with the perfect qualities for a specific discipline. For instance, an eventing sport horse would tend more toward the refinement and athleticism of a thoroughbred, while a fox hunter would tend more toward its drafty origins. A sport horse will quickly show which way his physical and mental disposition leans—toward the hot blood or the cold blood in him. You can choose which will suit you best. Some sport horses are the Irish, bred from the Irish draught and the Irish thoroughbred, and the Canadian, bred from the Clydesdale and the thoroughbred. Percheron and shire crosses are gaining popularity in the eastern United States as well.

A popular cross-bred is the Appendix quarter horse. It is a quarter horse-thoroughbred cross, which relegates this horse to the "appendix" of the quarter horse registry. Like all cross-bred horses, this one can tend more toward the "light" or the "heavy," and might be less likely to inherit genetic faults of conformation and disease common to one breed or the other.

Quarter Horse

The quarter horse developed in the American West. All the competitive sports in which he reigns supreme, such as team penning and roping, barrel racing, and Western pleasure riding, derive from the attributes he needed to perform his working duties involving livestock. He is conformed "down hill" and low to the ground, with a powerful rear end that gives him the ability for short bursts of intense speed, quick cornering and turning ability, and all around great agility. Quarter horses are among the most commonly used horses for pleasure riders who want a fast, rugged, even tempered, sure-footed trail horse. These attributes often make them a good choice for someone who wants an all-around horse.

The Morgan Horse

The Morgan is popular in the northeastern region of America, with the highest concentration of admirers in Vermont, the place of its origin. The Morgan is thought of as one of the heartiest, most agreeable, and versatile horses in the world. They usually lack the refined gaits of the thoroughbred or warm blood and tend to have a hotter temperament than the quarter horse. They are generally around 15 hands, although many breeders these days are trying to get a little more height into the breed. Morgan horses are most often shown in Western division competition and make a great all-purpose horse. Their tendency for high front action makes them a good candidate for a light carriage horse as well.

The Gaited Horse

Gaited horses were developed and bred specifically for ranch and plantation workers and owners so they could cover long distances at a fast and comfortable pace. Their movement is back and forth, which doesn't require posting, rather than a trot, whose motion is up and down, which requires a rider to post for a comfortable ride. They can have up to five gaits, ranging from a walk to what in some breeds is called a flying pace, which can be as fast as another horse's gallop. Some gaited horses are the Icelandic of Iceland, the Tennessee Walker and Standard Bred of North America, the Peruvian Paso of South America, and the Paso Fino of Spanish origin.

FACT

The Icelandic horse is enjoying increasing popularity in the eastern United States as a pleasure mount. They are generally kindly disposed, stoic, brave, hearty, bold, and intractable. One of the oldest breeds of horse, their disposition is uniformly consistent, quite unlike any other breed of horse.

Today, gaited horses are mainly used in breed specific competition, with the Standard Bred exclusively bred for harness racing. The smooth gait of most gaited horses makes them excellent trail horses, especially for someone with a bad back. However, they are sometimes limited by conformation, and these horses might have trouble performing the canter or over jumps. Though they are genetically disposed toward their gait, they must be constantly maintained in it in order to perform properly. This will require discipline and diligence on your part, and perhaps the hiring of a trainer from time to time.

Seeking Professional Help

This is a must for the amateur horse buyer. There is simply too much to consider when buying a horse, and many pitfalls lie along the way. There is no substitute for experience and expertise when you enter into the process of buying a horse. A professional's trained eye will notice faults and potential in a horse that are too subtle for the novice to see. A general rule is that the horse you are seeing for the first time is not the horse you will be taking home. A horse's true personality might not come out until he is comfortable in his new surroundings. It might be a few days or a few months until he shows his true colors. Vices and lameness might also not be apparent for days or weeks after purchase. There are too many factors that determine a horse's behavior in a given situation to adequately judge him in just a few hours, no matter how many times you go back to see him. However, an experienced horse person will have a pretty good idea and will ask the right questions to scope out the horse's true nature.

QUESTION?

Should I avoid horses that have "pig eye"?
It is a popular belief among people in the horse profession that a horse with a small eye, or "pig eye," is undesirable. This is more or less a superstition, with no scientific basis. However, if there is a strong historical bias against a horse with this feature, then that is worth considering. That said, a horse should be judged on her merits first, and her character determined by her quality, and not by the size or shape of her eye.

Your trainer might be a good person to bring with you to see and try a horse that you are thinking about buying. She knows your riding style and capability and will have a vested interest in finding you the right horse. After all, she will have to live with the decision also. However, it is not uncommon that a trainer will purposely find the wrong horse for a client. An over-mounted client can increase his dependency on a trainer. Such a horse will create business in the form of extra training and lessons. Both horse and rider will be under the trainer's control. Likewise, an under-mounted client will soon be looking for another horse, which will be another commission or two for the trainer. Keep ulterior motives and agendas in mind, and always try to have a second or third opinion from a knowledgeable friend.

Vetting the Horse

A standard pre-purchase exam on the horse you've chosen to buy is worth the money and could prevent you from making the wrong decision. The veterinarian should be independent from the seller of the horse to prevent a conflict of interest. How thoroughly he checks the horse will be a financial matter, and this should depend on how much you are spending on the horse. A checkup like the one listed below should suffice for a horse that is being sold for between $5,000 and $10,000.

Figure 2.1:
The Parts of
the Horse

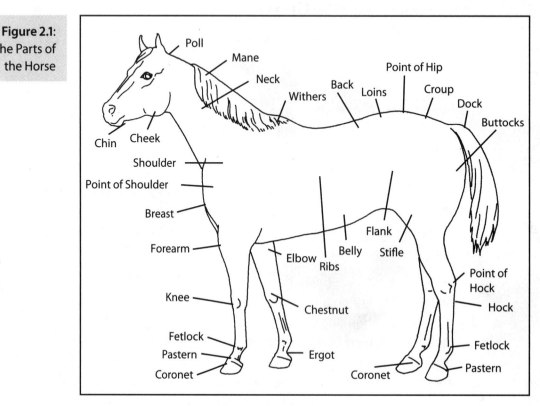

Get the History

What you see when you go to look at or try a horse you want to buy is not often what you get. Obtain all of a horse's veterinary records. Ask if the horse is prone to any illnesses or whether he has any chronic lameness issues. These can often be masked for days, weeks, or much longer with drugs or special care. A horse that is prone to colic, for instance, will show no signs of this for months or years even, but will be very stressful to take care of on a regular basis, and possibly costly. A cribber might not be indulging in his vice at the farm where you are seeing him because the fences are protected with special paint or are electrified. If you know to ask these kinds of questions about the horse, you will most likely be told the truth.

Tests and Other Observations

The vet will probably be able to tell previous and current problems the horse has had, has, or might develop, such as bowed tendons, quarter cracks, splints, and founder, and whether these problems might be a factor in the job you've chosen for your horse. The veterinarian's opinion should be strongly taken into consideration in your final decision to buy the horse.

Conformation

The vet will check the horse's conformation and movement to see if there is lameness or potential lameness from any evident conformation faults. He will also advise you, with your riding discipline in mind, if a conformation fault might become an issue. For instance, a horse with long pasterns might not hold up to a rigorous jumping program.

Flex Test

A "flex" test will further determine if the horse is prone to common joint problems, primarily of the hock, knee, or stifle. This is a simple field test where the vet folds the leg of the horse back on itself and holds it there for thirty seconds for a front leg, one minute for a back leg. The horse is then asked to trot off, which he should do "soundly." If not, he might have or could develop a problem.

Heart and Lungs

The horse's heart and lungs will be tested before and after exercise with his age, type, and level of fitness in mind. If undue strain or fatigue is apparent after exercise, this could be a sign of an unhealthy horse and would call for further testing.

Teeth

The vet will check the teeth, which can yield plenty of information about a horse's history, age, previous care, and whether he cribs. Cribbing horses should be avoided. Cribbing will be discussed further in Chapter 12, Horse Faults.

Blood

A blood test will check for healthy thyroid function and disease. This is especially important for certain breeds that are prone to specific diseases.

X-ray

An x-ray will help check for navicular changes and hock changes among other diseases (congenital or otherwise), and non-conformities that are a condition of arthritis, as well as fractures and bone chips, which can be difficult or impossible to notice otherwise.

Hoof Color

It is commonly thought that a white foot is inferior in integrity to a dark foot. Some horse dealers and auctioneers have been known to paint white feet black to conceal a white foot while they try to sell the horse. In some white feet, the consistency of the horn is weaker than in a dark foot, but this is not an absolute. Some professionals would even call this theory a mythical bias, like judging a horse's character by the size of his eye. However, like all prevailing biases, there is probably a reason why this one exists, and it is worth considering.

Buying from a Dealer

As in most professions, there are honest horse dealers and dishonest ones. Regardless of which one you find, your motto should be "buyer beware." It is strongly recommended that you bring a professional horse person, who can help pick a good horse from the many possibilities and negotiate a price, with you to a horse dealer. Most dealers won't allow a non-professional a trial period, but might extend this courtesy to a professional. You are often given the option of bringing the horse back if you're not happy, but only in return for another horse, not your money back. You might save money and purchase a fine horse by having a professional's advice. So many horses pass through a dealer's hands that a professional with a good eye might very well see potential in a horse that has eluded the dealer's notice. This is very tricky business, so be careful.

Common Pitfalls to Avoid

There are a handful of common mistakes that become the stories you will hear over and over as you hang around in horsy circles. Common sense and a little education will help you to not become one of the taken.

The Green Horse

A common mistake first time horse buyers make is to think they are saving money by buying a green horse as opposed to one that is trained and perhaps more expensive. In these circumstances, the owner often ends up "over-mounted," which is no fun and often dangerous. Any savings, and then some, are usually spent having the horse professionally trained. A good rule is that you don't want your horse to know less than you. He will almost surely take advantage of this situation and both of you will be the worse for the experience. Let the professionals do the training.

Trial Period

Another common mistake is to buy a horse without taking it on an adequate trial basis. A trial should last from a week to one month; the length of the trial period will probably be determined by how much money is involved. During this period, you can get an idea of the horse's true personality, level of training, soundness, and vices. Most of all, this trial period will give you the opportunity to see if he is a horse that you want to invest your time, energy, and money in.

What You Want versus What You Need

Although you will likely have a certain look or color in mind for the horse you wish to own, these preferences should not limit you in your decision. Such superficial qualities of a horse tell you nothing about him. What you want might not be what you need. The best horse for you might not look like what you imagine you want. That said, with the right combination of time, money, and sense of purpose, you will find a horse that is exactly what you want and what you need. In terms of looking out for the specific look or color you have in mind, it might be best to keep it to yourself. Such information in the hands of a horse dealer might end up weighing too heavily in what he will try to sell you and ultimately in your purchase decision.

Commissions

It is best to buy your horse as directly as possible from the seller. Often, when buying a horse indirectly, such as through a show barn, so many people have been involved in some way in the sale, and each takes a commission, that a $5,000 horse ends up being sold for $10,000. If you are spending $10,000, make sure the horse is worth $10,000 once you take it out of the place where you bought it.

Strangles

A disease known as "strangles" is sometimes carried by dealer or sale barn horses because of the high turnover rate at such establishments. Strangles, a serious upper respiratory infection, has a dormancy period in the horse, and it can remain active for up to eight months in an area where an infected horse has been. So, infected horses are passed on to other barns before they are symptomatic. Strangles is highly contagious through touch and sharing of water or food. This will often infect many of the horses in a barn before you can do anything about it and can require time-consuming quarantines of all the horses that occupy a barn with an infected one, as well as very expensive medicines. Beware of this very serious disease: Strangles can be lethal.

Chapter 3

Systems of the Horse's Body

In order to properly provide for the nutritional and health needs of your horse, you must have a basic knowledge of her body systems. Since you will be responsible for the exercise, food, water, and, at times, the air your horse takes in, an understanding of her skeletal, digestive, circulatory, epidermal, and respiratory systems can help you keep her healthy and prevent complications of her care.

The Digestive System

The digestive system of a horse is composed of the stomach, small intestine, and the large intestine, which involves the cecum, large and small colon, rectum, and anus. The most important thing for you to remember is that what goes into the horse and cannot be utilized by his system, must come out as manure.

The horse's digestive system is designed so that food is not permitted back up into the esophagus once it's passed through a one-way muscular valve. Therefore, a horse cannot vomit when he has eaten something disagreeable or indigestible. It must pass as manure.

Upper Digestive Tract

The processing of food material begins in the mouth where grass, hay, or grain is mixed with saliva and ground into a digestive pulp. Unhealthy or uneven teeth will inhibit this process.

The esophagus moves food matter toward the stomach by a series of wave-like contractions. This food enters the stomach through a one-way valve. Glands in the stomach begin digestion by combining enzymes, bacteria, and acid with the food material.

Some fruits, especially carrots, should be broken up before they are fed, because they will sometimes get lodged in a horse's throat and cause him to choke.

Figure 3.1:
The Digestive
System

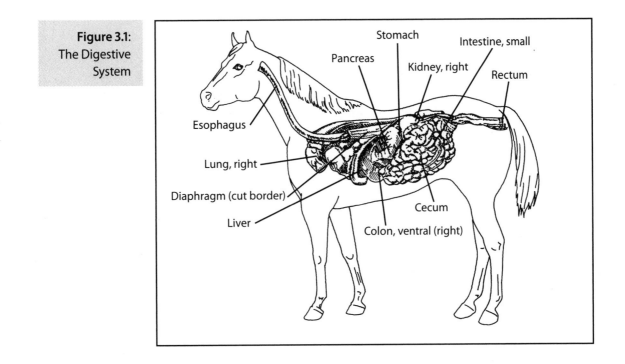

Lower Digestive Tract

From the stomach, digested material moves on to the small intestine, where it is broken down further into fats, protein, and carbohydrates. These broken-down materials are taken up by the blood to be used by the body as energy and for growth. The small intestine connects with the large intestine, where microbes in the cecum continue the breakdown of nutritional material.

The liver, which is a gland, receives processed food from the small intestine through the blood. The liver removes poisons and stores vitamins and sugar. The liver also regulates the body's amount of proteins, carbohydrates, and fats.

Broken down material moves on to the colon, which is about twelve feet long. Here, fecal balls are formed, which are constituted mainly of indigestible matter. These are eventually passed through the rectum as manure.

Illnesses of the Digestive System

If laid out in a straight line, the length of a horse's gut would be about 100 feet long. The large intestine occupies about 60 percent of this figure, while the stomach is disproportionately small, only about 10 percent or about the size of a football. It is easy to see why the digestive system is prone to illness.

Colic

Colic is a broad term used for any intestinal upset or dysfunction. Symptoms can range from mild to severe, with the latter resulting in a twisted gut, or an impaction in the intestine. Food moves through the intestine at the fast rate of twelve inches per minute. Because of this rapid movement of material through a horse's system, too much grain or a sudden change in diet can mean that not properly digested material is passed on to the cecum and colon. There, rapid fermentation causes gas, which is another cause of colic. Colic, its symptoms, and treatments will be discussed in-depth in Chapter 7, Most Common Ailments.

A horse's digestive system is designed to process small amounts of food throughout the day and night. Too much food at one time can cause sickness or sap energy and nutrients. So, divide your feeding schedule into at least three feedings in a twenty-four-hour period.

Laminitis

The most common cause of laminitis, or "founder" as it is more commonly referred to, is the consumption of high amounts of rich grass or an excessive amount of grain. Make sure that you acclimate your horse to grass, especially in the spring when it is most rich. Start at fifteen minutes, and work up to about an hour by the end of the week. After two weeks, he should be able to graze full-time. Pasture-kept horses will acclimate themselves, as the first grass that is available to them will be weak, left over from winter, and only gradually grow in richness. Laminitis will be discussed further in Chapter 5, Hoof and Foot.

ALERT!

Unless a new horse has come to you with feeding instructions, assume he has never had grain and acclimate him slowly. Start with a handful for about a week and work your way up. His digestive system will not only need to get used to the extra protein in his diet, but his energy level will be dramatically increased by feeding grain. If the energy level is not raised gradually, it could mean trouble for anyone who is handling or riding him.

Respiratory System

The function of the respiratory system is to take in oxygen and expel carbon dioxide. Oxygen is essential for life and is involved in all bodily functions. Carbon dioxide is given off as waste. A healthy respiratory tract will exhibit itself by relaxed, rhythmic, and quiet breaths. At rest, a horse typically takes ten to fourteen breaths per minute. Each of these breaths will be followed by a pause. Exercise will cause a sharp rise in respiration, but a healthy horse should return to his resting rate within ten minutes. You can easily check your horse's respiration at rest by counting the rise and fall of his flanks for one minute. The horse's lungs are large and take up a good portion of the chest cavity. To give you an idea of size, the lungs of a horse can hold up to thirty quarts of air, equivalent to seven and a half gallons. Structures involved in the passage of air into the lungs are the nostrils, pharynx, larynx, esophagus, trachea, and diaphragm.

A well-known disease of the larynx, known commonly as "roaring," is caused by the degeneration of the nerves that support the muscles that open and close the larynx. The sound a horse makes upon inhalation when afflicted with this disease sounds like a roar. This can be nothing to worry about. If, however, the noise is accompanied by any exercise intolerance, your veterinarian should examine the horse.

Circulatory System

The heart, blood, lymph nodes, and blood and lymph vessels comprise the circulatory system. The heart, located off center toward the left in the chest cavity, is a muscular organ. It pumps blood, which transports oxygen and nutrients to every part of the body. The blood also collects waste located in the tissues of the body. Veins bring blood into the heart, while arteries, which are larger and have thicker walls, carry blood away from the heart. The expansion and contraction of the artery walls can be felt externally as the pulse.

The maximum heart rate of a thoroughbred at peak performance is 225 to 240 beats per minute. You can listen to the heartbeat of a horse with a stethoscope placed on the left side of the horse, just behind the elbow.

The blood also transports hormones and regulates the balance of water and electrolytes. Its clotting capabilities protect the vascular system from losing large volumes of blood after an injury. The lymphatic system of a horse keeps excess fluid from collecting in any one part of the body. Lymph, which is a clear or slightly yellow fluid, contains white blood cells and circulates throughout the body, helping to fight infection. Lymph removes bacteria and some proteins from the tissues. An example of its malfunction would be the evidence of edema, swelling, or lymphanghitis.

FACT

Each teaspoon of blood from a horse would contain approximately 3,000,000 red blood cells to every one white cell. These red blood cells carry oxygen throughout her body, which is essential for all bodily functions.

Skeletal System

The skeleton of a horse is the framework of his body. It supports and protects his organs and soft tissue with 206 bones of all shapes, sizes, and structural and mechanistic purposes. Bone is living tissue, supplied with blood vessels and nerves. Toward its surface it is hard, while the inner bone is spongier, which gives the bone its lightness and resilience. Tendons and ligaments are elastic fibrous bands that help support and stabilize the bones. They are attached to the bone via the periosteum, which is a thin layer of tissue that covers and protects the bone. Perforation of the periosteum, which can happen with punctures wounds and breaks, can prevent proper healing.

Figure 3.2:
The Skeletal
System

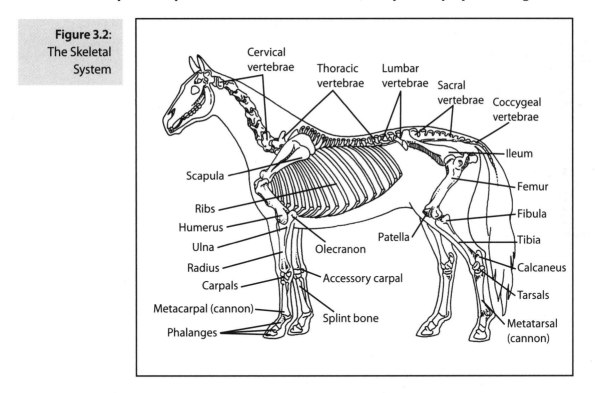

A working knowledge of your horse's skeletal system and anatomy can help you determine when and where your horse is having a lameness issue, or at least be able to convey what you are seeing to a vet, using the appropriate terminology. The quicker and more accurately you can close in on a problem, the more likely you are to save your horse from unnecessary discomfort, while saving yourself time and money.

A thin-skinned horse, such as an Arabian or thoroughbred, can afford you a better observation of the skeleton and points of a horse. Such a horse in motion can remove the abstraction of science and really give you an appreciation of how the skeletal system actually carries a horse.

One of his many adaptations for speed and endurance, a horse's skull has large sinus cavities that not only make his head less of a weight burden by decreasing heavy bone, but are also capable of holding and passing great amounts of oxygen into his system, which is then translated into energy.

The Horse's Teeth

At maturity, a horse has at least thirty-six permanent teeth. Incisors are used for the cutting action of grazing, while molars are for grinding roughage and grain into finer material, which is the first stage of digestion. Up to four inches of a permanent tooth is imbedded in his jaw bone, and it grows out from there throughout his life. A lot of information can be had by a good look at a horse's teeth—his age, general health, and history of diet and possible vices, just to name a few things you can learn from his teeth.

Dental Care

Good and properly cared for teeth are essential to your horse's general well-being. Differences in the diet of most domestic horses, in contrast with that of a horse in his natural state of twenty-four-hour grazing on all different types of grasses and legumes, means that his teeth need to be filed or "floated" by an equine dentist about once a year.

Dental Care for Young Horses

The replacement of a horse's first teeth, or "milk teeth," with his permanent teeth can be a difficult transition. The new teeth coming through are often very sharp and must force the temporary teeth out. Depending on the breed, this process will take about two to four years. Young horses should be floated at least twice a year while in this process.

FACT

Uneven tooth wear can inhibit a horse's ability to properly grind, take in, and digest his food. This will cause sharp tooth edges and result in weight loss. The sharp edges cut the horse's cheek and tongue and might cause a horse under saddle to hang his head to one side or refuse to "take the bit." Proper floating about once a year, along with removal of his "wolf teeth" (a pre-molar that some horses have), will keep him happy with or without a bit in his mouth.

Dental Care for the Older Horse

Uneven grinding surfaces are often endemic to older horses. The upper and lower jaws need to oppose each other correctly for proper grinding action and even wear of teeth to take place. Misaligned or missing teeth can upset this reciprocity, causing irregular grinding surfaces. This can lead to poor digestion and loss of food, which leads to loss of weight and dental decay from food that accumulates in crevices of the mouth. Older horses should be looked at twice a year by a dentist.

Determining Age from His Teeth

The growing horse is easy to age, as yearly changes in his teeth are apparent. After the age of five, determining age from his teeth becomes more difficult. If your horse isn't papered or tattooed, there are marks and changes that occur after five years of age that can help you determine his age fairly accurately. However, after ten years of age, even a vet or dentist might not be able to give you an exact age for your horse.

The best way to get proficient at reading a horse's mouth is to look inside every horse's mouth you come in contact with. With practice, determining age this way can be fun and add another skill to your bank of horse knowledge.

To look in the horse's mouth, stand to one side of your horse's head. Steady the head, and with your opposite hand, reach in the horse's mouth through the area without teeth. Grab the tongue and pull it out the side of his mouth. Now, with the tongue out of the way, you can see the teeth on that side without obstruction.

Figure 3.3:
The Horse's
Teeth

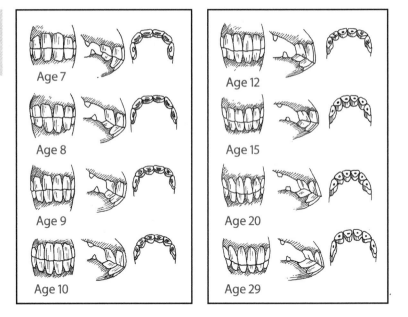

Age 7

Age 8

Age 9

Age 10

Age 12

Age 15

Age 20

Age 29

- **Age One:** She will have a full mouth of temporary teeth, including molars, six upper and six lower incisors.
- **Age Two and a Half:** The first two central incisors appear. These can be identified by their shape, size, and color.
- **Age Three and a Half:** The lateral permanent incisors have erupted. By four and a half, the corner incisors are in as well.
- **Age Six:** The "cups" are present on the grinding surface of the teeth.

- **Age Seven:** The cups in the central incisors have begun to grow out and therefore are of lighter color.
- **Age Eight:** The cups in the lateral incisors have changed as well. The appearance of what is called a "dental star" is apparent on the top of the central incisors.
- **Age Nine:** The cups are no longer visible, but a hook can now be seen on the upper incisor caused by grinding. Also, "galvaynes groove" appears, which is helpful to aging the horse from ten years of age onward. It is a dark stripe or groove located on the upper corner incisor that grows down the tooth. By age twelve, this groove will be about three-eighths of an inch long.
- **Age Fifteen:** Small circular dental stars can be seen on all incisors. Galvaynes groove is the length of half the tooth.
- **Age Twenty:** The galvaynes groove will extend all the way to the bottom of the incisor. At age thirty, the groove has grown off the tooth entirely. The front incisors will begin to slope forward.

Skin and Hair

A lot can be learned about a horse by taking a look at the condition of his hair and skin. A shiny coat and skin free of skin flakes is a good sign that your horse is healthy. Skin is the first line of defense against the elements, many types of harmful organisms and bacteria, cuts, scratches, and puncture wounds. A balanced diet and daily grooming is the best way to maintain your horse's hair and skin. Giving your horse a daily dose of sunshine is perhaps the best thing you can do to encourage his own natural maintenance and immunity to skin-borne problems.

Function of Skin

The skin has many functions. It serves to protect the internal parts of a horse. It also helps to regulate body temperature. Skin is attached in some areas to muscles beneath the skin. An example of this connection is a horse's ability to twitch his skin to ward off insects. The skin is an acutely sensitive organ, housing nerve endings that respond to touch and temperature. In cold weather, the skin can raise the hair, thus creating a layer of insulation that works to trap warmth coming off his body, a function of pilorector muscles. The skin also produces vitamin D, which allows the body to utilize calcium and phosphorous.

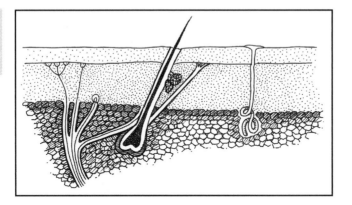

Figure 3.4:
The Horse's Skin and Hair

Care in Warmer Months

The warmer months make caring for the hair and skin easier. Horses "shed out" in the warmer months, so hair is short, making it easier to wash the horse after exercise and drastically reducing drying time. But short hair and warm weather makes horses more susceptible to cuts and scratches, as well as insects and allergens. So you must be vigilant with your grooming habits. Inspect your horse on a daily basis and protect him against insects.

Fly Control

Certain horses never seem to be bothered by conditions of the skin or the insult of biting flies, while others are miserable no matter what efforts you make. Fly control is a must if you wish to keep your horse comfortable in the summer, whether or not he is sensitive to insects.

There are many products that do a good job of reducing fly numbers around the barn, such as fly tape or traps that attract flies into them. There are many daily fly sprays that are effective for most horses. There are products similar to "Frontline" (used for dogs and cats) that need only be applied once a month and might do the trick for your horse. Fly sheets and mesh face bonnets will further protect your horse. It can't hurt to experiment with the many products that are on the market to see which ones work best for your barn or horse.

FACT

Icelandic horses are often genetically disposed toward fly-related allergies because they come from a place that has no naturally occurring flies. Because of Iceland's horse import laws, which ban importing of horses or returning any horse that has left the island, these horses are one of, if not the most, genetically homogeneous breeds of horse in the world.

For horses that are ultra-sensitive to flies—to the point where their mental and physical well-being is at risk—oral and topical steroidal drugs such as prednisone are available. Such horses might also benefit from night turnout, when flies are less active. But remember, although flies are not as prevalent at night as during the heat of day, dawn and dusk are when flies are the worst.

Skin Conditions

There are a variety of skin conditions that your horse might contract through flies, viruses, allergies, or neglect.

Ventral Midline Dermatitis/Summer Eczema

These are actually two different skin afflictions, which are very similar in cause and effect. The ventral midline is located along the chest and lower belly. There is not much hair in the area of the midline, and it is difficult for a horse to reach there in order to scratch or swish with his tail, so it is particularly affected by insects. A raw, scaly strip of irritated skin will develop on the midline. A horse affected with eczema or ventral midline dermatitis may also have an allergy to the saliva of flies, which makes the problem doubly difficult.

Any lesions on a horse must be kept clean and dry. Moisture is a further irritant to the damaged skin, so towel dry any washed areas. Corticosteroid and other antibiotic creams are helpful for easing irritation, but unless the horse's exposure to insects is controlled, the problem will continue.

Hives

Occasional hives are called "feed bumps." Hives are the skin's reaction to an external, or systemic, allergen. They can appear spontaneously and disappear after a few hours. If an antihistamine is administered, the hives will subside usually after a few minutes. Hives are, more often than not, nothing to worry about.

Papular Dermatitis

This condition of the skin is caused by a virus. It is exhibited as raised bumps, usually located in the area of the saddle. After some days, a scab will form over the bump and eventually be shed, leaving a bare patch of skin. This virus will run its course in a few weeks.

Papillomatosis (Warts)

Warts are another viral condition in horses, only seen in the young horse and not after the age of two. A horse can have a few to a hundred warts located on the muzzle and lips. They are contagious to other young horses and will normally spread throughout a group or herd of yearlings living together.

Let the virus run its course. The warts will fall off in a few months. In the meantime, they won't bother most horses unless the horse irritates them by scratching against something.

Ringworm

Ringworm is a fungal skin condition. It is very contagious, and any horse suspected of having ringworm should be quarantined. Ringworm can be noticed as a raised circle of skin, often seen on the neck, shoulder, or base of the tail. These lesions can be anywhere on the skin, and the horse will normally have more than one eruption. To properly diagnose ringworm, your vet should be called out. Anti-fungal cream can treat this condition. Treatment can last up to two weeks.

Rain Rot/Mud Fever

Rain rot is a bacterial condition of the skin, usually occurring along the back, shoulders, and rump. Mud fever is usually found on the lower legs. These bacteria gain entrance through the skin, when the skin has been exposed to prolonged wet conditions. The condition is seen more often in the fall, winter, and early spring due to wet and cool temperatures. Lesions are scaly and patchy, with puss-like material under the scabs. Hair appears matted where skin is affected.

Thoroughly wash the area with betadine, and towel dry. Any healing antibiotic salve can be used to soothe raw skin. Hair can also be clipped to make treatment of the area easier, and promote dryness.

Chapter 4
Feeding and Nutrition

Proper nutrition gives a horse the energy to fuel his body processes, such as building and sustaining healthy muscle and bone, blood circulation, tissue repair, and digestion. The nutritional needs of a horse are really very simple, yet during the latter half of the twentieth century, and especially during the last twenty years, horse nutrition has developed into a complicated and sometimes confusing science.

What Horses Need

In order to survive, horses need water and good quality grass or hay containing fiber, protein, fats, starches, sugar, vitamins, and minerals. However, adequate size and quality pasture is often hard to come by in domestic situations. Also, we often ask more of our horses in domestic situations, and this requires them to have more energy than a nonworking horse that just roams the plains. Therefore, grains are supplemented to a horse's diet. Most horses generally have very similar dietary requirements, but today we can specialize a horse's diet to her exact needs, which might differ according to the type and breed of horse, and the kind and amount of work she does.

Grains are composed of four basic elements, all of which are taken up by your horse's body differently and which perform different and necessary tasks within her to produce energy.

- **Insoluble Carbohydrates.** These make up the bulk of most grains. They are a low-energy, coarse, fibrous material. Digestion of these occurs mainly in the hindgut, where fewer enzymes are present, causing a more gradual breakdown of these materials, and consequently a slow uptake of these nutrients.
- **Soluble Carbohydrates and Sugars.** These are taken up almost immediately and entirely in the small intestines in the form of glucose, which accounts for most of a horse's available energy. Good pasture grass and legumes can contain up to 30 percent glucose—just to give you an idea of the quantity of sugar horses can and must process.
- **Starches.** Starch naturally occurs in grass, but is far more prominent in grains. Most grains are extruded, or modified, to make the starches in them more accessible to digestion. For example, oats are crimped, corn is cracked, and barley is rolled.

Energy Requirements

Every horse is an individual with his own energy requirements. However, you might be able to make generalizations about the energy requirements of a horse by his type, size, temperament, and workload.

Hot Bloods, Cold Bloods, and Ponies

A hot-blooded horse, such as a thoroughbred, that is involved in a rigorous exercise routine such as eventing or racing might eat ten quarts of grain throughout a day. The same horse that is not working for whatever reason might need less than half that amount, or even just a handful of grain, to remain in good flesh and energy. A "heavy horse" such as a draft, or some cross-breds, might have a slower metabolism and require less grain and protein to sustain his workload.

Small horses and ponies, even in heavy work, will never be on a feeding program like that of the racing thoroughbred, which eats ten quarts of grain a day. For a "heavy" pony, such as an Icelandic, a handful will more than likely suffice. A "light" pony with a hotter temperament might require a quart or even two a day to meet his energy needs. It is always better to be on the safe side and feed less than you think until you have found your horse's perfect ration.

Making it Easy

If you're a little confused, fortunately there are feed and grain companies in your area that have done all this work for you and have developed many different kinds of grains with the right balances to suit the needs of most any horse. These companies have trained and knowledgeable professionals whose job it is to help you figure out which grain is best for your horse. Especially if you have to experiment a little to find a feed that you and your horse are happy with, these professional equine nutritionists will be a great asset. So use them.

Good Pasture for a Healthy Horse

As previously noted, good pasture is all your horse really needs. But good pasture often needs to be created and maintained in order to contain the nutrients necessary for a healthy horse. All too often, horses will be left to their own devices on pastures that appear to have plenty of grass; however, they have eaten all the grasses that are nutritious to horses and left other grasses and weeds. The horse will eventually eat these grasses if desperate, but they are unpalatable, non-nutritious, and sometimes unhealthy. A horse subsisting on pasture only will need about three acres of healthy pasture during the growing season and supplemental hay through the winter.

Soil Quality

The quality and quantity of grass you can grow is only as good as the soil upon which it is growing. Your local agricultural extension agent will advise you how to collect soil samples from your pasture, and he or she will analyze the samples for a nominal fee. This will tell you what fertilizer and conditioners must be added to your pasture to be a fertile environment for the kind of grasses you want to grow. A prime pasture is rich in:

- **Nitrogen.** Nitrogen encourages grass growth. A good balance of nitrogen can double the quantity of grass in a pasture.
- **Phosphorus.** Phosphorus promotes root development and gives grasses a sweet taste. This encourages horses to eat nutritious grasses that they might otherwise find unpalatable.
- **Potassium.** Potassium helps grasses increase their natural resistance to drought and disease.

Soil Preparation

If you do not want to disturb an existing pasture, then the least you can do is to aerate the soil. This will loosen the soil and allow for existing grass and grass seedlings to take easier and more profitable root. Any fertilizer can be broadcast on top and allowed to leach into the ground. Horses should be kept off any fertilized area until after a couple of good rains.

It will take one growing season for grass to properly establish itself. If you can afford the time and space to start a brand new pasture, then the ground should be completely turned over with the fertilizer, and then raked smooth. You might try to enlist the services of your local farmer, who might have a cultivator which can do all these tasks, including drilling grass seed, in a single pass.

Which Grasses and Legumes to Encourage

Since weather and growth conditions vary in most places from year to year, you will want a mix of grasses in your pasture that thrive under different conditions and that mature at different rates. Tall fescue will thrive in wet or dry conditions and will stand up to a lot of horse traffic. Some other hardy perennials you can encourage are timothy, rye grass, wheatgrass, brome grass, bluegrass, and orchard grass. Orchard grass will not thrive in either excessively dry or wet conditions nor in an alkaline soil. Brome grass and wheatgrass can tolerate drought. All will lose digestible nutrients as they mature.

A pasture seeded entirely of legumes is impractical. Alfalfa and clover are very nutritious, but too rich and not hardy enough to exist alone in pasture. They should make up no more than 25 percent of a pasture.

Hay Is for Horses

Hay varies in price and quality each year, depending on how much rain falls. Hay needs to dry in a field for three days after it has been cut. Incessant rain can inhibit this drying time. Insufficient rain, of course, doesn't encourage grass to grow. This is why your hay farmer will probably be complaining in all weather conditions the whole year long. The kinds of grasses or legumes that compose your local hay will be determined mainly by what region of the country you live in. Timothy, orchard grass, fescue, and brome grass are very popular and are often mixed with other indigenous grasses of your area. Legumes, such as clovers and alfalfa, are often mixed in with grasses at about a 15 percent ratio. Although some still prefer straight alfalfa for their high-performance horse, such as racehorses, alfalfa is considered too protein rich for most horse's systems to feed it straight. Alfalfa cubes, obtained from your local feed store, are a good amendment to your horse's diet of grass hay. Your horse will think so too.

Quality

A good hay farmer whom you can trust will make your life easier. Sometimes determining the quality of hay is more of an art than a science. Nevertheless, there are telltale signs of good and bad hay. Upon delivery, open a bale. Be aware of any dust or smoke that is released from it. This could mean that the bale, and maybe much of the entire delivery, is dusty or moldy. Before you jump to conclusions, carefully check each bale over the next few days for smoke or wet or white spots in the bale, which will signify mold. Dust will irritate your horse's respiratory system and cause other general health problems. Improperly cured or stored hay creates mold. Mold is toxic to a horse even in small amounts. The hay should smell good, even sweet. Grab a handful from the middle of the bale. It should be soft and leafy, not stalky, because the digestible nutrients are mostly in the leaf.

FACT

Color is not necessarily an indication of good quality hay. However, hay that has lost its natural greenish color and is completely yellow might be on the old side and have lost much of its nutritional value.

The terms *first cut*, *second cut*, and even *third cut* hay refer to the seasonal order by which hay is harvested from a field. First cut hay is simply the first cutting from a field and includes whatever was left of the nutrient depleted grass that lived through winter, plus the next couple months of new growth. In most regions of the country, first cutting takes place from late spring to early summer. The growing season is not typically as long or wet for the second cut from the same field, so it takes more grass to make a bale of hay. For this reason, and because it is better quality since it is all new growth from that growing season, second cut is more expensive. Depending on the length of the growing season where you live and the rainfall, there might be third cut hay, which is typically an even better quality than second cut.

How Much To Feed

When hay is being baled, it is automatically divided into flakes. A flake will vary in size and weight according to how the bale was made and its size and weight, which is also variable (about forty to sixty pounds). An average horse, about 800 pounds, would normally consume twenty-five to thirty pounds of hay per day, so about half a bale or about six flakes. But each horse is an individual and should be fed according to his needs. You might have to do some experimenting to find the right amount of hay to feed your horse to keep him in good flesh. His size, type, disposition, and work regime might determine how much he needs (or might not). A "good doer" is a horse that easily remains in good flesh, while a high-strung or nervous horse might require twice the amount of hay and still have trouble keeping weight on.

ALERT!

A very common no-no that you should not practice, and discourage others from doing with your horse or horses in your barn, is feeding treats by hand. This will encourage biting behavior or bad ground manners in general. Feed treats in feed tubs or on the ground.

Is Your Horse Getting Enough Food?

Your horse should have a good covering of flesh over his frame. His ribs should not be visible to the eye, but if you run your hand over his barrel, you should just be able to define them. A horse that appears boney, or hollow of flank or hip, is probably too skinny. However, a horse that is too fat will have trouble performing and will be inclined to lameness.

Lots of Fresh Water

A horse's make-up is about seventy percent water. She must always have fresh water available to her, whether in her stall or in the paddock or pasture. If dehydrated only to a factor of twenty percent (about two to three days), she could die. Water aids in cleansing the horse's body of toxins, lubricates and aids the digestive process, which helps to avoid impaction colic, and helps to distribute nutrients throughout the body.

How Much

Body weight, body type, breed, workload, and weather can be determining factors in how much a horse will drink—but not necessarily. Generally speaking, a normal size horse will drink about seven to ten gallons of water per day. A hardworking horse might lose four to five gallons of sweat a day and require twice the amount of water as the average nonworking horse.

FACT

Although she is not exercising, a lactating mare will require significantly more water than a relatively idle horse of the same type. She is producing milk to feed a foal and requires a disproportionately high amount of water to body weight.

Body Type

A bigger horse does not necessarily drink more water than one that is smaller. Fat and muscle mass are factors in water consumption, but every horse is an individual and will probably find his own balance. However, a 2,000-pound draft horse must maintain his approximately 1,500 pounds of water mass, and so he will probably drink more than a 700-pound thoroughbred involved in a similar work regime.

Breed

Some horses indigenous to or developed in hot or arid climates like the Arabian will sweat less and have adapted to a lesser water requirement than other types of horses. Otherwise, there is no definitive water requirement according to breed.

Weather

Horses will require less and drink less water in colder weather. Sometimes, they are more apt to dehydrate in cold weather because they are often worked less and feel less inclined to drink. Also, very cold water is not agreeable to a horse and might prevent some horses from drinking. A salt block in the stall or paddock will generate thirst and is a good idea for winter as well as summer.

Watering Tips

A horse that is "hot" during or after work should not be allowed free access to water. He could cramp up or even develop colic. However, short drinks, about three seconds long every once in a while, will help him stay hydrated and healthy during a workout.

QUESTION?

What do I do if my horse is not sick but refuses to drink?
Horses might reject water from a different source than they are used to. "Flavoring" their current water with peppermint oil or molasses, and their new source with the same, might help them acclimate.

Very cold water should be heated up with heating elements in buckets or water troughs to around 40 degrees. This will encourage a horse to drink, as well as make it less taxing on his body temperature during the colder months. If heating is not a possibility, water buckets or troughs should be changed out with fresh water a couple times a day. Water coming from a ground source will be between 35–45 degrees in the wintertime.

For pasture kept horses that get their water from natural sources on the property, it is important to have the water tested for potability (whether or not it is safe to drink). You never know what is going in the water upstream from you. Also, this source must be checked regularly in both very cold and very hot temperatures to make sure it isn't inaccessible because of freezing, drought, or obstructions up stream.

Feeding Tips

Since we have taken the horse out of his natural environment, and in most cases either limited his natural diet or have introduced grains in a quantity he would never find naturally, we are responsible for his nutritional well-being. Here are a few points to keep in mind when feeding your horse.

Hay and Grain

Always feed hay along with grain, but preferably before grain. Hay is roughage that helps a horse move grain through his digestive track and is important for digestion.

Some horses develop the bad habit of "bolting" their grain. This habit could cause a condition in horses called "choke," or colic. Special feeding tubs are available to deter a horse that bolts his grain. For outside ground feeders, a large, smooth stone can be placed in the feed tub to slow the over-zealous eater.

Break Up Feedings

As a grazing herbivore with a relatively small stomach, a horse's digestive system has adapted to continual food processing. This doesn't mean we have to feed them all through the day and night, but small helpings of hay and grain should be split up into at least two, and preferably four, feedings throughout the day and night.

The processing of food is how a horse generates energy to stay warm. This is another reason to feed several times throughout the day and night, rather than just once. Unlike grain, a horse's digestive system can process great amounts of hay without danger of colic.

Be Consistent

Horses might become nervous if their routine is upset. These stresses can manifest themselves in a change in acidity levels and digestion-aiding bacteria in the gut. So be consistent with the kind of food, the amount, and the time you feed. This will help prevent digestive disorders such as colic and laminitis.

Feeding Around Work

Never feed or let drink a horse that is "hot" from activity. Likewise, never work a horse directly after he has eaten a full ration of grain. The general rule is to wait one hour from work to feed and vice versa.

Using Supplements

A horse that is being fed a balanced diet of good hay and grain or grazes in a healthy pasture should not need supplements. New products appear on the shelves of tack and feed stores every year, and marketers are quick to convince you that your horse must be lacking something. Your horse will tell you by his overall condition if he is lacking something essential in his diet. For some horses that are, for one reason or another, deficient, supplements are, literally, a life saver. At the very least, supplements can make it possible for him to perform in his job. For others, supplements pass through an already complete system with no or little benefit, or can even upset his natural balance and cause him harm.

ALERT!

All supplements should be prescribed and approved by a vet. Always consider a supplement as merely a Band-Aid; a more serious health issue might underlie his need for a supplement. Unknowledgeable supplementation to a horse's diet can do more harm than good.

When to Supplement

There are horses that develop problems throughout their lives, or have congenital diseases, that could otherwise not live a happy, active life without supplements. Horses stressed from work demands or environmental conditions are good candidates for certain supplements. There are a plethora of supplements to aid in the health and comfort of aging horses, who might not be able to process food as in their younger days, or are simply beyond the condition that a horse in a wild state would exist. A horse recuperating from illness or injury can often progress more rapidly back to health with the aid of supplements. A horse with a poor coat or a foot condition might call for the addition of a supplement to his grain ration. A horse that's not eating his grain or drinking enough water can have his grain and water supplemented.

Is It Working?

Once you have started your horse on a supplement, you might not see results right away. Many supplements can take from one to three months to show benefit to your horse or might never be blatantly apparent. A supplement might work for one horse and not for another. After the supplement has begun to make a difference, you should evaluate his situation with the help of a vet to determine if you have made the right choice and dosage of supplement. Some experimentation might be necessary.

Feeding the Young Horse

The nutritional needs of a young horse that is growing and developing will be very different from any maintenance diet you would feed to an already grown horse. Along with exercise, playmates, and general socialization, the young horse's diet must provide the essential nutrients to build a strong and healthy body, mind, and immune system.

FACT

A horse's legs at birth are already two-thirds the length they will be at maturity. This is an important advantage in the wild, because it allows them to stand, nurse, and run within a few hours of being born.

A Foal's Nutrition

The foal can receive all his nutrition from his mother's milk, provided she is healthy. The milk that a mare produces within the first few hours after birth contains colostrum that a foal needs in order to be able to resist disease. It takes several months for him to build up his own antibodies against disease. He will continue to nurse and receive most of his nutrients from his mother for about six months. However, as early as a few weeks old he will begin to experiment with eating grass, hay, and even his mother's grain if it is available.

Hay and Grain

Gradual introduction of hay and grain is the safest way to ensure your growing foal will make the transition to weanling with little difficulty of emotional or gut upset. Hay and grain can be fed "free choice." A creep feeder is an apparatus that allows the foal to eat grain through an opening that is too small for a full grown horse to access. This will ensure that his mother doesn't eat the grain you intend for him.

ALERT!

Horses cannot eat off round bales left outside like cows, or off paddock feeders that are not restocked every day with clean, dry hay. A cow's stomach has four chambers and can break down mold and other bacteria in a way that a horse's gut cannot. If moldy hay is a horse's only option, he will probably eat it and get very sick.

Legume hay is excellent for the growing horse. Its high protein, calcium, and phosphorus content helps to build strong bones and muscle. Too much protein, however, can lead to epiphacytus, an inflammation of the growth plates in a young horse's knees or ankles. This is a sign to back off from a high protein diet until a vet counsels you how to proceed. A horse's protein requirements are:

- **Foal:** 10 percent to 12 percent
- **Weanling:** 12 percent to 14 percent
- **Yearling:** 12 percent to 14 percent
- **Two-year-old:** 10 percent to 14 percent
- **Mature horse:** 10 percent to 12 percent

Vaccinations and Worming

It is important not to overload a new foal with too many vaccinations. Tetanus and equine influenza should be given in his first week of life. The first worming can be given after about a month, as a foal can get worms from mother's milk or from grazing. A vet will describe your new foal's vaccination schedule to you.

Feeding an Older Horse

At about the age of fifteen, the caring requirements for your horse will change. She is now a senior and will need to be fed differently to maintain good health and an active life. Worn down or uneven grinding surfaces in the older horse's mouth will make chewing more difficult and affect the way he breaks down and processes his food. In conjunction with general systemic changes that affect the way he utilizes his nutrients, this problem can radically alter his weight and health.

Grain

One of the first changes needed in your older horse's diet will be a more palatable, easier to digest grain. Many good "senior feeds" are available today. They are a little more costly, but well worth the expense. These feeds are specifically designed to provide the older horse with a balanced diet. They often have a beet pulp base, which is found to be useful in the maintenance of weight and energy. Increasing his ration, as well as the frequency of feedings, might help him to best utilize his grain.

Hay

Your aged equine will have more difficulty chewing hay as well. Softer grasses and leafy legumes will make it easier on him. Your hay man should be able to get you an ideal hay for an older horse. Pasture can be a great supplement to his diet and be beneficial to his general happiness and well-being, but the pasture should not be his only source of nutrition.

An older horse might have difficulty maintaining her body temperature in cold weather. Lower energy levels means that she won't be moving around as much as she used to, which means that she won't be generating as much body heat. Therefore, she might require a turnout blanket. She might otherwise lose weight and condition, using energy instead to stay warm.

Signs Your Horse Is Having Trouble

So much of horse care is observation and common sense. Ask yourself a few questions to determine whether your older horse's diet is inadequate so that he might be ready for a senior diet.

- Is he leaving part of his grain ration in the feed tub?
- Is undigested grain showing up in his manure?
- Are you finding wet, matted clumps of hay on the stall floor? This is a telltale sign that he is having trouble grinding his hay into material that he can swallow. These clumps can also gather between his upper cheek and gum, noticeable as a bump on the cheek of the horse.
- Is he dropping weight or losing condition despite a good diet?

Joint Supplements

An older horse will more than likely have arthritis to some extent. Whether it is debilitating or just uncomfortable, arthritis, among other discomforts, can affect your horse's overall appearance and ability to thrive. Old injuries are particularly susceptible to arthritis, which might require a cortisone injection once in a while. But for daily maintenance, one of the many joint supplements on the market can greatly improve your aging horse's quality of life. These mostly consist of glucosamine, with a carrying vehicle called chondroitin. Anti-inflammatories, either in conjunction with joint supplements or used by themselves, might also make the difference between a sound horse and a lame one.

Feed Storage

The quality of what you feed your horse will be dependent on, among other things, its proper storage. Whether inside your barn or in a separate building, feed and hay should be in a clean, dry, ventilated place, closed off from your horse.

Feed Room

It is of utmost importance that grain be stored where a horse cannot get to it. A horse that gets into an unlimited store of grain can easily eat himself to death or serious illness by colic or founder. Loose horses are a fact of barn life, so plan your feed room so that it is securely closed to them in any and all circumstances. Grain can spoil if left in the sun or mold if kept in a damp environment. It should be kept in a covered, metal-lined bin or in metal trashcans with cover locks.

Hay

It is common to store hay in the loft of a barn. A well-designed barn loft will already have the most important requirements for hay storage. It will be easily accessible by truck, have a wood—not cement—floor, have good ventilation, be dry in order to prevent mold, and give protection from the sun so that the nutrients are not depleted.

FACT

A ton of hay (2,000 pounds) will be about thirty to forty bales, which would fit in a square space as wide, long, and tall as an average man. An average horse, whose diet is not supplemented with pasture, will go through three to four tons of hay a year.

However, hay creates dust and can also create and fuel fires. Therefore, you should consider building a hay barn that is separate from your horse barn, yet conveniently close. Ventilation and protection from the elements are the primary concern. Dormers, overhangs, or other protrusions from the barn might prevent a hay truck from getting right up next to the opening of the barn, where it needs to be for delivery. Size might be a matter of preference, available space, or cost. It is generally cheaper to buy hay, as well as bagged bedding, by the ton, rather than by the bale or bag. So, the more you get, the less you pay. For this reason, you might want a larger space. Fewer deliveries will cause less commotion and be less cumbersome in winter ice or spring mud.

Rodents

You will most likely have a constant battle with rodents and varmints around your barn. They can make a mess, be unsanitary, and carry diseases to your horses, such as rabies or wobbles. Rats, when unchecked, can create a network of tunnels under your barn, which can undermine the soundness of the structure. Metal rather than plastic storage bins, which can be securely locked from the prying hands of raccoons and the gnawing teeth of rats and mice, will protect the grain. You can drastically reduce a rodent problem by simply keeping your feed room and horse stalls clean. A good barn cat can keep a rat or mouse population in check. Rat poison can expeditiously wipe out a rat problem, but must be used cautiously so that your horses and pets won't be able to get to it.

Chapter 5

Hoof and Foot

The foot of a horse is a complex and dynamic mechanism that must bear the full weight of a horse throughout his life, sustaining the concussion of this big, fast, and powerful animal. Needless to say, proper care must be taken to ensure healthy feet and hooves for your horse, especially when diseases and ailments threaten their integrity. The foot and hoof need attention on a daily basis from you or your caretaker and also must be tended to by a farrier.

Dynamics of the Hoof and Foot

The foot of a horse is made up of bone, cartilage, joint surfaces, and sensitive and insensitive laminae. The coffin bone, navicular bone, and the end of the short pastern bone comprise its basic support structure. A healthy front foot should be round, straight, and open at the heel. The width at the heel allows room for the frog. The front feet support more of the horse's weight (about 60 percent). The hind feet are slightly elongated. This shape allows them to act as a power source for propulsion.

Figure 5.1:
The Horse's
Hoof

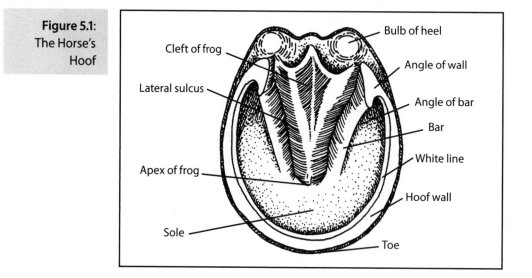

Cleft of frog
Lateral sulcus
Apex of frog
Sole
Bulb of heel
Angle of wall
Angle of bar
Bar
White line
Hoof wall
Toe

Hoof

The hoof is the horny covering of the foot, including the bars, sole, and frog. The hoof is non-vascular, which means it does not contain the blood supply. The hoof wall should be glossy and free of cracks and ridges. You should be able to draw an imaginary line down the center of the knee through the cannon bone through the middle of the hoof to the ground. The hoof should be of equal size on both sides of that line. When looking from the side, a line should follow the middle of the pastern, on a 45 degree angle to the ground.

The Corium

The sensitive structure of the foot is referred to as the corium. The corium is a vascular inner layer of tissue. The growth of the corium initiates at the coronary band, which is located where the hair of the leg meets the top of the hoof. It can be felt as soft and wax-like.

FACT

A hoof grows approximately one-fourth to one-half inch per month, with a little extra growth occurring in the spring and fall. It takes about nine to twelve months for a horse to grow a completely new hoof wall. So, a crack in the coronary band might take a year to grow out.

How the Hoof and Foot Bear Weight

The hoof wall, bars, and frog are considered weight-bearing structures of the foot. These must all work together for healthy hoof function. The elastic properties of the hoof allow it to absorb concussion. Moisture is also vital, because it too helps the foot remain elastic. The following list describes the parts of the hoof.

- **The Sole:** The sole is hard, slightly concave, and bears only a small amount of weight. Its main function is to protect the inner sensitive part of the foot.
- **The Frog:** The frog, the V-shaped portion of the hoof separated from the sole by the bars, is the circulatory receptor of the foot. It is made of a material called keratin, which is similar to what your nails are made of. When the frog makes contact with the ground, it acts as a pump, helping to recirculate blood back up the leg.
- **Bars:** The bars separate the frog from the sole and help to bear weight and concussion.

Hoof Angles

A horse's hooves are as individual as people's feet. They are naturally shaped according to a horse's conformation and whatever kind of work the breed of horse was meant for. However, there are general angles and shapes that can be assumed to apply to most horses.

Front hooves slope at about a 50 degree angle, while rear hooves slope at about 60 degrees. The pastern angle should be about the same as the angle of the front of the hoof. The distance to the ground of the coronary band on the front of the hoof (measured straight down) is twice the distance of the coronary band to the ground at the back of the foot. The hoof wall is thicker at the toe than at the heel.

Hoof Maintenance and Care

A healthy foot is the foundation for a healthy horse. Whether you choose to keep your horse shod or unshod, his feet must be cared for by a farrier every four to six weeks. It is of utmost importance that the horse's feet be level and balanced so that he can bear his weight evenly. Uneven feet will lead to favoring of one leg and can cause a range of soundness problems, not just in his feet, but throughout the horse. There is no good way for a horse to adequately rest his feet for any therapeutic duration of time, so care and prevention are that much more important.

Shoeing

Shoeing is not always necessary, but it does protect the hoof from wear and provides the hoof with a better grip on some surfaces. Shoes also protect a horse's foot from rocks or other objects on the trail or in turnout fields. These objects could cause bruises and abscesses that could put your horse out of service for up to a month. Shoes also give the horse's foot protection from cracks that can work their way up the hoof and cause eventual lameness.

Corrective Shoeing

If your horse has a congenital abnormality in his foot or has developed another kind of problem, corrective shoeing can make a tremendous difference. Good corrective shoeing can be the difference between a lame or sound horse. A good farrier can help a horse to have better balance, support, and movement by the way he trims and shoes your horse.

A horse that is used to having shoes will become extremely vulnerable to bruises and abscesses if he is suddenly made to go without them. Likewise, a horse that is used to going without shoes becomes inured to foot injuries. Hoof and sole toughening products can help harden the foot of a horse that goes without shoes.

No matter what type of hoof conformation your horse has, his hoof needs to be balanced. Corrective shoeing can help a horse with a conformation fault to be better balanced, but such changes should be subtle, not radical, which could adversely affect the entire limb. This is one reason to find a good farrier who will get to know your horse, and do a consistent job. Corrective shoeing will be discussed in detail in Chapter 6, Farrier Care and Natural Hoof Care.

Importance of Picking the Hoof

It is important to pick the hoof to make sure your horse didn't pick up a stone or sharp object while you were riding or in turnout and also to keep the hoof clean of debris. It is a good idea to scrub the sole, frog, bars, and heels once a month with betadine, and more often if your horse's stabling conditions are poor. This will help keep this most important part of your horse clean, healthy, and strong.

It is important to pick the foot after a ride to check for stones and pine shavings among other kinds of bedding which can have a drying effect on the hoof. However. it might be advantageous for your horse to retain the important moisture in the hoof by leaving his hoof packed with the dirt or mud he picked up on a ride or in turnout. This is a judgment call and is strongly dependent on your horse's hoof care needs.

Hoof picking also gives you a chance to inspect the foot and hoof for general health, which will be discussed further in this chapter. The only tool you need is a hoof pick, preferably with a brush on the end. To pick the hoof:

- Ask your horse for his foot or encourage him to give it to you by gently tugging or touching his cannon bone or fetlock. Shifting his weight onto the "off" foot will also incline him to give you the leg you are asking for.
- Start just in front of the bulb of the heel. Clean all debris from the hoof, the frog, and between the bar and the sole, otherwise referred to as the "cleft" of the foot. A pushing-out motion will give you more leverage than pulling in.
- With a stiff brush (often the pick is equipped with a brush), brush out the frog, the cleft of the frog, and any space where the shoe overextends toward the bulb of the heel, leaving a space between the shoe and the foot.
- Gently release the leg and move on to the back leg of the same side; repeat with each foot on the other side.

Pulling a Loose Shoe

A loose shoe can come off and potentially injure a horse. The clip on the shoe can be sharp and end up stabbing the horse in the sole of his foot or elsewhere. Also, nails used to keep the shoe on will remain on the shoe once it has come off or has partially come off, causing injury. Every barn should have a rasp, pullers, and nippers for pulling a shoe. How to remove a shoe:

- First, rasp the clinches, which are the nail heads visible on the outside of the hoof wall. This is necessary because they have been bent and so locked in place by the farrier.
- Next, pick up the foot, supporting the leg between your knees and supporting the hoof with one hand. Begin at the heel. With the nippers, remove one nail at a time from the bottom of the shoe. This will become easier as the shoe becomes looser.
- Finally, with the pullers, grasp the end of the shoe and pull down toward the toe, being careful to alternate sides, until the shoe is gradually loosened and freed from the hoof. If done properly, you will not lose any hoof in the process.

Hoof Oil

Since moisture conditions in the wild change gradually, a wild or pasture-kept horse almost never has trouble maintaining a good moisture balance in his hoof. A healthy hoof need not be artificially moisturized. Since the conditions we often keep horses under are variable, like bedding that can dry a hoof or a muddy paddock with nowhere else to go, it is sometimes necessary to use hoof oil. Hoof oil will moisturize the hoof and keep that moisture sealed in during constantly changing conditions. Hoof oil can be applied about three times per week depending on the needs of your horse.

Common Foot Conditions and Ailments

If you can recognize the signs of an oncoming foot problem, by catching it early you can potentially save your horse a full-blown injury, thus saving yourself time and money. However, the hoof is resilient and, if given time and care, can recover from most ailments.

Foot Abscesses

An abscess in the foot will be very painful to a horse and will usually cause dramatic lameness. Heat will usually be present in the foot as well, and if the abscess is close to the sole, a reddish bruise might be apparent.

An abscess will usually be caused by a horse stepping on a stone or anything that might cause a trauma to the foot. Applying pressure to different areas of the foot with a hoof tester can often pinpoint the area of infection.

Have your vet or blacksmith attempt to locate a soft area which, when trimmed, or dug out, will usually initiate draining. If a hole is left in the sole from this procedure, it will have to be kept clean and possibly packed with icthamol to continue to draw out the infection and keep debris from getting up into the sole. A horse might then need to wear a wrap or boot. The horse will instantly have relief in most cases. If no draining site can be found, removing the shoe and soaking the foot in Epsom salts is recommended. This will drain heat away from the foot and relieve excess pressure, hopefully opening a site to drain infection. Low doses of phenylbutazolidin (also called bute) might also be used. A poultice wrap can also draw out the infection and expedite healing.

Thrush

Thrush is a bacterial condition of the feet often caused by unsanitary environmental conditions. This condition will be more common in a horse that is kept in a stall rather than turned out. Some horses seem predisposed to thrush through the conformation of their feet or other sensitivities. Keeping the foot picked, cleaned on a daily basis, and dry, along with a good scrubbing monthly with betadine, will help to avoid this condition. Thrush is identified by a foul odor when picking the foot and the presence of black, sticky looking matter, often in the heel area or clefts of the foot.

Thrush can affect the frog, bars, and heel area of the foot. It is most often caused by unsanitary conditions in the stall or pasture. It is more common with stall-bound horses, rather than horses that are turned out most of the day or night, and is more common to horses with deep clefts.

Careful and thorough treatment of thrush is crucial. First, have a farrier remove any dead tissue on the frog. Scrub the frog and frog clefts vigorously with betadine. Once the foot is clean and dry, apply 4 percent iodine, diluted bleach solution, or any number of thrush medicines available to the frog, frog bars, and bulb. It won't hurt or help to get any on the sole of his foot, but don't get any on the hair or skin, because it will burn. If there are deep pockets in the frog or in the cleft of the bars, you can soak cotton in these medicines and pack the infected areas. A foot wrap will keep the packs in. The horse's stall should be kept clean and his feet picked out several times a day. Keep the foot clean and dry, so that healing can begin. The foot should be treated daily with medicine until improvement is seen. Rarely, infection can set into the foot, which must be treated by a veterinarian with antibiotics.

A daily routine of picking your horse's feet will not only promote a healthy foot and hoof, but will alert you to problems or pending problems of the foot. These problems could be thrush, which could be very easy to treat in its early stages, or a stone being held to the sole by mud or manure, which could cause a bruise.

Hoof Cracks

Cracks in the hoof, or quarter cracks, develop from several causes, but mainly from dry hoof walls. They can begin at the coronet band traveling downward or at the bottom of the horn and traveling up toward the coronet band. Quarter cracks do not necessarily make a horse lame, but quarter cracks that go above the coronet band can be big trouble.

There is very little you can do about a quarter crack once it occurs, except to prevent it from spreading. There are many hoof supplements that can be used to strengthen and improve your horse's foot if it is unhealthy. Most contain biotin, which also encourages hair growth. Consult with your veterinarian or farrier on what supplement to use. Hoof oil can also be applied to cracks to improve moisture. There are some tricks a farrier can perform on cracks to inhibit their migration, such as "notching" or "stapling." Eventually, in most cases, the crack will grow out without a trace.

Contracted Heels

A contracted heel develops over time and is usually caused by improper shoeing. It is defined by a narrowing of the bulb of the heel, with the frog becoming compromised, which causes shrinkage. Sometimes, the entire hoof will appear smaller. This condition doesn't necessarily cause lameness, but will surely limit the horse's activity. Quarter horses are genetically predisposed to this condition.

Is it better for a horse to have a black foot or a white one?
There is no positive evidence that the color of the hoof affects its quality. Often you will hear horsemen say a white hoof doesn't have the integrity of a black one. While it might be something to keep in the back of your mind, there is no factual basis for this common belief.

This condition can be improved and cured over time if the cause is improper shoeing. A good farrier will reopen the heel area over several shoeings to promote widening at the heel, thus allowing the frog to once again make contact with the ground. This will take up to a year, depending on the severity of the ailment.

Corns

A corn develops from repeated pressure on the small portion of the sole. Its cause is often improper shoeing or a shoe that is left on too long. A corn can be very painful, but will heal over time if recognized and the cause alleviated. Pads are recommended during the healing process. Corns aren't visible, unless an infection sets in and they begin to drain.

Bruised Sole

A bruise most often occurs somewhere on the sole, but can occur anywhere on the hoof. It is caused by trauma to the hoof. A horse could land on a stone in the wrong way, or a stone could get wedged between the shoe and hoof, and this could cause bruising. A farrier can also cause bruising by driving a nail too close to the "white line" on the hoof. Bruising will almost always cause lameness.

Initial treatment is to reduce pain with an anti-inflammatory medicine like phenylbutazolidin or bamamine. The shoe might have to be pulled off to administer further treatment. If heat is present in the hoof, cold hosing can be effective. Soaking the foot daily in Epson salts or the application of a poultice preparation to the hoof will eventually draw out an abscess. This is done by packing the hoof with poultice. A piece of cardboard roughly in the shape of the hoof will hold the poultice in place before you apply a foot wrap. This application should be changed every day. If the abscess is "shallow" or close to the sole, a farrier might be able to dig it out. This will leave a hole in the sole that must be packed with a medicine such as furacin or ichtamol to prevent infection. A cotton ball can then be used to fill the hole and kept in place with a foot wrap.

Laminitis/Founder

Laminitis, more commonly referred to as founder, is an extremely serious condition that requires prompt treatment for the best possible outcome. With founder, the sensitive laminae of the hoof become inflamed. In the early stages of founder, the horse will rock back onto his hind legs in an attempt to relieve pressure off the front feet (where it most likely occurs). As the disease progresses, he might refuse to walk or eat. Symptoms include heat at the coronary band and a strong pulse that can be felt at the ankle. The pain is often intense and will probably be accompanied by a sickly or stressed appearance.

Early detection can prevent extensive and irreversible death of laminae tissue. If laminae tissue is damaged like this, the foot will not be able to support the coffin bone, resulting in the downward rotation of that bone. If discovered too late or left untreated, permanent damage to the supporting structure of the foot will result. This can often mean the end of a horse's usefulness and/or the beginning of a chronic condition.

Early Warning Signs

The onset of laminitis will cause extreme pain to your horse's feet. Usually, it is the front feet that are affected, but it is not unheard of in the hind feet. Your horse will rock back onto his hind legs in an exaggerated pose, attempting to remove all weight off the front feet. He will be reluctant to walk and might even lie down. He might show further signs of pain such as sweating, rapid breathing, and he could possibly run a temperature. The feet will be very warm to the touch and a strong pulse can be felt in the digital artery, located over the fetlock joint.

FACT

Arteries run down either side of the leg and can be seen on the inside and outside of the fetlock. To feel for a horse's "digital pulse," place two fingers on either one of these arteries. A strong throbbing is an indication that there is a problem in the foot, since inflammation will cause constriction of blood vessels. On a healthy horse, this pulse is steady and barely noticeable.

Possible Causes

Laminitis can be a secondary sickness, occurring after surgery, a major illness, or from a high temperature. But the most common causes of laminitis are:

- **Grain Founder:** 90 percent of all founder is grain founder. It is an ingestion of above normal, spoiled, or a different type of grain than a horse is used to. This is common when a horse gets loose overnight and gets into the feed room. Like a dog, a horse will eat himself sick. However, unlike a dog, the horse cannot vomit to relieve himself.
- **Water Founder:** Laminitis can be triggered by ingestion of water when a horse is still hot from exercise. This is common when an overworked horse that has lost a lot of electrolytes through excessive sweating is immediately placed back in a paddock or stall with water available to him.
- **Grass Founder:** This is caused by ingestion of too much rich pasture or legume hay, such as alfalfa. This is common in the spring, when horses that have been without any grass all winter are indiscriminately placed on pasture or paddock grass instead of being slowly acclimated to this feed. Also, rich second cut legume hay should be mixed with grass hay, at least until the horse is used to it.

- **Road Founder:** This is less common, but occurs by repeated and excessive pounding on a hard surface for long distances. City bound horses, such as police and carriage horses, are subject to road founder.

Treatment

Time is of the essence and often determines whether laminitis will be cured or will become chronic. A veterinarian should be called out at any sign of possible founder. In all cases, grain should be removed from the horse's diet. Oils can be given orally to purge the system of toxins. Removing the shoes and soaking the feet in ice water every twenty minutes can relieve some of the pain and swelling. An anti-inflammatory should be administered. Forcing the horse to walk in short intervals can also help to increase blood flow to the foot and hoof, as will medications such as isocsoprene. If founder is caught within the first twenty-four hours, administering antihistamines can be enormously beneficial, since founder is caused by a release of histamines that are ever present in the bloodstream of a horse. A horse with chronic laminitis can benefit from corrective shoeing and can remain "pasture sound" or serviceably sound for many years. Ponies are particularly sensitive to laminitis.

Navicular

Navicular is considered to be more of a disease than an ailment. It is defined as a degenerative and inflammatory condition that affects the surface of the navicular bone. The navicular bone is situated between the deep-flexor tendon and the coffin bone and acts as a fulcrum between the two. Lack of blood flow accompanies degeneration of this bone and the surrounding deep-flexor tendon and navicular bursa, which is the space between the bone and tendon, creating channels throughout the bone. Most often, it will affect the front feet, causing lameness in varying degrees. A navicular horse might walk short strided, stabbing the ground with his front feet, to avoid putting pressure on the back part of the foot where the navicular bone is located.

Perhaps the best thing you can do for a horse with navicular, after finding the right medicine or combination of medicines, is to keep her fit and active. This is good medicine that will help to keep any horse healthy in body, mind, and spirit.

The jury is still out on how navicular develops. It occurs quite frequently to some degree in all breeds, and some researchers think that it might be genetic. Some horses, primarily quarter horses, do have a high rate of occurrence of navicular. However, this might be more on account of down hill conformation and feet that are often too small for their bodies. Large horses, particularly finer-boned warm bloods, also are disposed to this disease. There is no cure for this disease, but it can be managed quite efficiently.

Symptoms

Early symptoms of navicular are sometimes hard to notice. A shortening of stride might warn of navicular. A horse in a more acute stage of navicular might stab the ground with his front feet when he walks, trying to relieve pressure on the back of the foot where the navicular bone resides. Heat from inflammation might or might not be present. It is typical for a navicular horse to start her exercise routine very sore on her front feet, perhaps tripping at first, but after a few minutes "warm out" of this soreness and perform like any other horse.

Managing Navicular

Just because your horse has navicular doesn't mean that he can't lead an active life. New farrier techniques and more sophisticated and precise medicines have made great advances in improving the quality of life for a horse with this disease.

There is no cure for navicular, but supportive care can usually keep a horse at least serviceably sound. This might include anti-inflammatory medicines, corrective shoeing, cortisone injections into the joint or surrounding joints, and/or medication to increase blood flow and cartilage growth in the foot. Radiographs must be taken to confirm a diagnosis. As a last resort, a vet might recommend a neurectomy. This is the severing of a part of the nerve that services the foot.

Corrective Shoeing

There are differing theories on corrective trimming and shoeing for the navicular horse. Bar shoes are standard, giving extra support to the back of the foot. A farrier might trim more toe and leave more heel, promoting extra cushion and an easier "break over" point at the toe. However, some farriers believe that a healthy foot is the key to navicular relief and that the best way to achieve a healthy foot is through corrective trimming, while the horse goes without shoes. There is no harm in experimenting, but in the end, whatever works for your particular horse is the answer. The best thing you might be able to do for your navicular horse is to keep him fit and otherwise healthy.

Medicines

Phenylbutazolidin, or "bute," is an anti-inflammatory that can give relief from swelling and soreness and might be all your horse needs to stay sound. Isocsoprene promotes blood flow to the navicular area, where lack of blood flow can often be the primary cause of lameness. Joint lubricants, usually involving glucosamine and chondroitin, help to relieve the soreness that is caused when cartilage is worn away between the navicular bone and the coffin joint. Cortisone injections into the coffin joint are often very effective and can last up to a year. But scar tissue will eventually build up where the needle goes in, making the injection into the coffin joint increasingly hard to give and possibly causing other problems. Also, advanced erosion of the joint spaces can make continuous injections difficult.

FACT

A neurectomy is a procedure that has been improved greatly in recent years. In the past, the nerves that were cut would sometimes grow back, which could be very painful to the horse. New technology prevents this from happening. This operation can add years of productive life to your severely navicular horse.

Nerving (Neurectomy)

When none of these treatments work, a last resort might be to cut the nerves to sensitive areas of the foot, so that the horse no longer feels the pain associated with the disease. Although the technology in this procedure has advanced greatly in the last several years, complications can occur, and you must be extra vigilant about foot care for the nerved horse, because he can no longer detect injury to certain parts of his foot.

Chapter 6

Farrier Care and Natural Hoof Care

Along with a veterinarian and a trainer for your horse, a farrier will be the most important professional you will need to hire. A healthy horse starts with a healthy foot, and a healthy foot depends on a smart, skilled, dependable, careful, and conscientious farrier. Along with choosing a farrier, you will also have to determine if your horse is better off with conventional metal shoes or barefoot, when he is due for shoes or trimming, and what kind of setup will suit him best.

Finding a Farrier

Like any profession, there are great farriers, for whom shoeing and trimming a horse's feet is an art that they take pride in; adequate farriers, who will get the job done, but might not be able to recognize the subtleties and nuances of every horse's foot; and poor farriers, who just don't know or care enough to do a good job. Finding one in your area might or might not be a challenge, depending on the concentration of horses. Determining the quality of your farrier once he has begun to shoe your horse will be another hurdle to making sure the horse has the best hoof and foot care possible.

Ask a Professional

Your vet might be the best person to ask for a referral. Vets are usually the least biased professional in the horse business, and they have the most diverse knowledge of who is shoeing in your area. Chances are, your vet will know if a local farrier is inconsistent or unknowledgeable. The vet might have been called on to diagnose and doctor the farrier's mistakes in the neighborhood.

Other horse or barn owners can also refer you to their farrier. He might be tried and true, but always get second and third references from others who use him.

Special Needs

If your horse has special shoeing or trimming requirements, you might want to locate a farrier who is known for shoeing horses with that particular special need. A navicular horse, for instance, will be better off being shoed by a farrier who has a lot of experience with this disease and who has had more successes than failures. A horse that suffers from the aftermath of laminitis might need corrective shoeing for the rest of his life. A farrier who has a lot of experience with such a horse can greatly improve the quality of his life.

The Farrier's Qualifications

Before you let a farrier work on your horse, find out what his qualifications are. Many young farriers these days are educated in schools to be farriers, while the majority of older farriers learned through apprenticeship. Formally educated farriers are usually enthusiastic for this profession and have an aptitude for it, which should make them good farriers. It also means that they are up to date on all the new technology that science and greater communication can provide in these rapidly changing times. Most farriers begin their careers with some form of apprenticeship. There is no substitute for the experience and tricks of the trade that get handed down from training through apprenticeships.

Shoeing is not a science, but rather an art. A good farrier looks at the whole horse, his conformation, and how he travels before he develops a shoeing plan for your horse. As he gets to know your horse, he can make subtle variations toward perfection.

When to Call Your Farrier

It might be up to you to determine when or how often your horse needs to be shoed or trimmed. Change in weather and varying terrain might mean that your horse can go longer than the standard six weeks before he needs to be attended to by a farrier or that your horse might need to be seen every month. There are certain telltale signs that your horse is ready for a trim or new shoes.

QUESTION?

How do I know when my horse needs new shoes or a hoof trimming?
The hoof of an average, healthy horse will grow a little faster in the spring and summer months, so you might want to call your farrier out every five or six weeks. Excessively muddy or wet conditions might also warrant early shoeing or trimming. Such conditions will make the hoof prone to bacteria, which trimming can ameliorate.

Six Weeks, Plus or Minus

Six weeks is the standard amount of time that a horse can wear shoes or go without trimming. Hoof growth is determined by your horse's diet, his environment, and the amount of exercise he is subject to. If your horse's exercise is primarily in a sand ring, this will do little to naturally file down the hoof, in contrast to when he is turned out or ridden in rocky or various terrain. This is a more natural environment, and the reason why horses in the wild can maintain healthy feet without shoes. Biotin, administered as a food supplement, will promote hoof growth as well as hoof health.

ALERT!

Quicking a horse is a term used when a shoeing nail is improperly driven into the white line and sensitive laminae of the foot. This will result in pain and lameness. The shoe will have to be removed. A "close nail" is when a nail comes close to the sensitive laminae, causing discomfort and pressure. The shoe should also be removed and first aid administered.

After six weeks, the foot grows "long," over the edges of the shoe, mostly in front. This can lead to problems such as stumbling, lameness, and your horse throwing a shoe in work or turnout. A foot that is used to shoes will not be tempered to rough terrain and might incur a stone bruise or other lameness when the horse throws a shoe. Also, a shoe might only partially come off and end up damaging the foot or stabbing the sole of the foot, which is a relatively common cause of injury. A contracted heel or foot is another sickness related to leaving shoes on too long.

Signs That Your Horse Is Overdue

Your horse will probably tell you in several different ways when she is overdue for shoes or trimming. The edges of her hoof might chip and crack just as your fingernails and toenails are susceptible to breakage when they get long.

FACT

The feet of some gaited horses, such as Tennessee walkers, are kept long on purpose. A longer foot tends to animate the gait in the same way that wearing flippers on the beach would give you a higher, more exaggerated step. This is desirable for the show ring and can also help a horse that is otherwise sloppy or inconsistent in his gait.

She might trip and stumble, especially at the walk or trot. The dynamics of a horse's locomotion warrant a natural "break over" point at the foot for natural, fluid movement. Some farriers encourage this by curbing the shoe slightly up around the toe. Long toes impede the break over and make it somewhat difficult if not uncomfortable for her to travel.

Harmful Preparation of Hoof for Shoes

Leaving too much heel or not enough heel when a farrier prepares the hoof for shoes can ruin the entire hoof mechanism by altering the angle at which the coffin bone is stressed. For a healthy hoof, the coffin bone must be "ground parallel," so that it receives even distribution of the weight of the horse. If the heel is left too high, the digital artery can get pinched, blocking blood flow and sensation to the hoof.

Shoes with Studs

Studs or caulks are cleats of various sizes that are permanently fixed to the shoe of your horse or temporarily screwed in for extra traction in wet, muddy, or icy field conditions. They are a necessary addition to shoes for serious field riding like fox hunting or eventing, but can have their drawbacks as well.

Why and When to Use Studs

It doesn't take much for a horse to trip and fall in certain conditions. Serious injuries to you and your horse can occur from a slip or fall, especially with bigger, less agile horses like warm bloods that are more prone to slipping and injury. When your horse slips and falls, you might not get thrown from the point of accident, but rather end up underneath the horse, which is more dangerous.

Horses can wear studs on all four feet, just the front feet, or just the back feet. Be consistent, however, and never put studs only on the one foot that might be unsound and the one he's slipping on. Also, be sure to check before you ride that none of the studs in his shoe has broken off, which will make for an uneven ride, and perhaps a lame horse.

Even a surface as seemingly benign as a field of grass before the morning dew has evaporated can be as slippery as ice for certain horses. Winter ice can form on roads and trails as well or can be just below the surface of snow or rainwater. In winter and spring of colder climates, a sunny day will sometimes thaw the top layer of ground, while just below the surface the ground is frozen or icy. Mud can also be very slippery. Studs can help prevent your horse from slipping and falling in these conditions. Studs can help your horse during turnout as well, if your paddock slopes or gets very icy in the wintertime.

When Studs Can Be Detrimental

While studs can be essential in certain conditions to prevent slipping and falling, they do slightly impede a horse's natural step. A horse naturally slides forward for shock absorption when his foot hits the ground, which is especially important when he is coming to a stop from a trot or canter. At the stop, a horse's front feet will slide about one-half inch, thus limiting the shock to the front feet and legs, where most of the burden of weight and concussion is.

Studs also focus the weight and concussion of a horse somewhat on those two points of a horse's foot, rather than promoting a distribution of weight over the whole surface area of the foot. In consistently soft ground this is less so, but if your turnout is hard, your field conditions are hard, or you do a lot of riding on roads (even dirt roads), then over time studs might have a detrimental effect on your horse's foot. This is especially true of horses with existing foot ailments or diseases like navicular, contracted heels, or chronic laminitis.

FACT

Most horses can wear permanent studs through the winter in colder climates without experiencing any lameness as a result. If you find that your horse requires studs in other seasons, then screw-in studs should be used. These studs can be put in for your ride and then taken out. However, the process of putting in and taking out studs can be time consuming and back breaking.

Shoes with Pads

Pads are made of plastic or leather and are used between the foot and the shoe for protection of the sole of the foot. "Snowball pads" prevent snow from balling up in the foot. Various other pads can give extra lift to the foot of a horse to exaggerate or encourage his gait or relieve pressure to the heel of the foot for corrective shoeing.

Protection of the Sole

In particularly rocky regions of the country or if your horse has very sensitive feet, he might benefit from protective pads. Pads on the front feet only will usually suffice. They can prevent lameness from stone bruises and provide extra cushion against concussion.

Snowball Pads

Snowball pads protect the sole as well, but also serve to prevent snow from accumulating in the bottom of the foot during rides and turnout. The center of the pad is a slightly raised, hollow bubble that compresses upon contact with the ground, acting to pop out any snow that's in the foot when the horse's weight is off the foot, and then the bubble returns to its normal, convex position.

Possible Negative Effects of Pads

Like with most equipment, medicines, or work regimes, different horses will react differently to having pads on their feet over time. There is no way to pick or clean the foot if debris gets between the pad and the foot. Some horses might develop thrush. When your farrier comes to give your horse new shoes and pads, he will tell you if the foot is healthy or if your horse's feet might need special attention or thrush preventative care. He might need to go without pads for a shoeing or two. Most horses do fine however, wearing pads throughout the year.

A barefoot horse will have no trouble with snow retention. It is the shoe that creates a hollow area in the foot that traps snow. Snowball pads might be ineffective on a horse that wears bar shoes, which, unlike regular horse shoes, make a full circle around the foot. A larger diameter bubble in the pad might help. Cooking spray on the pad before a ride might also help to keep snow out of the foot.

Pads and shoes protect the foot. However, over time, this protection can actually weaken the foot. Just as our skin develops calluses in places where it is constantly in contact with rougher surfaces, a horse's sole and hoof also harden when left unprotected. If your horse is used to shoes or pads and must go without for some reason, then iodine applied regularly to the hoof and sole of the foot can toughen those areas.

Natural Hoof Care

Natural hoof care describes a system of hoof care that relies on special trimming techniques to promote hoof and horse health, instead of using metal shoes. Developed by Hiltrud Strasser, a German veterinarian, it is thought of as a relatively new idea. The technique is about thirteen years old in Europe and has been stirring controversy in America among vets and farriers for about five years. While many horse owners in this country and around the world never use metal shoes on their horses and swear by the integrity and function of a natural hoof, metal shoes have been commonly used for about 1,000 years.

Horse cultures in the late centuries B.C. and early centuries of the first millennium used horses for all manner of work and war mongering, covering great distances in various climates and terrain. From the ancient Hittites' famous chariot horses, to Xenophon in the fourth century B.C., to Alexander the Great, and for the duration of the Roman Empire, there is no mention of metal shoes in the ancient historical texts, and curiously no mention of the common foot ailments that became a factor when metal shoes were introduced to the world.

FACT

Saucy Night, a Steeplechase racehorse once described as having the worst form in England, went on to win at Folkestone immediately after his trainer put him on the barefoot program. His trainer said his physical, emotional, and mental states were drastically improved.

The premise for natural hoof care over metal shoes is basically that the preparation of the hoof for shoes ruins the natural architecture of the foot. The addition of metal shoes then causes a further breakdown of hoof strength, blood flow to the foot, and natural shock absorption, leading to lameness and disease in the horse. This in conjunction with the unnatural conditions in which many horses are kept contribute to the lameness, ailments, and diseases in horses that we consider to be common and acceptable, yet need not be. Natural hoof care is a holistic approach to horse health, strengthening the immune system and rehabilitating the foot from degenerative ailments and disease such as navicular, founder, ring bone, and contracted hoof. Natural hoof care can be utilized for any kind of horse and for any discipline of riding.

Advantages of Natural Hoof Care

The hoof of a horse is naturally designed to absorb most of the shock and concussion that he receives. An elastic hoof capsule expands upon contact with the ground. As well, the frog on a natural hoof will make contact with the ground. Both actions serve to absorb shock and as a pump to circulate blood back up the horse's leg all the way to his heart. Proponents of natural hoof care consider the hoof of a horse to be a second heart, as it functions in very much the same way—to pump blood through this large and rangy animal. The horse's actual heart is relatively small for its size and mass.

Problems with Metal Shoes

Not only does a metal shoe artificially protect the foot and prevent its natural toughening, which actually weakens the foot, but it inhibits the natural shock absorption of the elastic hoof by an estimated eighty percent. The rest of the horse's body, specifically his joints and spine, must then absorb excess shock that they were not meant to deal with.

Some riders who have switched their horse over to natural hoof care say that their horses are much more comfortable to ride because the natural hoof absorbs the concussion of locomotion. Otherwise, the concussion is absorbed by other parts of the horse's body that were not made for shock absorption and by the rider's body.

A metal shoe likewise prevents the proper blood flow to the foot by inhibiting the frog. This in turn reduces the flow of oxygen to the foot, which makes for inferior tissue growth. Not only does inferior tissue growth over time weaken the foot, but the weakened or diseased foot will have trouble healing without the proper blood flow to that area.

A horse's traction will be compromised with metal shoes. On smooth, icy, or slick surfaces, he won't have enough traction, while on softer surfaces, he might have too much. Metal shoes do not allow for a small degree of slide that is necessary for shock absorption.

Nails driven into the hoof wall to fasten metal shoes to the hoof can damage the integrity of the hoof wall over time and cause dehydration of the white line horn, as well as compromise the hoof's natural insulation by conducting cold into the foot. The nails also might allow for bacteria, fungus, or dirt to enter with the nail and get deep inside the hoof wall. The metal shoe and nails also conduct vibration up into the foot like a tuning fork, which can negatively affect the horn and corium, and lead to compromised coffin bone suspension.

FACT

The technology of protective boots for horses has come a long way in recent years and can substitute for a metal shoe or a weak foot. You might want to use them when you ride while your horse is making her transition from metal shoes to natural hoof care or to support her feet even after she has made the transition.

The tactics farriers use to aid a horse that has a pre-existing foot disease such as navicular or laminitis might help in the short run, but might only cause more damage down the line. Bar shoes, which make a full circle around the hoof rather than a three-quarter circle, will give extra support to the heel and area under the navicular and coffin bone, but will also cause further nerve damage in that area. Pads will provide artificial protection to the sole, but prevent the sole from getting tough so that it can do its job to protect the foot.

Unnatural Conditions

Another tenet of natural hoof care is that the health of a horse's hooves depends on the conditions under which she is kept. Horses have evolved in and adapted to some of the most extreme and various climates in the world. Yet the environments they are kept in as domestic animals, while seeming to be kind, often can be unnatural and unhealthy, especially for the foot of a horse.

Horses are grazing animals, which means that their physical and mental well-being depends on constant movement and gradual eating habits.

Confining a horse to a stall prevents this necessity, and for some horses might cause sickness or disease. Rich food in the form of grains and cereals can create unnatural concentrations of toxins in the horse's body, which can cause difficulty in the horse's gut and feet especially.

If a horse is kept in a stall, he is limited in movement and exercise. A wild horse will range on average about twenty miles per day. Bedding can also be too soft and unnaturally dry the hoof. A horse confined in a stall might be standing in the bacteria of his urine and feces, which can weaken the hoof.

In the winter when nutrition is scarcer, a naturally kept horse, meaning one that is wild or turned out to pasture, will shed body fat. This is a natural and healthy process of detoxification that horses undergo if left to their natural devices. So, a horse coming into the spring should be lean.

In the wild, horses travel over various terrains, so if the domestic horse's only exercise is in a soft sand ring or on hard pavement, then his hoof will neither get the wear it needs nor the varied footing it needs for proper circulation. The hoof needs concussion on hard surfaces to stimulate circulation for the production of healthy hoof tissue and healthy cartilage, ligaments, tendons, and bones. Likewise, paddocks can be uniformly dry and hard or wet and muddy, leaving the horse no choice or variation of footing as he would encounter in the wild.

Chapter 7

Most Common Ailments

Horses are typically very hardy animals. Their successful adaptation over time is a testament to the kinds of conditions and situations they can thrive in. However, modern-day horses are often asked to live and perform very differently from their wild counterparts. This change has attributed to a host of ailments and conditions we now consider to be common. Also, selective breeding has predisposed certain horses and breeds to ailments that were seldom experienced in the horse's past.

Fever

Fever is not an ailment in itself, but rather an indication that your horse might be fighting off an ailment or be otherwise in distress. Some horses will let you know right away when they are running a temperature. They might hang their head, refuse to eat (especially grain), and generally look pathetic. A horse running a high fever might lie down and breathe heavily and rapidly. On the other hand, some horses are "stoic," not showing any outward sign of the temperature they are running, or for that matter, any sickness until it becomes dire. Discomfort would usually show up in such a horse when asked to work, however.

ALERT!

Before inserting a thermometer in the horse's anus, make sure to lubricate it with a water-based lubricant. Also, tie a string to the end of the thermometer so that it doesn't disappear in there.

Fever should not be ignored, nor is it a reason to panic. The normal temperature for a horse ranges from 99.5 to 101.5 degrees. You should know if your horse when healthy is on the high side of normal or the low side. As mentioned above, the horse's temperature is taken with a thermometer in the anus. Generally, a horse with a slight fever should be isolated from other horses, given rest, and allowed to rebound without medication. A fever of 102 degrees or higher requires a call to your vet, and fever reducing medication such as banamine might be indicated.

Upper Respiratory Ailments

Whenever your horse is stressed due to changes in routine such as moving to a new stable, travel, or the stress of competition, his immune response might become compromised, opening the door to respiratory distress. Respiratory ailments are often accompanied by a dry or moist cough, a fever, and lethargy. Rest, fever reducing medication, and administration of a cough expectorant might be indicated. Occasionally broad-spectrum antibiotics, such as

Sulfathiazole, commonly known as SMZ tablets, will also be recommended for five days to two weeks.

Heaves

Heaves can be defined as the horse's inability to empty his lungs of air. It is considered a disease of the respiratory system and has no cure. It is thought to develop from reaction to mold, dusty living situations, or the effects of consistent hard work on a horse that hasn't had the proper conditioning.

Once a horse has heaves, supportive care is the only treatment you can offer, along with a dust and mold free environment. A pasture or full turnout situation is better than a stall environment. In mild cases, his hay can be soaked with water to remove any dust. In more severe cases, hay should be eliminated from his diet, and a complete feed given instead. Medications called bronchial dilators can also be successful in treating the horse with heaves. Clenbuterol is one such product that has been very beneficial and can be obtained only from your veterinarian.

Laryngeal Hemiplegia (Roaring)

This condition might be hereditary. Roaring is a dorsal displacement of the soft palate, a collapse of the pharyngeal walls, or laryngeal semi-paresis. The wasting away or paralysis of the cricoarytenoid muscle causes the "roaring noise" or whistling associated with the condition. It is important to determine the exact cause for the noise that is heard during exercise, since not all horses that make a noise will have airway obstruction. However, some horses with this condition will have a partial blockage, limiting the amount of air being allowed into the lungs during strenuous exercise. This condition usually develops in horses between the ages of two and seven and is seen more in the larger breeds. As stated, initial symptoms are a noise during strenuous exercise with or without poor performance. There might be a change in the neigh of the horse, and he might have a slight cough.

Proper diagnosis is the first step to determining the best way to treat this condition. This is done by your vet with an endoscope. If there is no airway obstruction, often no treatment is recommended. For the horse that has exercise intolerance and obvious obstruction that limits the air intake, surgery is often recommended. This procedure ties back the paralyzed muscle so that it cannot collapse into the airway.

As with so many health issues that can confront the horse owner, a determining factor of accurate and timely care is how well you know your horse when he is healthy, so that you can recognize when he is not.

Gastric Ulcers

Gastric ulcers are an irritation and ulceration of the lining of the stomach. Some studies suggest that ulcers can be hereditary. Foals and young horses are particularly susceptible to ulcers; however, any horse under stressful conditions, especially hot tempered and nervous horses, can develop ulcers. Post-surgical horses are also candidates for ulcers.

A horse that has developed ulcers might grind his teeth and act colicky. He might paw the ground or lie down and attempt to roll on his back to relieve discomfort. A full-blown ulcer can be extremely painful for a horse. She might suddenly throw herself down on the ground, so be careful working around a horse suffering from an active ulcer.

FACT

Some ailments are related to a horse's breeding. For example, thoroughbreds more than any other horse are disposed to suffer from colic, while certain gaited horses will be prone to diseases and breakdown of the hock.

Initial treatment is to relieve the pain that she is in. Medications are available to relieve symptoms and aid in the healing of ulcers, such as "gastro guard" which coats the stomach. A horse that suffers from ulcers might be prone to them, so long-term treatment and preventative care should be prescribed by a vet.

Leg Ailments

Horses are particularly susceptible to ailments and injuries of their bones and joints, especially in the long and sensitive leg area. These are some of the more common leg ailments you are likely to see in your horse.

Wind Puffs

This is a broad term used to describe swelling at the back of the cannon bone or ankle area. Wind puffs are usually seen after hard work or after the horse is stalled for a period of time, such as overnight. The swelling is leakage of synovial fluid, which distends the leg. This condition is not serious and usually produces no heat. The condition can be helped or alleviated with standing bandages or an alcohol rubdown of the legs until swelling disperses.

Splints

Splints refer to a condition where new bone growth is laid down after trauma or irritation that results from work stress or faulty conformation. Splints can be found in the front or hind cannon bones. Protein load might also predispose a young horse to develop a splint. Splints are most prevalent in young developing horses. The location of a splint is important in determining the severity of the problem. A high splint, one located close to the knee joint, might cause permanent lameness. Most splints, however, once treated and cooled will not cause lameness and are considered a blemish. Splints are identified by heat and swelling located between the second and third, or third and fourth, metacarpal bone. To confirm diagnosis and rule out a fracture of the splint bone, radiographs are a good idea.

About a month of rest is recommended, depending on the severity of the splint. The goal is to remove the heat from the area. Wrapping with a pressure bandage can reduce the swelling and injection of a corticosteroid will often reduce the amount of new bone growth.

Ring Bone

Ring bone is an inflammatory condition of the pastern and can affect any part of the joint surface. Often, it is caused by trauma, but poor conformation predisposes a horse to develop the chronic inflammation that leads to new bone growth. For example, a horse with short, upright pasterns will be a candidate for ring bone due to constant stress on the ankle. Symptoms are heat, swelling, and lameness. A diagnosis must be made by radiograph. If left untreated, permanent arthritis and lameness will result.

In the early stages of ring bone, a corticoid steroid can be injected into the affected area. Recuperation is slow, and any growth of new bone layer is permanent.

Hock Problems

Soreness in the hocks is quite common in performance horses due to the stress of jumping or collective work. There are conditions of the hock that can result in permanent blemish without lameness. There are also conditions that lead to arthritis and permanent damage to the joint.

Capped Hock

This is bursitis located at the point of the hock caused by trauma, often from a horse that kicks the wall of his stall or other unforgiving surfaces. Another cause might be getting up from a sitting position off a hard surface. If treated promptly with cold hosing, salve, and possible bandaging, this condition can heal quickly. If not treated aggressively, fibrous tissue will form, and a blemish will remain at the site. In most cases, a capped hock will not cause lameness.

Stringhalt

Stringhalt is an involuntary over flexion of one or both hocks. It doesn't cause pain or swelling. The condition will be more noticeable when the horse first leaves his stall after rest. Stringhalt results from lesions that develop on the articular surface of the hock or on nerves in the hock area. This condition can be treated surgically.

Bone Spavin

Bone spavin is a term used to describe arthritis in the joint spaces of the hock. In advanced cases, the joint spaces will fill in with bone, and the affected joint will fuse. This fusion will normally alleviate pain associated with spavin, but the hock will be less elastic. Early treatment would include reduction of pain and swelling and an increase in rest until inflammation decreases. In the early stages, a horse will often leave her stall stiff, but will eventually work out of the stiffness within ten minutes or so. Swelling and pain are prevalent. Spavin is easily seen as lameness in the hock when the horse jogs off.

FACT

Spavin is inheritable, and certain breeds and type of conformation, such as sickled or cow-hocked horses, will be more inclined to develop spavin. There is a diagnostic test for spavin that a vet can perform, which consists of hock flexion for a few minutes, then jogging the horse out of the flex position.

Many treatments are used to lessen the discomfort of spavin, such as joint injection and anti-inflammatory drugs. Occasionally, surgical fusion of the joint is recommended. This will often return the horse to usefulness. Eventually the hock will fuse on its own anyway, but this could take up to a year or longer.

Upward Fixation of the Patella (Stifle)

This occurs when the horse's patella catches on the medial condyle of the femur. This locks the leg in extension. It is often noticed as a hitching of the hind leg when the horse moves. Straight hind leg conformation can predispose a horse to this condition. Trauma to the hind leg can also be a cause.

If the condition is not severe, for example, the catching of the patella is partial, the veterinarian might suggest that the owner give the horse time to recover. This would include a regime of very light trotting daily on level ground. To keep a horse with this condition stalled would only make him stiffer. Light work could strengthen the patella and relieve the condition. A veterinarian could sedate the horse and attempt to snap the patella back in place. Startling the horse into moving quickly backward might also snap the patella back into place. For severe cases, or if the leg is locked in extension, surgery is recommended. The procedure is called a patellar desmotomy.

Back Soreness

The causes of pain along the horse's back vary greatly. Pain can result from an ill-fitting saddle, too much work, the stress of jumping, collection, or an unbalanced rider. Whatever the cause, the horse should be rested while the cause of his problem is discovered. A sore back can make a horse uncomfortable throughout his body and can therefore lead to secondary injuries. You might be able to find the point of soreness, and from that the cause by running your hand down either side of the spine from wither to rump with even pressure. But it is very difficult to locate the exact point of soreness. X-rays are helpful, but because of the thickness of the horse's back muscles and the depth of his body, they have imperfect results. Often, as a horse gets on in years, the bones of the spine, especially in the lumbar region, tend to fuse together. This process can cause her pain until the fusion is complete.

A sacroiliac injury occurs at the junction of the backbone and the pelvis. They are most common in large horses with weakened hind quarters from lack of conditioning, improper riding, poor conformation, or old age.

A vet, horse masseur, or acupuncturist can in most cases determine the source of the problem and speed healing. A slow return to work, once the horse is feeling better, is wise. Horse acupuncture will be discussed further in Chapter 11, Alternative Health Care.

Colic

Colic refers to intestinal upset accompanied by pain. A vet should be called in all cases of colic. This ailment can come on suddenly and should always be considered a serious threat to your horse's health. The two most common types of colic are gas colic and impaction colic. An impaction is when digested matter builds up somewhere in the intestine but is not passing through and out as manure. Gas colic is just as it sounds. The symptoms of colic are:

- Repeated rolling or pawing the ground
- Sweating
- Loss of interest in surroundings
- Loss of appetite
- Pale gums
- Depressed demeanor, glazed over eyes
- Rapid pulse
- Kicking at belly with hind leg
- Looking back at belly

A "twisted gut" is a cause of colic or a complication of other forms of colic brought about by rolling. It occurs when a portion of the small intestine becomes wrapped around itself, forming a twist. In such cases, the blood supply becomes cut off, or "strangulated," producing pain and possible shock. Intestinal strangulation requires surgery. If the problem isn't corrected within six to eight hours, that portion of the bowel must be permanently removed.

Steps Toward Treatment

After a vet is summoned, the horse owner should attempt to keep the horse as quiet as possible. Any feed and hay should be removed from the stall. If possible the horse should be kept standing, as repeated rolling can cause the intestines to twist. An agitated horse should be walked for short intervals until a vet arrives. Based on your description of the horse's condition, a vet might recommend that you medicate the horse for pain reduction with a low dose of banamine until the vet can get to you. Occasionally, your veterinarian might suggest a tranquilizer such as Ace promazine if the horse is in danger of hurting itself. With colic the choice of drugs is important, because some medications that suppress a horse's system can complicate matters.

ALERT!

It is a common belief among amateur horse owners that a horse that is colicking should be given banamine. Banamine is an anti-inflammatory as well as a smooth muscle relaxer, which includes the gut muscles. Depending on the kind of colic your horse is suffering from, a relaxation of his gut muscles could be fatal. This is a prescribed medicine. Leave it up to a vet.

When the vet arrives, he might determine the colic to be benign and just ask you to keep a close eye on the horse, make sure he doesn't roll, and keep track of his manure piles, or lack of them. The vet will want to know about the horse's manure piles so he can determine what kind of colic the horse suffers from and how severe it might be. Depending on the symptoms, he might give the horse a rectal examination. This will give the vet an indication of the condition of the intestines, and he will be able to see if fecal matter is present. He will listen for gut sounds, take the horse's pulse, and check his gums. He might pass a stomach tube and administer mineral oil in an attempt to get food moving. If dehydration is suspected, fluids might be administered. He will administer medication for pain relief as well.

A colicky horse must be watched even after symptoms seem to subside. Colic can often reoccur within twenty-four hours.

Causes of Colic

Worms are the most common cause of colic. Poor feed, moldy hay, stress, confinement in a stall without the ability to move around, abrupt changes in diet, improper cooling after work, and allowing a horse that is hot from exercise to gulp water or eat grain are some other common causes.

FACT

Sand colic is an impaction that is caused from ingestion of sand. It is most prevalent when horses are fed their hay on sandy soil or riding rings. Paddock rotation is a good deterrent, as well as hay nets or hay barrels. Product feed supplements that are specifically meant to prevent sand colic can also help.

Melanoma

Melanomas are tumors of pigment producing cells. Most often these tumors occur in gray or light colored horses. The tumors tend to be benign. Their appearance is solid and black in color. They can be found anywhere on the body, but tumors are more commonly found around the anus, sheath, and abdomen.

Melanomas are often no larger than a quarter, and veterinarians often advise to leave them alone. Removal is most often not necessary. These tumors should be watched as they can ulcerate, which would require topical treatment until the ulcer heals.

Heart Murmur

Heart murmurs, which can be congenital, are not uncommon in horses and might be an indication of cardiac disease. A heart murmur has nonspecific symptoms, noticeable perhaps through exercise intolerance or from a routine examination from your vet. To diagnose it properly, an echocardiographic exam must be administered so that the heart can be looked at carefully. Unless specified by your vet, your horse should remain in use if there are no outward signs of disability.

Lyme Disease

Lyme disease is a bacterial illness transmitted by the bite of an infected deer tick. Symptoms of Lyme are numerous and can come and go. The most common symptom is joint pain; less common are lameness and changes in the horse's behavior.

Lyme disease is diagnosed by a blood test. If the test is positive and the horse has symptoms of the disease, a series of antibiotics is most often recommended. A blood test only tests for antibodies, however, so it is not uncommon to get a false positive or a false negative result. Sometimes, if a vet notices symptoms of Lyme disease, she will begin antibiotic treatment before the blood test results are in. Usually an infected horse will then show signs of improvement.

Some horses, like some dogs and some people, have a natural immunity to Lyme disease. So don't worry too much about this ailment. Other than careful grooming habits, there is not much you can do to prevent Lyme disease.

Daily grooming and removal of ticks can greatly reduce the chances your horse will contract Lyme disease. An infected tick needs to be feeding for twelve to twenty-four hours before bacteria can be passed. Tick repellent when your horse is out in the field is another preventive.

Cushing's Disease

This is a disease of the endocrine system caused by a tumor on the pituitary gland. This disease most often affects ponies and older horses, but it has been diagnosed in horses as young as ten. This tumor causes the pituitary gland to produce excessive amounts of the hormone cortisol. This produces symptoms such as excessive water intake, increased appetite, increased urination, lethargy, and a thick, wavy hair coat that does not shed in the spring. Some horses that have this disease will also be more susceptible to bouts of laminitis.

There is no cure for Cushing's disease. With daily medication to balance the horse's symptoms, affected horses can usually lead a normal life. Other ways to help the horse with this disease are to keep his daily stress to a minimum. Don't change his routine. Avoid turning him out with aggressive horses. Keep him on a high quality, easily digestible diet. Also, clipping the hair coat will give him relief as the weather turns warm.

Chapter 8
Medical Emergencies

In this chapter, you will learn how to notice and give a first response to some of the most commonly encountered medical emergencies you will run into. Often, you will be responsible for recognizing that your horse has a problem and for the administration of first aid. The quality of that first aid, before a vet is able to arrive on the scene, can be a deciding factor in his success in treating your horse. With knowledge, attention, and common sense, you can be an expert first responder to your horse.

Choke

Choke refers to an object lodged in the esophagus that the horse cannot pass. This could be a piece of wood or other foreign material, but most often it is a large amount of dry food matter. Choke is more common in older horses whose teeth are poor. A horse exhibiting choke will have an anxious expression and will repeatedly swallow in the attempt to move the mass. Saliva and food might be expelled through the nostrils.

FACT

Carrots are a common cause of choke in horses. It's easy to get carried away giving your horse treats and for your horse to get carried away eating them. If you do feed large amounts of carrots, break them into pieces first, which will make them easier to swallow.

A horse with signs of an obstruction should have food and water removed. The horse should be kept quiet, as occasionally with repeated swallowing the obstruction can be passed due to the softening properties of saliva. Your veterinarian should be called as choke is a serious threat to your horse. The longer the mass remains, the more damage and swelling will develop in the wall of the esophagus. Your horse will also become more stressed as time progresses when he isn't able to pass the obstruction. Your veterinarian will give your horse medication to increase salivation. He might also administer a tranquilizer and muscle relaxant to reduce spasms that can occur in the esophagus. He might also pass a stomach tube and add water in the hope of moving the mass toward the stomach. Flushing the esophagus with water will usually relieve choke.

Heat Exhaustion

This is a collapse of the circulatory system caused by exposure to high heat and humidity for a prolonged period. High temperature without proper ventilation can also cause heat exhaustion in horses. The horse will appear starry-eyed and distant. He will have a rapid pulse and might or might not be sweating depending on the stage of exhaustion he is in. The horse will be very weak and could be found lying down.

A quick response is necessary to avoid shock if you suspect your horse is suffering from heat exhaustion. Hosing the horse with cool water and standing him in ice or in a stream will begin to reduce the body temperature. Fans to get the air moving in your barn might also be helpful. The horse should be offered water to drink and electrolyte therapy is often indicated.

Dehydration

This is a condition that develops when the horse is losing more body water than is being taken in. You might notice that your horse's eyes are sunken, his third eyelid is protruded, or the normal salmon pink color of his gums will have turned white, signifying anemia. Also, his skin, which is usually elastic, will "tent" when pinched, taking up to a few seconds to lie back down. By the time outward signs of dehydration are noticeable, your horse will have already lost about 5 percent of his body water.

What Can Cause Dehydration

Summer and winter are the times your horse is most likely to get dehydrated. A tough exercise regime or one that is unusual for your horse could upset his balance of water intake, compared to how much he sweats in hot weather, and cause dehydration. Loose stool from sickness or nervousness might upset this balance as well. Keep in mind that water becomes foul easily in hot weather, and you should change his water every day. Also, if your horse's water source is from a stream or river that runs through a pasture, then you must be vigilant in checking that the water hasn't dried up from summer drought or isn't being excessively diverted for irrigation upstream, or for that matter polluted.

In cold weather, your horse might simply not be thirsty and decline to drink a sufficient amount of water. Icy cold water might disencline him further from drinking. Make sure that the source of your horse's winter water is not frozen and, if possible, heated to about 40 degrees.

A horse can die of dehydration after only three days without water. Therefore, it is imperative that your horse's water source be diligently checked to ensure that water is available, accessible, and potable.

What to Do

To correct dehydration, fluids and electrolytes are administered intravenously by a vet. You can prevent this condition by taking note of how much water your horse is drinking. Each horse has his own needs as far as water is concerned, so what you are looking out for is a change in his drinking habits. A salt block or electrolytes in his feed should keep him drinking water. If not, a vet should be summoned to determine if his refusal to drink water is secondary to a different problem.

Shock

Shock is an acute and progressive failure of the circulatory system. It can result from blood loss, severe trauma, and hypothermia secondary to colic or surgery, or an allergic reaction to a toxin. Shock is a red alert emergency! A horse in shock will demonstrate great distress. The gums will be pale or even have a bluish tint with slow capillary refill time. Her tongue will be dry, her pulse will be low and maybe faint, and her body temperature will drop.

FACT

Normal body temperature for a horse is 100.5 degrees, give or take about a degree. You should know your particular horse's temperature when he is healthy so you will know if he is on the high or low side of normal.

If you are dealing with shock, the horse should be kept warm with blankets and preferably kept in a stall. Any grain should be removed from his reach; however, hay can be offered if he'll eat it. This might help to warm and calm him. A vet should start intravenous fluids as soon as possible. If the shock is from blood loss, in addition to fluids, plasma and antibiotics will be given.

Puncture Wounds

Puncture wounds can amount to a very serious situation and can occur anywhere on your horse. Punctures of any kind require vigilant care and treatment, as improper healing will often create pockets of deep infection. Punctures into the foot or joint space can permanently affect the usefulness of your horse. Punctures are wounds that appear small but open up larger in the interior. Because of this, they often are wounds prone to infection.

ALERT!

In the event that your horse steps on a nail, contrary to your initial inclination do not remove the nail. The point of entry must be obvious to the vet so he can clean and treat the wound, possibly opening it up to do so. Pulling the nail might make it hard for him to locate the puncture. Immobilize the horse and make an emergency call to your vet.

A puncture should be treated initially by your vet, who will clean it and possibly open it up so draining is initiated. A course of antibiotics is usually recommended to further deter swelling. You will then be responsible for the follow-up care of making sure the site remains clean and heals from the inside out.

Eye Injuries

Any ailment or injury to the eye should be taken seriously. It will be difficult for a layperson to tell if the eye is ulcerated; therefore, a vet should be called if you suspect a problem. Symptoms of a problem in the eye will be swelling around the eye or inner lids. The horse might hold the eye closed. The eye might tear and be ultra-sensitive to light.

FACT

The eye's mucous membranes should be salmon pink in color. Yellowness in these might indicate jaundice, while paleness might indicate anemia and blue might indicate shock. The third eyelid is a common area where cancerous growths could form.

You can flush the eye with sterile saline if the horse will stand for it. This will clear the eye of any foreign bodies that might be causing the problem. A vet will put a stain in the eye that will illuminate an ulcer. The surrounding structures of the eye can be examined with an otoscope. Deeper structures of the eye can be examined with an ophthalmoscope. A vet might give your horse a sight test by leading him over unfamiliar obstacles with one eye covered at a time. A horse with impaired vision will be very sensitive to sound, moving his ears back and forth. He will also exaggerate his walk, lifting his legs high over poles or other ground obstacles.

Profuse Bleeding

If the blood coming from a wound is bright red and pumping or spurting out, this is an indication that an artery has been severed. Immediate veterinary attention is a must. Pressure can be applied to the wound with a clean towel or gauze. A tourniquet might be required if blood loss cannot be slowed or a vet is not immediately available. Remember, a tourniquet must be removed every twenty minutes or tissue below the tourniquet could die.

Nosebleed

Horses can bleed from the nose for a variety of reasons. Usually, cold weather exercise can be the cause of a ruptured blood vessel in his nose. This will produce mild bleeding in one nostril. If bleeding occurs in both nostrils, this is an indication that the origin of the rupture is further up in the head. This is a potentially serious condition requiring vet care.

Snake Bite

Snake bites are fairly common in certain parts of the country. You should familiarize yourself with the poisonous snakes that inhabit your part of the country and learn about their habits so you can avoid them. Rattlesnakes, copperheads, and water moccasins are the most common culprits of snake bites to horses in America. Horses are usually bitten on the legs, chest, and most seriously the head. Bites will cause extreme swelling to the leg, to the point of incapacitation. If bitten on the head, the eyes might swell shut, and the ears will swell and droop. Breathing will be labored, and the horse will be visibly weak.

A horse that has been bitten should be moved as little as possible. Movement will only make the venom move through his system faster. Any bite from a poisonous snake can be fatal.

ALERT!

If you are in a high risk area of the country for poisonous snakes, primarily the south and southwest, then a snake bite kit should be a permanent fixture in your saddle bag.

It might be difficult, if not impossible, to rely on vet care in the wilderness. If a vet is summoned in time, she will administer anti-venom, a tetanus booster, an anti-inflammatory, antibiotics, and possible fluid therapy to combat the shock that might set in. If possible, an incision can be made at a fresh bite site, and the venom sucked out. If the bite is on the leg of the horse, a tourniquet can be applied above the bite to slow the venom from progressing through his system. Remember, a tourniquet must be released every twenty minutes to allow blood flow to the limb.

Azoturia (Tying Up)

Azoturia, more commonly referred to as tying up, is a syndrome that affects a horse's muscles. It has various causes and degrees of severity. It is most commonly caused by overfeeding, or giving a working horse that is out of work his normal feed rations. It is sometimes called "Monday morning disease" because draft horses that are hard at work all week and then have Sunday off sometimes would come down with this condition on Monday.

Carefully observe your horse at all times, so you can identify when something is wrong. Sometimes the problem is shockingly apparent, and you must be cool and confident in your knowledge of how to respond. At other times, the signs that your horse is unhealthy are so subtle that they can go unnoticed for days, weeks, or months.

Over exercising a horse just returning to work or an unfit horse can also cause tying up. A long trip in a horse van or airplane can also bring on azoturia.

Symptoms can range from mild muscle stiffness to a reluctance or complete inability to move. The horse might pass dark, brownish urine as a result of toxins being released from damaged muscle. Blood tests can be taken to clinically determine azoturia and gauge the degree of muscle damage.

The horse might be in great pain from this condition. It is important not to move him in severe cases of azoturia until he is treated by a vet. A vet will administer a muscle relaxer, painkiller, anti-inflammatory, electrolytes, and prescribe rest. For a horse that is prone to tying up, electrolytes can be added to his grain ration. Electrolyte paste would be a good product to have on hand as well. This is a fast way for it to enter his system.

Chapter 9

The Horse's First Aid Kit

Every horse caretaker should be prepared to treat a wound or injury when it occurs. There are basic supplies that must always be on hand. Immediate and knowledgeable application of topical medicines, disinfecting solutions, and sterile dressings can prevent an otherwise harmless injury from becoming a danger to your horse and a big and expensive headache for you.

Prescription Medicines

Prescription medicines must be obtained from your veterinarian. The two most prescribed prescription drugs to have around are phenylbutazolidin, known commonly as bute, and Flunixin meglumine, known commonly as banamine. Bute is a nonsteroidal anti-inflammatory. Banamine is an anti-inflammatory, smooth muscle relaxer (it will affect muscles such as those in the gut) and an anti pyretic (fever reducer). They are both available in paste, tablets, and as injectibles. Unless you've been instructed on how and when to give an intramuscular (IM) injection and are comfortable doing it, the other forms of administration will usually suffice.

ALERT!

Generally speaking, pony breeds do not tolerate bute well, although a small dose once in a while should be okay. Consistent or long-term use of bute on any horse should be addressed by a vet, since it can cause irritation to the lining of the stomach. One-half a bute a day, or one-half gram, is usually a safe level for an average size horse.

Intramuscular Injection, Paste, or Pills

Intramuscular injection is the fastest way to reduce swelling and get pain relief to you horse. With a severe injury, or one in which the horse is in obvious pain, has acute swelling, or in the case of severe colic, an IM injection is the best choice.

Dosing with paste by mouth is the second quickest way to relieve pain and swelling. It will take about forty-five minutes to take effect, but the paste will last longer than an IM shot due to a slower absorption rate. This is ideal for an injury where swelling must be controlled but the pain is not acute.

Crushing pills over your horse's grain is the slowest, yet longest lasting application. You would use this method on a mild injury. Dosing in the feed is a way to continue medication if needed for a prolonged time after injection or initial paste dose.

A mortar and pestle is a convenient way to crush up pills for feed dosing. Grinding pills into a fine powder will ensure complete take up of medicine added to feed. Some smart horses will actually eat around unpalatable pills that are only snapped in half or quartered.

Dosage

The medical dose is determined by the weight of the horse. An average-sized horse will weigh about 900 pounds. An average pony will weigh about half that. A warm blood will weigh about 1,300 pounds. Draft horses vary greatly in stature but can weigh upward of 2,000 pounds. Your vet can help you estimate the weight of your horse if you have trouble figuring this out.

Each medication will have dosing instructions on their label, but your vet might instruct you to dose slightly differently, depending on the horse and the nature of his injury. For example, the recommended dose for IM Flunixin meglumine, more commonly known as banamine, is 1.1 mg per kilogram of bodyweight. The initial oral dose of bute is 2 grams in the morning and 2 grams in the evening on the first day, then 1 gram in the morning and 1 gram in the evening on the second day. The dosage is lessened as the symptoms decrease.

How to Give an Intramuscular Injection

You will need a sterile six or twelve cc syringe, and a sterile 20-gauge one and one-half-inch hypodermic needle. The most common site for intramuscular injection is the lateral muscle of the neck. This muscle is large and easily accessible to the handler.

FACT

In the event that you do use a needle and syringe to administer medication, keep them in a container and give them to your vet the next time she is in your barn so she can dispose of them for you. This is medical waste and might not, by law, be disposed of in your regular garbage.

First, have a handler hold the horse in his stall, or somewhere he feels safe and is somewhat immobile. Next, distract the horse by lightly tapping with your fist at the site where you will inject the medicine. After the last pat, the needle should be inserted. Then pull back slightly on the syringe to make sure you do not aspirate blood. This would indicate that the needle is in a blood vessel and should be removed. Intramuscular medications are not meant to be administered in the vein. This mistake can be catastrophic. Slowly inject the medicine into the muscle. To avoid the possibility of a knot forming at the injection site, you could massage the site gently with your hand for a few minutes.

How to Administer Paste

Paste medications are contained within a plastic syringe with dosage measured out on the plunger. Administering medication by this method is the same as paste worming as explained in Chapter 10, Routine Immunizations. The horse's mouth should be cleared of food matter. After dosage is determined and measured, the tip of the syringe is inserted into the interdental space, and then passed toward the back of the tongue.

Non-Prescription Medicines

Most of what you need to have on hand can be purchased at your local pharmacy, tack, or livestock supply store. These items should be kept in a dry place that is easily accessible to you, but not to your horse.

Topical Treatments

A large portion of your medical supplies will consist of balms, salves, and other soothing medicines used to treat skin irritations and other topical (as opposed to internal) ailments. For example, furacin spray and ointment is a soothing salve with antibacterial properties. It is useful after initial healing has begun when a wound is open to the air but needs to be kept clean. Furacin is also beneficial under a wrap used for its heat creating properties. The heat that is generated will increase blood flow to the area and promote healing.

All medications have an expiration date after which they will tend to lose potency and effectiveness. So, keep stock of the contents of your medicine cabinet and replace medicines that have expired. If you have a friendly vet, she might take commonly used medicines within a month or two of their expiration in exchange for newer medicines.

Other important topical medicines to have on hand are:

- **Novasan Cream.** This is also an antibacterial salve with antiseptic properties. It is a little more expensive than furacin and used for wounds that are more serious.
- **Triple Antibiotic Cream.** This can be used for minor cuts and scrapes. It keeps the skin soft while it is healing.
- **Mineral Ice.** Mineral ice is an intense cooling gel used for bruises, sprains, and any swelling that causes heat and therefore lack of blood flow. It should not be applied to open wounds.
- **Poultice.** This is clay that is used to draw the heat and moisture out of an injury. It is most commonly used to draw an abscess from an injured foot.
- **Epsom Salts.** Dissolved in warm water, Epsom salts is used to soak the feet, drawing out infection and abscess, reducing pain and swelling, and for general cleansing.
- **Betadine.** This is most often used as a cleansing antiseptic for all wound care. It can be used liberally as a first defense against infection of an open wound.
- **Sterile Saline.** This is used to flush a deep wound to clean and remove debris without irritating tissue.
- **Witch Hazel.** This is applied to unbroken skin as an antiseptic and skin toughener. It can also relieve itching.
- **Benadryl Cream/Aveeno Anti-Itch Cream.** Anti-itch medicines are useful to relieve itching from bug bites or allergies where a horse might be rubbing himself raw.
- **Caustic Powder.** This is indicated for certain wounds to reduce scarring. It is applied only after initial healing has taken place.

- **Desitin.** Desitin is used to provide a moisture barrier to wounds. It is very useful for a condition called "scratches." "Scratches" develops in the healing area and is often caused by too much moisture.

Eyewash

Eyewash is a sterile irrigating solution used to flush the eye to remove a suspected foreign body. When administering eyewash to the eye, hold the upper and lower lid open. Flush across the eye from the outside toward the tear duct. Do not point the tip of the syringe, or the applicator, of the medicine directly into the eye, as a sudden movement from your horse could cause him injury.

Equipment and Supplies

Effective care of wounds or injuries not only depends on having the right medical supplies available, but on having the necessary items with which to administer and sustain your care.

Thermometer

A thermometer is used to take a horse's temperature. This is often the first thing you can do to determine if your horse might be sick. There are different types of thermometers that can be used for your horse. Some horse owners prefer digital thermometers, because they are inexpensive and easier to read than mercury thermometers. Mercury thermometers are also known to be dangerous, especially since they could break and leave mercury in the stall. However, the accuracy of digital thermometers is often questioned in the horse business, and they can run out of batteries.

Wound Care

Keep in mind, for a wound to heal with as little scarring as possible, it must be tended to daily until healing is complete. Scar tissue can interfere with the skin's elastic nature and cause problems in a horse, especially around joint areas such as the ankle. To properly care for your horse's wounds, you will need a clean stainless steel bucket for wound care. The bucket should be used only for this purpose and kept clean when not in use. You will also need rolls of cotton for wound cleaning (in conjunction with betadine) as well as the following supplies:

- Soft cold packs
- Conform gauze
- Sterile four-inch gauze pads
- Vetwrap
- Bandaging scissors
- Cotton quilts

Applying Treatment

Medicines are used to reduce pain, swelling, itching, and to aid in the healing process. To be effective, however, they must be administered properly. Improper administration can not only be ineffective, but can cause further injury to your horse.

Step One: Water

Before any medicines can be applied to a wound, the wound should be flushed with water to remove any debris that might otherwise remain inside. A wound not properly cleansed can develop infection, despite topical medications.

Step Two: Betadine

The wound can now be disinfected by washing it with warm water, betadine scrub, and pieces of cotton torn into hand size sections. Squeeze betadine onto moistened cotton and gently wash the wound in the direction of the hair. This way, if there is still any debris in the wound, you will be moving it out and not scrubbing in new debris from the hair or scrubbing in hair itself. Continue to wash until your cotton comes clean off the wound site.

Although cold therapy on an injury in the way of ice packs, hydro-boots, or cold hosing can be very beneficial, it should not be administered for more than twenty minutes on an open wound because it can kill that tissue.

Step Three: Saline Solution

Now the injury is ready to be flushed with sterile water or saline solution. Once clean, the wound can be examined closely to determine its severity. If it still bleeds, apply pressure. A puncture can look like a small surface wound, but might be deeper than it is wide. Therefore after flushing and cleansing, the wound should be looked at closely. The wound can heal over foreign bodies that get trapped inside, which will most likely cause infection. If the bone is scratched or damaged in the accident, surgery might be required.

What Not to Do

If you suspect that a wound might need to be sutured by a vet, do not apply ointment because that would contaminate the site. If you've decided that the wound won't need sutures, there are many topical ointments you can use. These minor wounds can be left open to the air and treated with triple antibiotic ointment, furacin, or novasan cream. After the wound looks dry, furacin spray can be used for a few additional days to continue to aid in the healing. It is important that any medication be washed off daily and a fresh application given to a clean and dry wound. A wound that requires some type of bandaging will benefit from triple antibiotic cream or novas an. Novasan is considered a disinfectant and antiseptic and works longer than other topical medicines to minimize bacteria at the wound site. Furacin creates heat and is not recommended for use under a bandage, unless a sweat treatment is later indicated.

It is important to record the time medication is administered, so you can know when the horse should be feeling relief. Also, you will want to know when the first dose was given in case further medication is needed.

Witch hazel is not used to treat wounds; use it as an antiseptic on unbroken skin. Witch hazel is good for itching, bug bites, and as a skin toughener. You might use it to toughen skin where a harness is worn or for a blanket rub, for example. A poultice application is excellent for reducing pain and swelling, and it can be applied with or without a bandage. A poultice is not recommended for open wounds but is a good choice for sprains, bruising, or foot soreness.

Chapter 10

Routine Immunizations

To protect your horse from known infectious diseases that can compromise his health or impede his performance, it is important to have a vaccination program. If your horse is stabled away from home, the management should have a herd health program in place for all resident horses. Ideally, all horses should be vaccinated at the same time to avoid confusion, which can result in missed or double vaccinations. New horses should be current on their vaccinations before mixing with an existing horse population.

Vaccinations

When and how often to administer vaccinations depends on the length of a vaccination's effectiveness, the requirements of show grounds or other facilities you might visit with your horse, how often horses come and go where your horse is stabled, and whether your horse is a breeding animal or a youngster. Certain vaccinations are recommended at certain times of the year; for example, the immunizations for Eastern and Western Encephalitis, or E.E.E., should be given in the spring, just before mosquito season. If your horse is kept at home, you should plan a suitable immunization program with the help of your vet. The vaccination schedule should be incorporated into your horse care regime along with yearly dental exams, a worming program, and farrier care.

FACT

Immunization usually begins when a foal is about three months of age, although most farms administer tetanus antitoxin at birth. Before this, a foal has immunity from his mother, or "dam," provided he was able to nurse within a few hours of his birth when colostrum is present in the dam's milk. Colostrum is the very important "first milk" that carries the antibodies the foal needs to have protection against disease.

Requirements for vaccinations might vary in different parts of the country, due to prevailing conditions such as the length of mosquito season, the horse's possible contact with other horses and livestock, and disease outbreaks, which might be more common to warmer climates and in areas with a large horse population. It should also be noted that the horses on a farm might each have different vaccination requirements. If your vet gives all your vaccinations, she will keep a record and probably remind you in the spring and fall that shots are due. Otherwise, if you give your own vaccinations, you must keep a record so that you stay up to date.

How Vaccinations Are Administered

Vaccinations are most often given by intramuscular injection (IM shots). Where in the muscle a vaccination is administered often depends on how reactive a vaccine is. Vaccines that tend to cause some soreness will often be administered into the hamstring muscle instead of the more common area of the neck. Foals and yearlings are often vaccinated in the hamstring due to their fractious nature. Most vets feel this is safer. Intranasal vaccination is another method being currently used for flu vaccines. It works well and is easy to administer. Administration of IM shots is explained in Chapter 9.

Combined Vaccinations

Some vaccinations are often combined by drug companies and can be given in one dose. This limits the times a horse will have to be stuck with a needle, which can be stressful to some horses. Keep in mind that there is always the chance of soreness and swelling at any injection site. You might want to consider the possible side effects of vaccination and plan it around your riding and showing schedule.

A popular technique for the application of intramuscular injection is to insert the needle first and then attach the syringe. A rambunctious horse can have time to settle down after the needle is inserted without the weight of the medicine-filled syringe to pull the needle out.

For most horses, receiving several medicines at once is safe. However, some horses will react to medications especially when given in combination. High fever and general illness might result. This is especially true of horses that have been living wild or semi-wild and have never been immunized. For such horses, you might want to break up the doses into several different shots over several days.

Live or Killed Vaccines

Vaccines are referred to as "live" or "killed." Live vaccines contain a non-infectious form of a live organism. The objective is to challenge the host—the horse—without causing disease. This will trigger an immune response in the horse, which will lead to immunity against a virus or disease. Killed vaccine is similar in its action, but it cannot become active.

Diseases to Vaccinate Against

The most common diseases which horses are susceptible to are preventable through vaccination. Because of effective vaccinations, these once most common diseases rarely occur in American horse populations, but they are by no means eradicated. So it is important to be faithful in your vaccination schedule, be flexible to changing conditions such as heavy or prolonged mosquito season, and to know how long a vaccine is effective for.

Tetanus

Tetanus is caused by the bacteria *clostridium tetani*. It is ubiquitous in a horse's natural environment, even present in the soil. This bacterium enters the body at the site of a wound, foot puncture, or umbilical cord stump in a foal. Its symptoms are a stiff, or locked, jaw, noticeable when your horse is trying to eat, along with muscle spasms.

Rabies

Rabies is a highly fatal viral infection of the central nervous system. It is transmitted through a bite from or the saliva of an infected animal. Its symptoms are general disorientation, excitability, increased salivation, and running blindly.

ALERT!

Be alert to potential carriers of rabies around your farm. Rabies is endemic to certain animals such as raccoons, skunks, bats, and coyotes. Such an animal will appear visibly sick and disoriented. Seeing one of these animals in the open during the day is an indication that it might be sick and should be destroyed for your safety, and that of your farm, house animals, and the neighborhood in general.

Equine Encephalitis

There are three forms of equine encephalitis: Eastern, Western, and Venezuelan. All horses in the United States should be vaccinated against the first two. It is recommended that horses living in New Mexico, Arizona, or California are vaccinated against Venezuelan encephalitis as well. Polo ponies also are often in close contact with horses from South America and should be vaccinated against Venezuelan encephalitis. Its symptoms are swelling of the brain that causes erratic behavior, high fever, and impaired vision. The decline of an infected horse will be rapid, most often ending in death.

Influenza

This is an upper respiratory disease similar to the flu that affects humans. Influenza is not often fatal, but can be troublesome for the very young or very old horse. The immune system of these horses might not be strong and can become weakened by influenza, inviting secondary infections such as pneumonia. Its symptoms are nasal discharge, cough, fever, lethargy, and loss of appetite.

FACT

Pneumonia is a common secondary infection of the lungs stemming from any number of other respiratory infections. Especially in a young horse, pneumonia can have devastating effects and cause permanent lung damage. So, it is important to catch and treat any respiratory infection expeditiously.

Rhinopneumoitus

This is also an upper respiratory disease, which is caused by herpes virus 1. It is most often seen in young horses in the late fall and early winter. "Rhino" is highly contagious and very dangerous on a breeding farm, because it can cause late term abortion in pregnant mares. Its symptoms are nasal discharge, cough, and fever. It is not fatal to most horses. If an outbreak is suspected, every effort should be made to isolate possibly infected horses.

Strangles

Strangles is a highly contagious upper respiratory infection. Vaccination against strangles is usually not necessary; however, if your horse is often exposed to other strange horses, you will want to vaccinate him. One situation that might require you to vaccinate is if your horse is in a sale barn where different horses are constantly moving in and out or if your paddock or pasture fence line borders a riding trail where your horse might come into contact with various other horses out of mutual curiosity.

Symptoms can vary from mild to severe. High temperature, lethargy, fast breathing, nasal discharge, and swelling of the lymph nodes under the jaw are the most common and noticeable. These nodes often abscess and drain. Treatment consists of antibiotics and care of the draining abscesses until healing occurs.

If strangles has entered your barn, it is irresponsible to hide the fact or to let it pass onto another farm through a horse that might have been infected at your barn and not quarantined. A casual attitude with regard to strangles, one of the most contagious and damaging equine diseases, is largely why it still remains in American and European horse populations.

Quarantine of sick horses is a must. The strangles bacteria can survive in the environment for several months to a year. Therefore, no horse should be allowed in or out of a barn where strangles has been present until all horses get a clean bill of health from your vet and areas where an infected horse has been have been disinfected. These might include stalls, wash stalls, horse trailers, wheelbarrows, tack, and aisle ways. After attending to a quarantined horse, your clothes and shoes must be changed and your hands thoroughly washed before touching another horse.

Equine Infectious Anemia

This is most often a fatal disease. It is contagious and is transmitted by bloodsucking insects. Current research connects the large horsefly as the possible vector. Its symptoms are sweating, fever, weakness, anemia, limb swelling, and rapid weight loss. Horses with this disease will often back off from consumption of water. Death can occur within one to two weeks of infection. Some horses can recover but will have reoccurring symptoms.

Potomac Fever

Potomac fever is an incurable, systemic disease. The vaccine is only currently recommended in high risk areas of the country, such as the east coast of the United States and Canada. Potomac fever is caused by *ehrlichia ristici*, which invade monocytes in the horse's bloodstream. How it is transmitted to a horse is unknown. Its symptoms are severe diarrhea, depression, dehydration, high white blood cell count, and loss of appetite. Laminitis often accompanies and complicates this disease. The prognosis for recovery from Potomac fever is poor. Vaccines offer short-term protection—from four to six months.

West Nile Virus

West Nile is a disease that is transmitted to a horse from the bite of an infected mosquito. Its symptoms are a swelling of the brain that can cause erratic behavior. This is a new disease, so the effectiveness of the vaccination is unknown. At any rate, vaccination is recommended where cases of West Nile have been reported in livestock, birds, and humans. Your local agricultural extension office or your vet will be informed of West Nile reports. In a few cases, West Nile will be fatal, but most horses will recover.

Coggins Test

A Coggins test determines the presence of equine infectious anemia mentioned above. All horses that travel in or are imported into the United States are required to have a negative Coggins test once a year or every six months, depending on the requirements of affairs you will visit with your horse. Once a horse tests negative, the vet will issue you a signed document that records his status; a copy of this should be carried with the horse whenever he travels.

There is some controversy over the Coggins test that requires any horse testing positive to be destroyed, even though in rare cases he might be healthy and never show symptoms of the disease. Cases of this disease are very rare, but a serious effort has been made to keep it out of the horse population in the United States.

Health Certificate

A health certificate is a form signed by your vet that states the present health of your horse within ten days of her traveling. It is required of all horses traveling across state lines when a horse is traveling on a commercial carrier or by air. Some horse shows also require a health certificate.

To minimize the introduction of disease to your horse, or from your horse to others, strict management practices should be adhered to. Such practices should include a sound vaccination and worming schedule, isolation of a new horse to your stable until his health is verified, a clean living environment, and separation of breeding stock from riding horses.

Parasites

Internal parasites pose a continual health threat throughout the life of a horse. Parasites are ever present in the horse's environment and in the horse. Although they can never be eliminated entirely from a horse's system, a consistent deworming schedule can significantly reduce their numbers and the threat to your horse's health. Since worm infestation develops through stages, it is important to interrupt the process with deworming medicine, thus limiting their development. There are many types of parasites that prevail in the environment, depending on what region of the country you live in. If left unchecked, these parasites can do damage to a horse's liver, lungs, circulatory system, stomach, and digestive tract.

Worms are the most common cause of colic in horses. It is estimated that about 90 percent of colic is due to current or previous worm damage to the lining of blood vessels in the bowel, which blocks blood flow to the area, causing pain and abnormality there.

Ascarids

These are the most common parasite found in all horses. The very young horse and the senior equine are most susceptible to detrimental effects from this worm. Their life cycle is three months. Horses ingest ascarids while grazing or eating hay from the ground. They migrate to a horse's liver and lungs if unchecked. A symptom of lung damage from this worm is a dry cough. Other symptoms are diarrhea, poor coat, a pot belly, and impaction.

Large Strongyles

These parasites effect all ages of horses. They are ingested when a horse grazes. The larvae travel to the large intestine, where they burrow into the wall before migrating throughout his body. They have an eleven-month life cycle.

A horse suffering from a worm problem will appear generally sick and haggard. His coat might be lackluster and patchy. The belly might look round and distended, his eyes might be dull, and his energy down. Another indication of a horse with a heavy worm load is that she will suffer chronic bouts of mild colic especially during feeding time.

Small Strongyles

These parasites only have a three-week life cycle and settle in the small intestine. Symptoms of infestation can be diarrhea, constipation, and an overall unthrifty condition.

Bot Flies

The bot fly lays her eggs on the insides of a horse's front legs. These will bother a horse, causing him to lick the eggs off, ingesting the eggs in the process. The larvae will burrow into the tongue and mouth, eventually migrating to the stomach, which takes about three weeks. In the stomach, bots will cause obstruction, ulcers, and anemia. If you notice these small, yellow eggs on your horse's legs, you can clean them off with a bot knife before your horse ingests them.

Pinworms

This parasite has a life cycle of five months. Ingested by grazing horses, pinworms can be detected by the intense itching they cause around the anus of the horse. Your horse might have this worm if you notice him rubbing his tail against a fence rail or in his stall. You might notice pinworms around the anus or under the tail.

Worming

There are over forty varieties of worms indigenous to the United States, so how do you protect your horse from them? A strict worming program begun the day a horse arrives at your farm will usually do the job. Worming every six weeks is standard, although a heavily worm infested paddock or pasture might require that you worm every month. This might be a paddock that has been in continual use without a break from horses in a long time. Also, your turnout might be heavily infested with parasites if it is small and not effectively managed. Pasture management, including the removal of manure and dragging as discussed in Chapter 19, along with regular worming is your best defense.

If you think your horse might have a worm problem, talk to your vet about an intensive deworming program, as a regular dose of paste will no longer suffice. Just giving her extra wormer or adding a daily wormer will not solve the problem, and will probably make her sicker.

Paste Worming

Paste worming is the most common method of deworming your horse. Paste wormer is available at tack and feed stores or from your veterinarian. Ask your vet to recommend a rotational program for you, so you know what products to rotate with and at what time of year. Deworming products have been developed to target different parasites, and these products need to be rotated in order to be effective. The parasites in a horse will become resistant to a wormer that is used over and over.

ALERT!

When choosing a worming product, keep in mind that a wormer is a mild poison, and some products are not recommended for pregnant mares or foals. However, there are alternatives for these horses. Ask your vet.

Paste wormer is fairly easy to administer. The product comes in a syringe with weight calibrations. The syringe is slipped into the side of the horse's mouth, and the wormer is deposited on the back of the tongue. The head is then kept lifted with a hand under the chin until the horse has swallowed the complete dose. The paste is sticky, and even if the horse tries to expel it from his mouth he will most likely get the full dose. However, if he has hay or grain in his mouth, the wormer will stick to that, which he will have no trouble expelling.

Daily Wormer

In additional to rotational worming, many horse owners choose to feed a continuous daily wormer. The most common product goes by the name "Strongid C"; its main ingredient is Pyrante tartrate. This comes in pelleted form and is fed according to the weight of the horse, and is top dressed in the daily grain ration. All horses seem to eat it readily. This product controls the infestation of large/small strongyles, ascarids, and pinworms. It becomes useless if even one day is skipped. Remember this product is in addition to paste worming, not a substitute for it.

FACT

The Strongid C daily worming program offers an insurance policy against colic if you purchase the product and initiate administration through a vet. This is a strong testament to the harmful effects of worm damage on your horse.

Worming a Foal

A foal is wormed for the first time at one month of age and occasionally younger. All horses on a breeding farm are usually wormed every month. Worming by stomach tube is still common on breeding farms, since this method is thought to be more effective than paste worming.

Fecal Test

A fecal sample from your horse, regardless of any apparent sickness, should be tested by your vet two times per year to check the effectiveness of your worming program. Have this test done just before your horse's scheduled worming. This will give you the opportunity to re-evaluate your worming program according to what kind of parasites show up in his manure.

The Extra Bonus of a Vet Visit

Having a vet around your barn once in a while can be very beneficial. Her trained and experienced eye might catch a subtle problem or oncoming problem in a horse that might otherwise seem healthy. She might diagnose a horse with the early stages of founder by the way he is standing in his stall. She might make other diagnoses by the way a horse eats, walks, or just by his general appearance or behavior. So it might pay to have your vet come around to your farm to administer dewormings every six weeks, even though it is a relatively easy application. Having your veterinarian visit, even just a few times a year, will be a benefit, as her trained eye might catch problems you might have overlooked.

Chapter 11

Alternative Health Care

Alternative therapies for horses, like alternative therapies for humans, have been around for centuries, long before conventional medicines were ever used. Many of them are available to horses living in the wild, like aromatherapy, natural herbs, and hydrotherapy, yet the environments we keep our domestic horses in are usually void of the space and variation that a wild horse could enjoy. Other natural therapies, like acupuncture, acupressure, and kinesiology, were applied to horses as humans developed a relationship with them through domestication.

Hydrotherapy

Hydrotherapy is a work regime of swimming specifically for horses that are injured or coming through an injury and cannot or should not bear their own weight. Swimming is excellent exercise for any horse. For an injured horse, it might be the only exercise he can undertake. Water suspends his weight and offers resistance so that a full cardiovascular workout can be accomplished and muscle tone maintained, making his return to regular work faster and easier.

Minerals in salt water and water used in therapy pools are also excellent for the feet, coat, and the skin, which synthesize vitamins that encourage the healing process. The coolness of water is also beneficial to the healing process. Inflammation at an injury site can impede the chemicals that the immune system releases to aid in healing. Inflamed tissue blocks oxygen-carrying blood also necessary for the regeneration of healthy tissue from entering the injury, causing a condition known as hypoxia. Cold therapy disperses and reduces inflammation so that healing can take place.

ALERT!

Horses are very capable swimmers. Most enjoy swimming once they are used to it. Be careful when swimming your horse however. Hang on to the mane just to his side. Don't try to ride him as if he were on land. It is easy to slip off the back and get inadvertently kicked by his working hind end.

Hydrotherapy can be practiced in any body of water, whether it is a pool designed specifically for that purpose, a lake, or the ocean. A gradual decline into submersion is required, which you will find at the beach. In a controlled environment, a therapist will walk along with the horse and lead him with a rope through his exercise. In some cases, a therapist can also swim the horse in a less formal body of water, controlling him with a swimming bridle.

Acupressure and Acupuncture

Acupressure is practiced along the lines or meridians of the body that channel its life force or "chi," as it is called in Chinese medicine. Imbalances or blockages in this energy can cause illness and malaise that can be corrected by manipulating certain points along these pathways to create a harmonious condition in the body so it can repair itself. Acupuncture is similar to acupressure. It works within the same philosophy of chi, restoring the body's balance of the two fundamental and opposing forces of nature, Yin and Yang.

Acupressure

There are fourteen main meridians that correspond to organs and glands of the body. Each organ serves several functions within the body. Equisonic is a device used by practitioners that emits infrasonic sound waves in the range of 8–14 hertz, which is about the same frequency that is naturally emitted from a chi gong master's hands. This breaks up blockages at the desired pressure point and clears the channel for the clear flow of chi.

FACT

Horses with navicular, arthritis, and other problems relating to the skeleton have benefited enormously from acupuncture. It is often beneficial as a treatment for allergies and used in conjunction with kinesiology.

A map of the meridians and pressure points and a guide to acupressure can help you in your practice of acupressure. Incorrect acupressure is benign, as the hertz are low and the applied pressure, between one and four pounds, is not enough to harm a horse if administered in the wrong place or applied to a healthy pressure point. When you are doing it right, you will probably see immediate effects on your horse. His lips and eyelids might droop, or he might yawn repeatedly. Acupressure can be effective on any injury or disease, whether skeletal, muscular, soft tissue, repertory, or faschel.

Acupuncture

Fine, hollow needles are inserted just below the skin at certain acupoints. This releases blockages in the energy pathways to restore a free flow of chi. Acupuncture is generally thought of as a more specific treatment for organ dysfunction than acupressure. It should only be practiced by a licensed acupuncturist, who must first be a licensed vet. It should not be attempted by a layperson.

Chiropractic and Massage

Chiropractors are mainly concerned with the manipulation of the spine for re-alignment in order to ease pressure that misalignment can apply to nerves to restore health and flexibility to the whole body. While some problems in a horse might originate in the skeleton and be fixed by a chiropractor, others might be inherently muscular and need to be treated with massage. Strained or chronically spasmed muscles will only pull a chiropractic adjustment of the bones back out of line.

A horse having regular exercise or that is allowed turnout will self-adjust 80 percent of the time. Taking her through all her gaits, including gallop, or letting her buck around the paddock a few times is her way of giving herself chiropractic treatment.

Chiropractic Treatment

Chiropractic treatment must be practiced by a licensed chiropractor; large animal certification takes seven years. In this method of treatment, sharp thrusts are applied at specific locations along the horse's back and neck, and the body is manipulated for the purpose of adjustment. Relief is often immediately apparent, and the long-term effects of chiropractic care can be dramatic. Horses that move or stand with crooked alignment or are unbalanced might be good candidates for chiropractic. The slightest misalignment in a horse's spine can misdirect thousands of pounds of pressure.

FACT

A muscle spasm happens where the muscle attaches to the bone. This tendinous fascial tissue tightens and holds the muscle from releasing from its contracted state. Muscle tightens up around a bone to protect it when it is weak or compromised from injury. Therefore, massage and chiropractic should be used in tandem.

Massage

Massage is a manipulation of muscles to keep them supple, elastic, and available to oxygen, which is carried by the blood. A masseur will use her fingers, fist, and elbow to penetrate deep into muscle and soft tissue to promote blood flow and balance and harmony between the muscles of the horse and the rest of his body.

Magnetic Therapy

Magnetic therapy can increase blood flow and stimulate new and healthy tissue growth. It has had great success in relieving pain from joint and muscle illnesses like arthritis, rheumatism, and navicular.

How It Works

The earth exerts a magnetic force that influences iron atoms in the blood of all beings to promote oxygen absorption and healthy cell function. Bipolar or multipolar magnets, set to certain frequencies depending on the location and injury on the body of a horse, mimic this natural magnetic field while intensifying and focusing it, which facilitates the healing situation.

ESSENTIAL

The premise of natural therapies is that nature provides all species on the planet with everything we need to be healthy. When we subject horses to unnatural living and working conditions, they might need our help to remain healthy.

How Magnets Are Applied

Magnetic therapy can be applied through blankets, leg wraps, or bell boots. Therapy can be recommended for a few hours, a few days, or constantly. The location of magnets and frequencies are specific, so get a professional opinion before starting magnetic therapy.

Reiki

Reiki is a non-invasive form of energetic healing that can enhance a horse's physical, spiritual, emotional, and mental well-being. Reiki translates universal energy through the therapist into the recipient, in this case a horse, in order to restore balance and harmony. Reiki is sometimes used on pre- and post-surgery patients in hospitals. It has been found to increase the success of surgery and the recovery time after surgery.

QUESTION?

What is kinesiology?
It is a kind of touch therapy combining Chinese acupuncture with western medical knowledge. A kinesiologist uses muscle testing to detect energy imbalances in the body that can cause many different kinds of physical and emotional illnesses (including phobias, allergies, and weight issues). Kinesiology balances the energy in the body by helping to reduce tension, eliminate toxins, and reinforce the body's immune system.

Reiki is practiced with hands on or just above the body of the horse. Any one with an aptitude and sensitivity for energy work can learn Reiki. The life force that heals does not come from the therapist, but rather through her. No harm can be done by a well intentioned amateur, but truly effective Reiki must be administered by a master.

Homeopathy

Homeopathy is the science of treating a sickness, disease, or allergy with a diluted tincture of the active agent causing the problem, or other toxic substance, in order to stimulate a healing response from the immune system.

FACT

Rhus tox is extracted from the poison ivy plant. It is a homeopathic treatment for arthritis, yet, in a healthy horse, rhus tox causes muscle stiffness.

How It Works

The premise of homeopathy is that substances in large doses might cause illness, but in small doses homeopathy can jumpstart the body's immune system into action; then the body can take the healing process from there. Conventional medical vaccines work upon the same premise. Some homeopathic substances are:

- **Echinacea:** Jumpstarts the immune system in the first stages of illness or infection.
- **Arnica:** Aids in the reduction of bruises and swelling. Can also be used as a substitute for bute.
- **Chamomilla:** Has a calming effect on a nervous horse.
- **Acetic acid, Abrotanum, and Iodum:** Used against diarrhea.
- **Aconite:** For horses in shock or that might go into shock.
- **Nux vomica:** Used to aid in the relief of the symptoms of colic and as a detoxifying agent to the organs and digestive system.
- **Hepar sulphuris calcareum:** For nasal discharge and coughs.
- **Colocynthis:** Used to ease the gut during or after colic.
- **Silica:** Used to restore hair growth from a scab or allergy.
- **Apis:** For swelling from an injury, allergy, or insect bite.
- **Lycopodium, bryonia (wild hops):** Used to ease gas or impaction colic.
- **Arsenicum album:** Used to treat Mud Fever, Rain Scald, and Sweet Itch.

- **Rhus toxicodendron (poison ivy):** For arthritis.
- **Sepia:** For hormonal imbalances.
- **Urtica urens:** Used to ease bee stings and nettle rash.
- **Belladonna (deadly nightshade):** For treating chronic laminitis.
- **Hypericum perfoliatum:** To reduce the risk of infection from cuts and puncture wounds.

Who Administers Homeopathy

The correct substances in the proper doses and applications and given for the right duration of time are necessary for the success and safety of homeopathy. Homeopathy is often practiced in conjunction with kinesiology by trained homeopaths. Most formulations are available in powders, liquids, or pills, and can be given as an injection, orally, or amended to a horse's feed. Once you have consulted a professional and have a diagnosis, then you can safely administer homeopathy.

Osteopathy

Osteopathy is a holistic approach to healing the entire body. Bones, muscles, connective tissue, and ligaments all work together in a body, so when one becomes strained, broken, or misaligned, all aspects of the body can suffer. Osteopathy addresses this interrelationship between the different structural systems of the body.

How It Is Practiced

Like all of the therapies discussed, osteopathy seeks to improve blood flow to areas of stress or tension to promote healthy tissue and restore harmony to the body. Osteopaths manipulate the skull, limbs, pelvis, neck, and tail of the horse, sometimes under sedation, to restore musculoskeletal balance.

How does physiotherapy work?
Physiotherapy is mostly a preventative therapy that examines a horse's conformation, movement, balance, and working discipline to predict what stress injuries might occur and where they might occur. The therapist then designs a specific regiment of exercise and stretches to improve balance and to compensate for potentially overstressed areas.

Could You Practice Osteopathy?

Osteopathy is an art as well as a science and should be practiced by a trained professional. However, you can administer many of the stretches and simpler manipulations. You can learn what stretches to practice on your horse by watching him practice them on his own during turnout or coming out of his stall in the morning. Holding treats at strategic locations around his body is a good way to make him do the work of stretching.

Aromatherapy

Aromatherapy utilizes the physical and emotional therapeutic properties of essential oils, which are extracted from nature and concentrated in a "carrier oil" such as walnut or almond oil. An aromatherapist or kinesiologist can help you determine which oils your horse might need or crave. However, the best judge of this will most often be the horse himself. Let him choose the oils you administer. Some aromatherapy oils and their uses are:

- **Rose:** For hormonal imbalances in mares, both in and out of season.
- **Neroli:** For a depressed horse, used proactively to prevent distress or depression from uncomfortable situations.
- **Arnica, Witch Hazel:** Used after hard work to prevent bruising and inflammation. Also used as a substitute for bute.
- **Lavender, Rosemary:** Used to ease stiff muscles after exercise and as an aid to the symptoms of arthritis. Lavender is popular for calming a horse before travel or shows as well.
- **Aloe Vera, Tea Tree, Vervain:** Used to treat wounds.

After an initial diagnosis by a professional aromatherapist or kinesiologist, you can offer aromatherapy to your horse. These therapies come in bottles and are either inhaled or rubbed into his skin, his muzzle, or forehead. Offer your horse her favorite oils for as long as she likes and responds to them. Her needs will probably change once the oils have done their job.

Bach Flower Remedies

Bach Flower Remedies are concentrations of non-poisonous flowers and plants that have natural healing powers and promote equilibrium and harmony. They are concentrated into water and applied onto treats or in feed. They can also be made into ointments and rubbed into the horse's skin.

Rescue Remedy is the most famous of all Bach's remedies. It can be used on all animals to calm the nerves, bring them out of shock, or keep them from going into shock after a traumatic experience. Many animal owners who have experience using it will tell you that it is, literally, a lifesaver.

Tellington Touch

Linda Tellington-Jones developed the Tellington Touch (T-Touch) system of therapeutic movement for horses by combining her knowledge of the physiology and the mental and emotional adaptation of animals with her knowledge of the Feldenkrais Method of Functional Integration. This therapy teaches a system of non-habitual body movements that could awaken unused brain cells and establish new neural pathways for people who have developed negative body patterns and postures resulting from trauma, dysfunction, and tension. The T-Touch system not only promotes performance, health, concentration, coordination, and general well-being in a horse, but it also fosters communication and trust between you and your horse. This system includes a number of different exercises involving massage, stretching, and acupressure that you might safely practice on your horse.

Clouded Leopard

This exercise is a circular movement holding your fingers slightly curved. It is used to increase circulation or ease stiff muscles. While pressing slightly into the horse's skin with your fingers, make circular, one-and-a-quarter revolutions all over the horse's body.

Python Lift

This is used to stimulate circulation and allay muscle spasm. The muscle is slightly pulled and lifted with one or both hands and held for four seconds.

Tail Pull

Pulling and rotating the tail acts to release tension in the neck and back. Your own weight can be used to pull the tail by gripping it firmly in both hands and then leaning back.

Ear Work

In Chinese medicine, the ear is a microcosm for the entire body. There are many acupressure points in the ear, so you really can't miss. Gently stroke and squeeze the entire ear. Rubbing the tips of the ears can calm a nervous horse. Rubbing the bottom of the ear can aid in digestion. This can calm a nervous horse among other benefits.

Leg Circles

This is an all around good stretch for your horse before or after exercise. It can be done by picking up a leg of the horse and flexing it backwards and forwards, making rotational movements.

Chapter 12

Horse Faults

The two most important faults to consider about your horse are his conformation and whether or not he has any vices. How a horse is structurally conformed will affect his appearance and way of moving. Faults in his conformation might induce stress to certain areas of his body and could lead to secondary conditions that might ultimately impede his usefulness. Every experience in the horse's life will have a positive or negative effect. It is the negative effect that can predispose a horse to develop a vice.

Vice and Conformation

A horse begins his life as an inquisitive animal; learning begins first from his dam and field mates. At the same time, the foal also begins to have interactions with people. As an owner, the worst thing you can do to a youngster is to isolate it from other young horses. The social behavior learned in a herd, no matter its size, is vital to his development. Most vices will develop from improper care or handling, neurosis, or boredom, but can also be picked up from other horses.

ALERT!

Horses are amenable creatures and want to please and to know their place. It is not recommended that the novice take on a horse with a vice without the help of a knowledgeable horseperson.

Many horse breeds have an evaluation system set up to assess a horse's conformation according to the breed standard. This is usually a numerical score from one to ten, with ten being perfect. However, it is rare to find a horse that has perfect conformation. It is also important to note that what one breed considers ideal conformation might be slightly different from other breed standards. This is similar to the standards set up for canine breeds. Horse breeders evaluate the best traits of their mares and choose a stallion that will complement or improve any weakness in conformation, hoping for a foal that will have the best attributes from both sire and dam.

Cribbing or Wind Sucking

These terms tend to be used interchangeably. Cribbing describes a horse that chews wood. Wind sucking refers to a horse that grabs an object with his teeth, such as a feed tub, water bucket, or fence, and gulps air. Cribbing seems to be quite addictive; the vice often develops from boredom, but can be picked up from observing another horse.

A horse with this vice tends to look in poor condition, thin with a poorly shaped neck from constant cribbing activity. The front incisors of a cribber will also wear unevenly, leading to unthriftiness (failing to put on or maintain weight with adequate food). It is easy to notice a horse that cribs either in the stall or in the field. The horse that gulps air can also be heard while engaging in this behavior.

Curing or lessening a bad behavior will depend on the patience and communication skills of the horse's handlers. The temperament of the horse and length of time a vice has been practiced will also be an important factor in your success.

To stop the behavior, most horsemen will recommend using a cribbing strap. This fastens around the throat of the horse and does not allow him to crib. Various styles are available at tack stores and are considered a humane deterrent to cribbing. While the horse is stalled, his feed tub and other objects he can grab should be removed. Exposed wood can be covered with metal or coated with crib-prevention paint. As with all vices, activity and a good health management program will keep your horse happier and healthier and less likely to pick up this vice.

Weaving

Weaving is a nervous actively in which the horse continuously rocks from one side to another, shifting weight from one front leg to another. High-strung, nervous, or ill disciplined horses or horses with a lot of energy can be prone to weave when bored or seeking attention.

A horse does not often weave when outside his stall, so giving the horse ample exercise is key. When the horse must be stalled, toys can be hung along the front of the stall where horses usually weave. The toys will occupy him and, if placed strategically, they will interrupt his back and forth activity. A horse that weaves puts additional stress on his front legs and will often be on the thin side from constant motion. Another possible solution is a stall companion such as a goat.

Pawing, Stall or Fence Walking

Some horses just never seem to be content. Often a horse that walks the stall or fence has an abundance of energy. A horse with this vice will leave the grass in a paddock untouched in favor of walking. This vice is very hard to cure, so it is important to take measures to stop the behavior as soon as it occurs. Pawing goes hand and hand with walking, as both are quite destructive vices to the floor of the stall and fence line. A horse can walk quite a deep trench along the fence, making it unsafe for him and anyone else using that field. Likewise the walker will waste bedding by churning up his stall. A dirt or clay floor will be destroyed by the horse that paws.

A stall walker can be given twenty-four hour turnout. A fence walker can be kept in his stall and hand walked or exercised rather than given turnout. Activity and company in general are recommended for this vice. A good workout will often take the nervous edge off a horse with vices. A concrete or rubber matted stall is also advisable.

Biting

Young horses are often mouthy, which can lead to biting if they are left undisciplined. Stallions and colts tend to nip more. This annoying and potentially dangerous habit is often ignored by the horse owner until biting has become a habit. A horse will not attempt to bite if he is clear about his place in the world. He must understand, just like a dog, that while biting might be okay with his turnout partners, it is not okay with humans. All nipping behavior must be corrected with a sharp "no!"

ALERT!

If you have a horse that is a known biter or kicker, you should not get casual with the ground rules of horsemanship. When you are around the horse, always position yourself close by his shoulder, or if you must be behind him, stand close by his rump where he cannot bite or kick you.

This is sometimes a curable habit. A horse that bites you doesn't respect you. The kind of respect a horse has for his alpha person is motivated in large part by fear of the consequences if he steps out of line. You must, by all means, put an end to this behavior using severe physical discipline, not to hurt, but rather to scare the horse. A biting horse should be made to fear you so that he accepts you as his alpha.

Kicking

This vice is often observed when the horse is in the stall or being saddled. A horse that kicks the wall of his stall is usually being possessive of his environment. If the stall has bars instead of a solid partition, it would be best to install a solid wall. If this is not possible, changing his neighbor might be the solution. Moving the horse to a quiet stall away from the horse traffic of the barn is often helpful as well. Horses that kick out when being saddled or girthed up might be protesting discomfort. A horse that has been pinched by the girth or had it tightened roughly or too quickly can develop this vice. Time and gentle handling when tacking up will ease or alleviate the vice.

A horse kicking out deliberately at you is exhibiting totally unacceptable behavior. But before you discipline him, make sure it wasn't your fault because you snuck up on him from his blind spot. Kicking and biting are potentially the most dangerous vices to a horse's caretaker. Either one can be fatal and happen often too quickly for you to get out of the way. Most professionals, even horse whisperers, will advocate beating a horse firmly but without anger in these instances.

Mounted Vices

Negative behavior under saddle results from poor communication between horse and rider. These behaviors can become habits when left uncorrected. The mounted vices result from the horse not understanding the demands of his mount. Being sore or tired can also lead the horse to act out. In the case of playful bucking, the horse might be trying to let off excess energy and a simple solution might be more time in the pasture. Whatever the cause, mounted vices can be eliminated with proper training. In fact, a horse with mounted vices that is being ridden by a professional often won't display his bad behavior!

Backing Up When Being Mounted

This is a vice that develops when the rider has held the reins too tight as he attempts to mount. It can also be a reaction to associating being ridden as something negative. Take some time to think about the cause of this vice. The horse should not dread his work! Are you demanding too much? Do you always bring your horse home tired? Do you mount roughly or pull yourself into the saddle, which can be uncomfortable to the horse? Mounting the horse with his rear to the barn wall or a fence will cure this bad habit in time.

ALERT!

A horse that kicks other horses in the field should be marked with a red ribbon on her tail. This behavior, more often exhibited by mares, can be dangerous to other horses and riders. A red ribbon will warn riders to keep their distance.

Bucking

A playful kicking up of the heels at the beginning of the ride is an indication your horse is feeling good. Bucking repeatedly, as if trying to unseat the rider, is another matter. The first thing to do is to check the fit of your saddle. A poor fitting saddle will make your horse very uncomfortable. Second, some horses are sensitive to the girth or cinch being tightened. Make sure you're taking your time when tacking up and tighten the girth slowly to alleviate pinching. A horse that bucks hard enough to unseat the rider has a serious vice. Only an experienced rider who can sit out the buck should deal with this behavior until it is cured. The correction for a buck is a strong half halt to bring the head up while strongly driving the horse forward with your leg. A horse cannot buck while moving well forward with his head up.

Bucking, rearing, and spinning are all defensive traits that a horse naturally possesses in order to free himself of a predatory cat, such as a lion or tiger that he might encounter in the wild. Along with their speed, these safety mechanisms protect horses in the wild.

Rearing

This vice is considered to be the most serious. There is no mistaking your horse's intention when he rears on you. He wants you off his back. A rider on a horse that rears could easily unbalance the horse, resulting in the horse falling over backward. Only a professional should work with a horse that attempts to rear. A martingale that binds the horse's head at a certain distance to his body, while appearing to prevent rearing, is not usually a good answer to this vice.

An often-repeated mistake that riders and trainers make with a rearing horse is to add a Standing Martingale on to the tack of the horse. This might act as a Band-Aid for the problem or might only make it worse by applying tension for him to react against. It is not at any rate a cure to rearing.

Shying

All horses shy from time to time. They are flight animals after all. If your horse trusts you, and you learn how to properly handle things that might frighten him, shying can be lessened or alleviated. If a horse shies repeatedly or suddenly begins shying, it would be wise to have the horse's eyes examined.

The alert rider will often anticipate what his mount will shy away from and prepare well in advance of the actual object by applying a strong and confident leg to encourage forward movement. The most important thing to remember is to ride your horse forward! The trot is a good gait to pass objects that you know might frighten your horse. As you ride past, you should turn the horse's head slightly away from the scary object. If you make a big deal by kicking, yelling, and forcing the horse to face his monster, you are only enforcing that this is something to fear. It is your confidence that will make your horse feel secure. Trust in the rider will reduce or alleviate shying.

Conformation Fault

A conformation fault is a physical trait that deviates from the breed ideal. Most horses will have at least one trait that could be considered a fault. The horse with perfect conformation is rare. A conformation fault might infrequently interfere with a horse's ability to be a useful animal, whatever his discipline. However, certain faults might decline a horse from a discipline, particularly when she tries to move up to the top levels of competition where the demands are great. For instance, a horse with excessively long pasterns might have no trouble as a pleasure jumper or low hunter, but the demands of high show jumping might stress the area past the point where he can remain sound. Similarly, a horse with hock non-conformities might not hold up to high-level dressage training, which is very demanding on that part of his body.

It is important to remember that the amount of heart a horse possesses is a far better indicator of how well he will perform than is perfect bone structure. Throughout the history of the horse, more stories have been told of the insurmountable odds that the horse have overcome, all because of heart.

The wise horse owner will evaluate his horse and design a training program that will allow him to develop to his full potential. As the training of your horse progresses, and horse and rider move up in competition, it will be up to the owner or trainer to determine if the horse can take the stress of advanced work.

Long Back

A horse with a back that is considered abnormally long will often look as if the front and hind end do not match. This horse will be more of a challenge to train and maintain in good muscle, because he will need the help of the rider to remain in proper balance. If ridden well and the muscles of the back have properly developed, the horse should be able to reach his full potential. But long backed horses will be harder to collect. Therefore, they are predisposed to soreness in the back from ill formed and overstressed back muscles, and the horses will have more difficulty balancing and supporting a rider, especially a large rider. However, many talented jumping horses have long backs!

Crooked Legs

This is a broad term, but refers to any limb that deviates from the norm. A horse should travel straight, with the hind leg following the path of the corresponding front leg. There tends to be more conformation faults in front legs. When looking at conformation, a line should be able to be drawn vertically down the horse's front legs, from the point of the shoulder to the ground. The limb should have equal distribution on either side of the line. Hind leg conformation is looked at a little differently. The line begins at the point of the hip traveling straight to the ground, bisecting the gaskin down to the center of the hoof. Viewed from the rear, a vertical line is drawn from the buttocks to the ground.

FACT

A farrier can be extremely helpful in keeping a horse with crooked legs balanced. When a farrier studies how a horse looks, stands, and travels, he can compensate for imbalances, among other nonconformities, with careful trimming and corrective shoeing.

Pole Nonconformity (the Occipital Crest)

The pole is a bone located just behind the horse's ears at the top of his head. It is important to have a well-conformed pole if you wish your horse to do collected work. It is at the pole that a horse must be able to flex. This is often referred to as the horse being "round" or "in a frame." This position will help a horse balance, engage his hind end, and accept the bit. Some horses whose pole is set on wrong will have difficulty being comfortable in a frame and might tend to invert or hollow out their backs. This will make the horse uncomfortable if not difficult to ride and will build up the wrong back muscles, instead of a healthy "top line" for proper support of his spine.

A horse's top line refers to the space from his wither to his rump. A desirable top line only slightly dips between these two points and appears muscular. An unhealthy top line is one that gives the horse an appearance of a swayed back and that does not support her barrel.

Sickle-Hocked and Cow-Hocked

A sickle-hocked horse refers to the angle of the hock as viewed from the side. This hock will be weaker than a well-set hock, and the limb will appear to be set under the body more. A horse that is sickle-hocked might be predisposed to a curb, bog spavin, or have trouble with bone spavin, and other arthritic changes in the hock. Secondary problems might develop in the hip and stifle.

Cow hock is a deviation of the hock as viewed from the rear of the horse. The hocks deviate inward and can appear to touch each other. Many horses are cow-hocked to some degree. This conformation fault will predispose the horse to bone spavin.

FACT

Many horses toe out to some degree. Less common is the horse that toes in, also called a pigeon-toed horse. These horses usually have no problem compensating for this conformation fault, but there will be increased stress on the pastern and fetlock joints to some degree.

Long Pasterns, Short Pasterns

Long pasterns can be easily seen by viewing the horse from the side. Pasterns that are long are a conformation fault that puts excessive stress on the flexor tendons, suspensory ligament, and the sesamoid bones. This horse, however, is often a beautiful, long mover, possessing extra suspension and shock absorption. Many gaited breeds of horse are purposely bred to have long rear pasterns. Unlike the front end of horses that practice an animated gait, the rear end must rather slide or shuffle along in order for them to gait properly.

Short pasterns are the opposite confirmation fault. Here there will be more stress on the bones, and the pastern will have less ability to act as a shock absorber. The horse with upright pasterns will often be bouncy and difficult or uncomfortable to sit on. Possible resulting conditions would be ringbone, navicular disease, and osselets, which are bony changes in the fetlock joint.

Chapter 13

Grooming for Health and Beauty

Grooming a horse is a necessary task for your horse's safety, comfort, and emotional well-being. For most caretakers, it is looked upon more as a joy than a chore. First and foremost, grooming keeps your horse clean, which is most important for his comfort, and for etiquette if you will be putting a saddle and bridle on him. Dirt between the horse and his tack can not only be uncomfortable for him, but also could cause rubs and sores that, among other things, might cause him to resist your putting tack on him.

Benefits of Grooming

Horses, as herd animals, are social beings that require touch and affection. It is how they form bonds of friendship and respect with each other. A consistent grooming practice will help to form such bonds between you and your horse while instilling in him your intentions of nurture and kindness toward him. Grooming can also be an opportunity for you to give him the pleasure of a massage that he will appreciate. Grooming is also an opportunity to assess your horse's health close up. You can look and feel for hidden puncture wounds, cuts, scratches, swollen areas, ticks, eye impediments, and healthy feet. That is why it is important to groom your horse on a daily basis.

FACT

Your horse will probably let you know if some part of his body is in pain by trying to prevent you from touching that area or by looking back at you when you do. It is an often-repeated saying of horse professionals that a horse will tell you when he is sick, if you pay attention and use common sense.

The Grooming Box

The tools and products you can assemble for your grooming box are available at your local tack or feed supply store. The choice and variety is seemingly endless, which is a testament to the importance of grooming. For instance, your horse might be thin skinned and not like a brush that is too stiff. With some experimentation, you'll find the equipment that is right for you and your horse.

A minimally equipped grooming box should contain:

- Hoof pick
- Mane and tail brush
- Curry
- Stiff brush
- Soft brush

- Shedding blade
- Towel

These tools will fit into a grooming box that can be kept in a tack trunk, stored on a shelf, or carried in one hand. If you have the room and inclination, you could easily get carried away at the store and make this list longer and more varied.

Grooming the Horse

Begin your daily grooming by picking out each of the horse's feet, and with a stiff brush knocking off the mud from the outside of his hoofs. This is a good opportunity to check if his feet are healthy, and if he is shod that his shoes are in good shape. (Foot and hoof care procedures are discussed in depth in Chapter 5, Hoof and Foot.)

Next, start at the shoulder and curry the entire horse with the exception of his lower legs and his face. Currying is done in a circular motion, which loosens caked on mud and brings dirt up to the surface. When grooming a horse, your free hand should always remain on the horse in order to comfort him.

A stiff brush is your next tool. It should be used in a short flicking motion to remove the loosened dirt, and this brush can be used on his legs. When grooming under his belly and lower areas, keep your head up for safety. If you are squatting or kneeling, you are less able to get clear of your horse if he is startled.

An equine vacuum is an excellent grooming tool and timesaving device. Most horses get used to the sound and feel of it quickly and even learn to enjoy being groomed in this way. However, they are expensive and they need maintenance and, of course, electricity.

Now, the mane and tail comb can be used. In order not to break his hair, hold his hair two inches from the end to work out knots and debris, working your way up. A full and healthy tail and mane are desirable and should be encouraged by constant care.

A soft brush will then flatten his coat, bring out the shine, and remove any fine dust left over. This is safe for use on his face and ears.

Finally, dampen a towel, wash his face, wipe out his ears and nostrils, and vigorously wipe down the entire horse for extra shine and removal of errant dust. Don't forget under his tail. Hoof conditioning oil can now be applied for aesthetic and health purposes.

Bathing the Horse

Unless you have a heated wash stall, you shouldn't bathe a horse if the temperature is below 55 degrees or on a blustery day. Before you begin bathing a horse, you must assemble the right equipment and, whenever possible, use warm water. Remember to keep these things from under a horse's feet or where he might otherwise step on them. You will need:

- Hose
- Bucket
- Sponge
- Soap
- Conditioner
- Sweat scraper
- A safe, obstacle free area or wash stall
- A cooler or sweat sheet to cover the horse if the weather is cool

First, curry off any mud that is caked on your horse's hair. It is more expedient to do this with a currycomb rather than with the hose. Fill a bucket with soap and water. Wet the horse down with a hose, taking care to soak her mane and tail thoroughly. Wash the mane and tail with soapy water. Rinse, then apply conditioner. This will give the conditioner the required time it needs to set in to the tail and mane while you are working on bathing the rest of the horse.

Wash the legs from the knee down. This might require some scrubbing, especially if he has white socks. Then, vigorously lather his entire body, working the sponge in a circular motion.

FACT

A horse that will not stand for bathing on cross ties can be held by another person with a lead rope instead. Sometimes, a lead rope attached to his halter and draped over his neck while on cross ties will help to keep him still. Once a horse gets used to being bathed, he will most likely realize there is nothing to be afraid of and stand still on cross ties.

Starting at the feet and working your way up, rinse the horse thoroughly with the hose, taking care not to aim it at his face, which will scare him unless he is used to it. Avoid his ears as well. He will not tolerate water in his ears, which can also be a health hazard.

To wash his face and forelock, use a more diluted mixture of soap and water with a clean sponge or cloth. Don't be afraid to hold his head down by the halter for this task to make it easier on yourself and so you don't get soap in his eyes. A grooming halter will come in handy here, as it will allow easier access to all areas of his face.

Use a sweat scraper to whisk the excess water from his body with short flicks of the wrist. He will dry faster, be less attractive to flies, and less susceptible to catching a chill. For his legs, he will appreciate you using your hand to perform the same function of a sweat scraper, which would hurt him in these sensitive areas. In cool weather, you might want to further dry him with a towel before covering him with a cooler or blanket to avoid him catching a chill.

Clipping Your Horse

Clipping is nothing more than a close haircut for your horse. It is not a necessary service to a horse but can be beneficial depending on your needs and the needs of your horse.

When to Clip

A horse's natural state is to have hair when it's cold and to shed out when the weather warms. In warm climates, and for the late spring, summer, and early fall of colder climates, a horse that is being worked might be clipped to keep cool while working and to dry off quicker after work. Long hair takes much longer to dry on its own and is much harder to towel dry than short hair. It is also considerably easier to groom a clipped horse. Short hair doesn't collect and hold dirt the way longer hair does. Horses in work through the winter in colder climates or seasons will sweat when working, and so they might also benefit from clipping. The horse can be bathed with warm water, dried, and blanketed expeditiously. This is a judgment call and should be based on your experience of your horse before, during, and after cold weather riding.

Benefits of Clipping

Although cold-blooded horses tend to have a thicker coat than light horses, any horse that has been living in a colder climate and is relocated to a warmer climate might have trouble shedding out in the spring, or might have trouble adjusting to heat in general. Such horses might benefit from a clip to help them stay cool. You might also need to clip your horse for a neater, more aesthetically pleasing appearance that's usually expected in the show ring. A clip will reveal the musculature of a horse and make it easier to keep him clean during a show.

Extra Precautions for Your Clipped Horse

Before you clip your horse, keep in mind that there are reasons he has his natural length of hair. You will need to compensate for removing it with extra, time-consuming care. Hair is grown for protection from sun, wind, cold, rain, snow, bugs, cuts, and scratches. If your turnout is rough, and your horses are out more than a few hours a day, or if you ride mostly in the field rather than in a ring, you might want to leave him the hair on his lower legs for protection from cuts and scratches. You might also leave him the hair on his face and in his ears for extra protection from flies. Likewise, you might want to leave him his whiskers. They protect his face and eyes from debris and aid his sensory perception of his environment. For these reasons and to prevent the horse from growing his hair back immediately, he should be blanketed with a turnout sheet or fly sheet in warm weather or a turnout blanket in cold weather, both inside his stall and during turnout.

FACT

A turnout sheet is worn on a clipped horse when the temperature is above 60 degrees. Below 60 degrees, the turnout should be switched from a sheet to a blanket. However, don't forget to let your horse receive a good dose of sunlight on his entire body at least every few days.

How to Clip

Unlike grooming, horses often don't like to be clipped. The noise, the smell, and the feel of clippers are offensive to them, yet most will learn to stand for it. It is not a difficult nor complicated task once you learn how to do it. However, there are many tricks and techniques that will make it easier on you and your horse, and so you might want to watch it being done by a professional the first time.

If you choose to go it alone, the basic motion is against the grain or direction of how his hair grows. The clippers must be kept clean and lubricated with petroleum products available at your tack store.

Trouble Spots and Solutions

A novice will have the most trouble with the legs, the face, and especially the ears for which you will need smaller, finer clippers. Clipping is a lot to ask of a horse, and you want his first few experiences to be as positive and stress free as possible. A small amount of tranquilizer will help, which can be obtained by your veterinarian. Administration of medication is covered in Chapter 9, The Horse's First Aid Kit.

A helpful tip for clipping is for you or an assistant to pick up one of the horse's legs. A horse can't take a step if you have immobilized one of his legs. Be careful! A horse in severe protest of clipping will probably hurt himself by trying to escape if you use this technique.

Care of the Mane and Tail

Many horse owners choose to "pull" their horse's mane routinely. This is a shortening of the mane by pulling out the longer hairs with a sharp "pulling comb" for a cleaner, groomed look. It also makes it easier to braid the mane, which exposes and accentuates the neck allowing show judges to see the whole horse. It should be noted that not all breeds of horses are judged by the same criteria, and some manes are never artificially shortened or braided for shows. You might also put a horse's mane in braids if it is a long, thick mane and it is very hot out. The tail is the same hair as the mane, and can simply be maintained by keeping it conditioned and brushed.

Mane Pulling

Like so many horse chores, pulling a mane to the desired length (about four to six inches) will take practice. It can be daunting if tried for the first time on a head tossing equine or on one with a long mane. If you want to learn this skill, it is best to try it on a very patient horse whose mane is maintained this way.

You will need:

- A pair of thin gloves (riding gloves are good)
- A pulling comb
- A step stool

To begin, tie your horse in the stall or put her on cross ties. Start at her least sensitive place, which will probably be either at her withers or at her poll. Don't shampoo the mane because it will become slippery and hard to handle. Thoroughly comb the mane, removing all tangles. Take a small section of hair about half an inch wide and put the comb into this section. Push the comb up toward the roots, which will get the already short hairs that don't need to be pulled out of the way. While holding those hairs with your left hand, re-insert the comb just above your left hand. Wrap the long hairs twice around the comb, then pull vigorously straight down. Work your way along the entire mane in this manner. Pulling the mane should take you about fifteen to thirty minutes, depending on your skill and the previous condition of her mane.

FACT

Routine mane pulling keeps the mane from becoming unruly, making maintenance easier. Also, your horse will get used to standing for it once he understands that it is a relatively short and painless procedure. A treat or two during and after clipping will go a long way toward making your horse stand for clipping.

Wrapping

There are several reasons why you might want or need to wrap a horse's lower legs, and there are different kinds and styles of wraps according to your purpose. A horse's legs are sensitive and prone to injury and illness, so wrapping must be done when it is needed and done correctly. The most common reasons to wrap are:

- To protect a wound from dirt, debris, and insects.
- To keep a cold pack or medication in place.
- To semi-immobilize an area where tissue needs to heal.
- To reduce soft tissue swelling.
- To support a sprain or strain.

The two most common and useful wraps are 1) the standing wrap, sometimes known as a shipping wrap, and 2) the support or pressure wrap.

Standing Wrap

The standing wrap should extend from just below the knee on a foreleg or the hock on a hind leg to the ankle. A quilt or three sheets of bandaging cotton should be used under the wrap.

If your horse requires wrapping for any length of time, the opposite leg should be wrapped as well. Horses tend to shift weight from an injured leg to the opposite healthy leg, which might create a problem in that leg as well.

To begin wrapping, the leg should be clean and dry. The quilt is held at the cannon bone just below the knee and wrapped clockwise around the leg. It should lay flat with no wrinkles. While holding the quilt in place, the bandage should be started at the cannon bone on top of the quilt and unrolled in a clockwise direction as well. Even pressure should be applied with every revolution around the leg. Go once around, and then begin to angle the wrap as you work your way down. Overlap one-third of the bandage each time. The bandage should be smooth with no gaps or wrinkles. Most bandages will go down to the ankle and back up to the knee where they are secured with Velcro, pins, or tape, depending on the wrap.

Support or Pressure Wrap

Begin this wrap with a thin quilt or two sheets of bandaging cotton. The bandage itself can be cotton or vet wrap, otherwise known as coflex. Begin and wrap following the same procedure as a standing wrap but continue down to the pastern, supporting the entire ankle. Vet wrap will make it easier to avoid gaps that might form around the ankle and will not restrict movement. When using a support wrap, tension should only be applied across the front of the cannon bone and not around the tendon.

A wrap that is pulled snug around the back of your horse's leg, which is his tendon, rather than the front of his leg, which is his cannon bone, could result in a bowed tendon. This is a serious injury and will take a long time to heal.

Bandages should be removed daily and also for turnout unless the horse is supervised. A bandage that comes loose and unravels will probably scare your horse, potentially causing more damage than good.

Chapter 14

Tack and Equipment

The equipment or tack we outfit our horses with has a dizzying array of options. The variety of choices in bits alone can be somewhat intimidating to the novice. The best advice is to simplify your choices. There will be no shortage of passionate opinions on just about every aspect of the horse business including tack from vets, trainers, and tack store workers. Everyone might be telling you something different, but consider their opinions and see what works for you and your horse.

Bridles

Bridles often come as a complete set, which includes a headstall, cheek pieces, brow band, noseband, and reins. There is a wide range in leather quality and stitching designs from single to triple stitched. The leather can be thin or wide, rolled or flat. Color is usually varying shades of brown or black. It would not be unusual to see twenty different bridle styles in a tack store. Having a price range in mind will help to narrow the choices. Have an idea of the size bridle you need. Sizes range from pony, Cob, horse, and warm blood. If you have an old bridle that you're replacing, bring it along. If not, you can measure the width of the forehead, length of the cheek, and muzzle of the horse beforehand.

Figure 14.1:
A Bridle

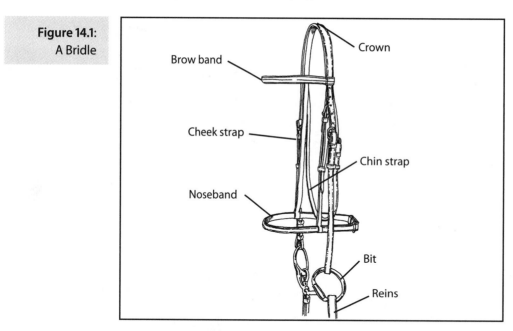

Nosebands

The two common noseband designs are the cavesson and the drop noseband. The band on a cavesson has no angle and sits two inches below the end of the cheekbone. The drop noseband is slightly thicker in the middle or angled. It sits lower to encircle the muzzle, fastening in the chin groove.

It is designed to keep the mouth from opening wide enough for the horse to get his tongue over the bit.

Reins

The most common leather reins are approximately three-quarters inch thick with a single length of lacing for additional grip. Riders are often quite particular as to the type of rein they prefer to use. Often dressage riders will use web reins, which are a combination of cloth and leather. Event riders often prefer a slightly thicker rein made of rubber. Brow bands can be plain, inlayed with lacing or metal, or even studded with rhinestones! The only common requirement of reins is that they should be long enough to have about a foot of potential slack so the horse can have his head to stretch and relax after a workout.

QUESTION?

How do I know what tack to buy?
Often the new owner of a horse will use the same type of tack the previous owner used. This is a good starting point if the horse seemed happy and well cared for. You can also take notice of what your fellow riders and others in your equestrian community are using for tack and equipment. Different areas of the country and different disciplines of riding might warrant specific kinds of equipment. Another way to get help is to ask your local professionals for advice.

Western Bridle

The most common Western bridle is the split eared type. This is a simple headstall that sits across the poll and over one ear. There is no throatlatch or noseband. It is simple and plain in appearance. Several choices of leather are available, and reins can be leather or rope in varying widths. Western reins are longer and not closed with a buckle.

Bridling Your Horse

To bridle a horse, you should stand on the left side of the horse near the shoulder. The reins are placed over the horse's head allowing you some control if the horse attempted to walk off before the bridle is fitted. Next, the headstall is lifted toward the poll, as the left hand cups the bit. The horse is encouraged to open his mouth by applying pressure to the toothless gum area on the side of the mouth. As soon as the horse takes the bit, the right hand should place the headstall over the far ear first, then the near one. The throatlatch and noseband are then secured. The reins should be taken over the head before the horse is led out of the barn.

Most horsemen agree that the coarser the head, the plainer the bridle should be. A really eye-catching bridle should be reserved for the finer headed horse.

Bits

Bits can come in different metals such as copper, nickel, and stainless steel, and even in rubber. They can be solid or hollow and come in different shapes and sizes to suit the needs of both horse and rider. Some types of bits will predominate in certain disciplines.

Snaffle Bit

The most common English bit is known as the snaffle. This can be single jointed or broken with various shaped inserts placed between the right and left mouthpiece. For example, sometimes there is a roller or flat piece made of copper, which is said to increase salivation.

The rings of the snaffle bit can come in many shapes, each with a slightly different purpose. The D-ring snaffle is known as a racing bit, while an Egg-butt is often used in riding schools for less experienced riders who haven't developed quiet hands.

The snaffle puts pressure on the bars of the mouth, cheeks, and slight pressure on the tongue. The thicker the mouthpiece on the snaffle bit, the softer the pressure will be on the mouth, and so the more mild the bit. Thinner mouthpieces are harsher. When fitting a snaffle, it should cause a single wrinkle in the corner of the horse's mouth. If the bit is too narrow, it will pinch and possibly cause sores. If it is too wide, the joint might hit the roof of the mouth. Most bits, snaffle or otherwise, measure between four-and-three-quarters and five-and-one-half inches long.

Curb Bit

A curb bit is often used for advanced training when more collection is desired. It is also used by field riders such as fox hunters, who require a stronger bit for more control. However, a curb bit can be damaging to the horse in the hands of an inexperienced rider, who might overflex the horse and develop in him a hard mouth. The action of the curb is on the bars of the mouth and tongue. The width of the mouthpiece and height of the port, which is the raised area in the center of the mouthpiece, determine the harshness of the bit. The longer the shanks on the curb bit, the more pressure is on the horse's mouth.

ALERT!

Professional advice should always be sought when stepping up to a harsher bit. Some bits can be harmful if used in the wrong way and are meant only for training purposes by a professional. Some horses are said to have shallow mouths, which can be a problem in bitting them properly.

The curb bit is usually used with a curb chain that sits in the groove of the chin. The chain should lie flat, not twisted, and should not be tight. You should be able to get two fingers in between the chain and the chin. The curb bit is designed to draw the chin in. In turn, the horse will flex at the poll.

The Pelham Bit

This bit is a cross between the snaffle and the curb bit. The shanks can be long or short. Two reins are used with a Pelham, which can be cumbersome to some riders. One rein acts on the bit, and the other on the curb. Pelhams are common in the hunt field and other cross-country events. Like the curb, they give more control to the rider.

The Kimberwick Bit

The Kimberwick bit is also used with a curb chain but has a single rein. The mouthpiece contains a port that can vary in height. The rings of the bit are shaped like a D.

These bits sit slightly lower in the horse's mouth and should not cause a wrinkle like with the fit of a snaffle.

ESSENTIAL

Any poorly fitted bit can cause sores, head shaking, unsteadiness with the head, and other resistance because the horse's mouth is extremely sensitive. If the horse is being properly put to the aides and is still resisting, a change of bit might be in order. Some of the softer metals can develop sharp edges or wear when the horse chews on the bit. All bits should be routinely checked for wear.

Western Bits

Western bits were developed with a specific job in mind. For example, the roping horse often uses a bit with curved shanks that join below the chin and are attached to a ring. This design keeps the reins from getting in the way when roping cattle. Traditionally, the Western bit is a curb, but snaffles are common too. The hackamore is common too which is a means of controlling the horse without a bit. Instead, pressure is put on the nose and chin with the action of long shanks.

Saddles

English tack offers three basic types of saddles: the flat or jumping saddle, the all-purpose or event saddle, and the Dressage saddle. Western saddles are usually some variety of stock saddle. There are less common varieties such as a saddle seat saddle, Icelandic saddle, race saddle, and still others. Saddles are available in several different leathers, even buffalo hide! Color is most often shades of brown or black. Lightweight saddles with cloth seat and flaps are available as well. Whatever saddle you choose, it must fit you and more importantly your horse. Sizes run from child to nineteen inches.

FACT

The saddle size is measured from the tack, which is on the side of the pommel, to the middle of the cantle. The saddle flap can also come in various lengths to accommodate a rider's long or short leg.

Saddle width is very important for the comfort of your horse, since most back problems can be traced to a poorly fitted saddle. You might love your saddle, but if it doesn't fit your current horse, a change is in order. Occasionally a horse will require a custom saddle made to accommodate his body type.

English Saddle

English saddles tend to give you a good sense of the horse underneath you, and allow you to ride out of the saddle in a half seat for jumping, cantering, and galloping. Some riders compare riding in an English saddle versus riding in a Western saddle to the difference between driving a sports car versus driving a truck.

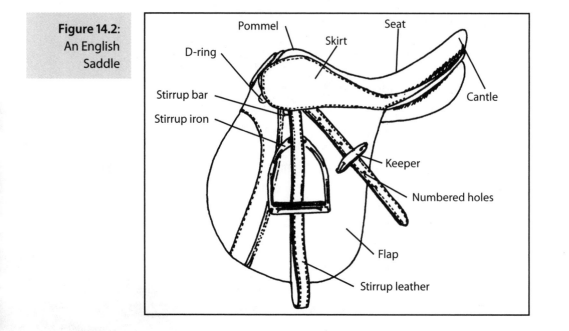

Figure 14.2:
An English
Saddle

Jumping Saddle

The jumping saddle's leg flaps are situated more toward the shoulder of the horse. It is designed to incline you slightly forward in the seat. This position is ideal for jumping, where you must close the angle of your hip to accommodate the horse as he jumps.

Dressage Saddle

The Dressage saddle is for exactly the opposite effect. Its leg flaps are long and straight, designed to situate you straight up in the saddle and encourage a long leg to maximize this most important of aids in Dressage.

FACT

Gaited horses most often require a Western or Dressage saddle in order to perform their gaits. Most gaited horses have a more exaggerated shoulder movement in their gaits, which are hindered by a jumping saddle whose leg flaps extent slightly onto the shoulder.

All-Purpose Saddle

The all-purpose saddle is simply a hybrid between a jumping saddle and a Dressage saddle. Eventers use them because they compete in both jumping and Dressage and for safety reasons: they jump from a more up and down position, rather than close to their hip angle. Pleasure riders often use an all-purpose saddle because it allows them the freedom to jump some field jumps while not being constantly thrust forward by a jumping saddle.

Western Saddle

The most common Western saddle is known as the stock saddle. Other styles are available, ranging from simple to ornate. Western saddles have a deep seat and encourage a long leg. The horn on a Western saddle can be convenient to hold on to in an emergency.

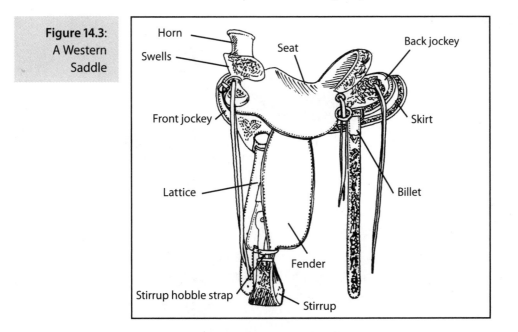

Figure 14.3: A Western Saddle

Western saddles are designed so that the weight of the rider is toward the cantle. They are also heavier than English saddles. The saddle flaps are long and come with stirrups attached (as shown in Figure 14.3). Stirrups are often made of wood or rawhide. Western saddles are available in several grades of leather, and they often have a good deal of tooling. These saddles are used with a square blanket, often in a Navajo design. The girth can be mohair or cord.

How to Fit a Saddle to a Horse

When the saddle is placed on the back of a horse, it should sit more or less level. Let the saddle sit where it wants to. That is to say, place it up toward the wither and slide it down to where it falls naturally, which is where it will probably end up anyway once you start to ride. The seat panels should rest on the fleshy muscles located on either side of the spine. It should be wide enough to not pinch the shoulders and high enough at the withers so two or three fingers can be placed between pommel and withers.

Saddle Pad

It is recommended that a pad be used between the saddle and the horse's back to keep the sweat off the leather of the saddle. There is also the benefit of some padding for the horse. Many styles are quilted, which offer a good cushion between saddle and horse. There are even materials like gel pads that have shock absorption ability. Other available materials are cloth, rubber, and sheepskin, to name a few. A pad must not wrinkle under the saddle and should extend beyond the saddle on all sides.

If you get thrown from your horse, you must fall clear of him. Shoes with smooth soles and heels are recommended for riding for just this reason: in the event of a fall, your foot doesn't get caught in or through the stirrup.

Stirrups and Leathers

The stirrup leathers and stirrups are sold separately. Leathers come in different sizes and widths. Stirrups have a few styles and should be large enough to leave an inch of room on either side of the foot. Fully enclosed stirrups can be dangerous in the event that you become unseated from the horse and your foot gets caught. Safety stirrups have an easily breakable rubber band, rather than metal, enclosing the outside of the stirrup.

The Girth

The girth secures the saddle on the horse by wrapping around her barrel and attaching to each side of the saddle. It can be leather, mohair, plastic, rope, or neoprene. Girths are a matter of preference, although some are thought to chafe less.

Girths are sold in various sizes. Forty inches is the average size for a large pony, forty-eight inches for the average horse, and fifty to fifty-two inches for the large warm bloods.

ALERT!

Some professionals recommend tightening your girth over the first few minutes of your ride for the sake of your horse's comfort. However, if your horse spooks or misbehaves before your girth is tight, your saddle could slip and you will fall off the horse.

Saddling the Horse

A saddle pad should be placed over a clean back, taking care that the pad is smooth. The saddle is then lifted and placed over the back, and allowed to settle in the natural depression of the horse's back. Make sure the stirrups are not dangling when you do this. If your pad has straps, they can now be attached to the billet straps located beneath the saddle flap. Next, the girth is attached on the off or right side of the horse. If your girth has one side that is elasticized, the elastic should end up on the left side where you will secure and adjust the girth. The girth should be securely but not tightly fastened. Instead the girth should be gradually tightened over a few minutes to avoid making the horse uncomfortable.

Accessories

Accessories to basic tack, like martingales, breastplates, and cruppers, customize the tack to the special needs of a horse and rider.

Martingales

There are two types of martingales, a standing martingale and a running martingale. The Western version of a martingale is called a "tie down." The martingale helps to stabilize the high-headed horse. It should be an aid but not a substitute for teaching the horse to carry his head properly. The standing martingale is a leather strap that attaches to the bridle on the underside of the cavesson and the underside of the girth. There is a yoke that goes around the horse's neck to keep the strap stabilized. The running martingale is similar in its makeup, but has two straps with rings on the end that are slipped on to each rein. This has a direct connection with the horse's mouth.

When fitting the horse for a martingale, allow the horse the freedom to use his head and neck naturally, in no way restricting the horse. Pressure should come into play only when the horse's head is above his natural carriage. Martingales are prohibited in some classes at horse shows. Those who misunderstand the purpose of a martingale might use one on a horse that rears. This will probably only make the problem worse and could, in effect, cause the horse to flip over backwards.

Breastplate

The purpose of using a breastplate is to keep a saddle from slipping back. It is attached on either side of the saddle to hooks and also to the underside of the girth.

Crupper

The crupper performs the opposite job as the breastplate. The crupper attaches to a ring on the cantle of the saddle and then has a padded leather strap, which is fastened under the tail; this keeps the saddle from slipping forward. Cruppers are used on ponies and horses conformed "down hill" or with low withers.

Horse Coverings

Horse coverings, of which there are many varieties, are a matter of convenience and comfort for you and your horse. You can use coverings to keep your horse clean, warm, or protect him from insects.

Anti-Sweat Sheet

The name can be slightly misleading. Anti-sweat sheets are usually made of very absorbent cotton woven in a mesh design. This design keeps the horse warm and draft free, but also initiates quick drying. They are useful after the horse works up a sweat through exercise or after you bathe him. Anti-draft sheets are also light enough to afford fly protection. This sheet comes with chest buckles and one or two surcingles to secure the cover. A horse should not be turned out with this cover because it is more fragile due to its design. Instead the horse should wear this cover after exercise on cross ties in the stall or while being hand grazed after a bath.

Blankets can be heavy, smelly, cumbersome, and time consuming to put on and take off. This is why lots of caretakers get lazy about taking them off. A horse's skin and coat should receive its all important sun and fresh air.

Sheets

Sheets are most often cotton, but they are also available in nylon and synthetic fabrics. Cotton is recommended since it breathes the best. Horse owners will sheet their horse in preparation for blanketing. A sheet can help to keep the coat down, as fluctuations in weather can cause the coat to pop out or grow in response to cold weather. They are useful in late spring and early fall when weather is less consistent. Some sheet styles are light enough so that they can be worn by the horse throughout the summer.

A fly sheet is for the hot months of fly season. It is therefore extremely breathable open mesh, which protects the horse's body from flies without insulating him. A rain sheet is a light waterproof sheet for use in warm but rainy weather.

Blankets

Blankets come in many thicknesses and materials such as cotton, nylon, or wool. Some are quilted and filled with polyfill, similar to your own winter jacket. These coverings provide the greatest protection against cold. Both sheets and blankets have similar closings. Typical closures are chest buckles and one or two surcingles. In addition, some sheets and blankets are permanently closed at the chest and must be put on over the head. Still others have a tail band, which further secures the blanket and prevents it slipping to one side. There are even blanket styles that come with a neck hood.

Turnout Blanket or Rug

A turnout blanket is invaluable to the horse that has been clipped. These are sturdy coverings made of canvas or nylon that can be quite heavy or very light depending on their purpose. They keep the horse warm when she is outside with the additional benefit of keeping her clean! They are usually waterproof, so they offer good protection against the elements. Closures are similar to blankets and sheets with the addition of leg straps. These straps are elastic and go between the hind legs to keep the cover from slipping.

E
ALERT!

A poorly fitted blanket can cause serious injury to a horse. A blanket that is too big for the horse can slip off in turnout or overnight in the stall. There is a good chance that some of the buckles and surcingles will still be fastened, resulting in the horse getting tangled in the blanket.

If you decide to use a covering for your horse, it must fit him well and be checked periodically for wear. It should also be kept reasonably clean. The horse should also be checked for blanket rubs, since thinner skinned horses can develop rubs from the friction a blanket causes. A cover should not be worn for twenty-four hours without being removed to allow the coat to receive air and sun. Attention must be paid to the daily weather predictions—it is unhealthy for a horse to sweat under a covering.

How to Blanket

To place a cover on the horse, it should first be folded in thirds, from the tail end to the withers. Now it can be placed over the head for closed chest styles or laid across the withers and fastened at the chest. Take care that surcingles are not dangling because they could hit the horse in the legs or frighten him. Finally, unfold and secure the blanket.

Chapter 15
Handling a Horse

When handling and approaching a horse, there are a few basic rules to follow in order to stay safe and be an effective handler. Horses have blind spots that must always be considered, especially the rear blind spot, which is their largest and most vulnerable. Because they have such a complete field of vision, a surprise from a blind spot is often met with an extreme reaction. For this reason, a horse should, if possible, be approached from the front, and should be approached slowly and calmly.

How to Approach a Horse

Horses have very good voice and tone recognition capabilities. You can speak to him to announce your presence, which might have a calming effect. Quick movements or catching him by surprise might initiate his natural instinct to kick, bite, or bolt, which can endanger both of you and undermine his trust in you.

FACT

It is customary to initiate all procedure from a horse's left side. This custom probably dates back to the days when horses were used mainly for warfare, and a rider's sword was worn on his left side. This meant that the horse had to be mounted from the left to avoid interference by the rider's sword. Today, there is no reason to do everything from the left, except that your horse was probably handled and trained that way and he is used to it.

When approaching, you must also consider the horse's personal space, an area about three yards in circumference around the horse, which he considers his own. Horses let people violate their personal space all the time as we handle, groom, and ride them. They also let each other enter it in play, mutual grooming, and general group companionship. However, one must always be aware that there are circumstances where they might be inclined to protect their space. These might include if he is injured, protecting food, a male who is proving ownership of a mare, a mare feeling the need to protect a foal, or if he is just plain ornery.

Catching a Horse

There are rules and methods to catching a horse. How you approach and secure your horse in the paddock or in a stall is important to your safety and a successful, positive experience.

In the Paddock

When walking into a paddock or field of horses to catch and bring one of them out of the group, it is important to be aware of all the horses and their possible reactions to you. Horses in a group act differently from a single horse and are somewhat unpredictable. You might be upsetting the order of the group. Or maybe the horse you have caught and are leading through the other horses has entered into the personal space of a more dominant horse. Perhaps one or more of the horses take your presence as an opportunity to incite the others to flee or play. Any of these circumstances can be dangerous to you and to the horses. Among horses, what they consider to be play is only a benign version of fighting. The kicks, bites, and rearing might be harmless among themselves when done in a playful manner, but to you they could be devastatingly powerful. To avoid the possible scenario of getting caught in the middle of a group of active horses, you must command the respect of the group by insisting on your personal space and that of the horse you lead. Your approach to the horse should be off center, preferably to his left shoulder.

Teaching a horse a "head down" command is helpful in this and other processes and even necessary with very tall horses. With this command, your horse will drop his head so that you don't have to stretch to reach his head, which would put you in an uncomfortable and vulnerable position. If you have to struggle with him before your ride, you will probably have to struggle with him during your ride.

Standing at his shoulder and facing in the same direction, bring the lead rope, which is already attached to the bottom ring of the nose strap of a halter, up and around his neck. This is a faster way to secure some control over him, so that if he bolts or shies away from the halter, you still have him. Next, bring the halter from his chest up to his face, sliding his nose in first. With both hands on the sides of the headstall, bring the halter up toward his ears. Fold each ear under the headstall. Finally, close the throatlatch.

In the Stall

Catching a horse in the stall follows most of the same basic rules as catching him in the paddock. He is alone, which can make it easier, but the confined space can present other dangers and difficulties.

He is more apt to sleep when in the stall, so whether he is facing you, or more particularly when he is facing away from you, never assume he is awake and knows you are there. Make sure you have his attention before going into the stall and that he is facing you. In the event that you do surprise him or you are otherwise caught behind a kicking horse, the closer you are to his rump, even if you are hugging it, the safer you are. This way, there is not the injury potential of a fully extended kick.

Leading a Horse

Leading a horse is like leading a dog on a leash. It allows you control over his speed and destination. Depending on where a horse thinks he's being led to, he might try to either drag behind or race ahead of you. So it is important to be positioned correctly to protect yourself from injury.

When leading, you should be at his left shoulder or slightly in front of it. Look in the direction where you are going. The horse should pay attention to your purpose and go off with you. Insist on consistency with voice commands. The voice command can be backed up with a sharp downward pressure on the lead rope or with a crop to encourage a more forward step. Don't allow laziness or disobedience. Leading is a simple but essential training exercise and will set the tone for further training.

The Lead Rope

The lead rope should be held by both hands, your right hand just below the horse's nose where the rope clips onto the halter, the left hand taking up the slack so the lead line doesn't drag on the ground. A dragging lead line can be stepped on by you or your horse, which might startle him toward flight or rearing. In such an instance, holding the lead rope close to his face without slack would limit the full power of his actions and might prevent the horse from getting loose.

Safety Precautions

For these reasons, and other variables or unforeseen circumstances that might arise during leading a horse, it is of utmost importance that the lead line is never wrapped around your hand, draped over your shoulder, or any other part of your body. In some situations, it might become necessary to release a horse rather than hold on and risk injury. Wrapping the lead line will keep you attached whether you want to be or not.

When leading a horse through a gate or into a stall, you must enter first with him close behind. Horses are most comfortable in wide-open spaces and could get nervous when asked to go through narrow spaces which contradicts their natural instincts. They are trusting you in such instances and should be given reassurance. An otherwise well-behaved horse might bolt through a gate or into his stall with no regard for you. Instead, he will feel more confident if you go first. Also, he is more apt to consider and avoid you if he does bolt if you are in front, rather than to his side.

Turning Out a Horse

The transferring of a horse from a stall or any confined or controlled space to a turnout area such as a paddock or pasture is called turning out. Many of the rules addressed above can be applied to turning out a horse. They look forward to turnout after being in a stall or after a ride. They are often eager to be turned out, equating the paddock to a playground. A horse might rush the gate of a paddock, pull away once he is in the paddock, or take off bucking. For these reasons among others, it is important to turn the horse around once inside the paddock so he is facing you before releasing him. Never turn your back on him to walk away; rather, let him move away from you. If you are turning out two horses simultaneously, or you and a friend are turning out horses together, let them go at the same time. One horse moving away might incite the other to pull away too.

Turning Out Difficult Horses

With a horse that bolts away from you immediately when you let him go, you might try turning him out first before any other horses are in the paddock. You can also stay with him for a minute or two after you have turned him around to face you, while petting or talking to him. This might alleviate the anticipation and habit of bolting away from you.

Horses that don't turn out well, whether from fear, bad habit, or disrespect for their handlers, must be handled with great care and consistency with the correct procedures. They are creatures of habit, so good habits must be taught, practiced, and enforced.

Single Turnout

Although horses are by nature social beings, there are some that don't mind being alone or even prefer to be alone. Sometimes they will take to a goat, a miniature horse, or another non-threatening, low impact farm animal. Otherwise, it is okay to give her solitude. Other than leaving her somewhat more vulnerable to predators, it is her preference to be alone and should be honored if it is convenient.

Some horses who are considered too valuable to risk the potential injuries that can occur from fighting or horsing around in a shared or group turnout situation, are usually fine alone as long as other horses or people are close by. Nervous horses should be closely monitored during turnout.

Group Turnout

When turning out horses together, it is not only important that you understand herd dynamics, but also that the horses that you are turning out together understand them as well. In domestic situations, you cannot always assume that a new horse being introduced to the group has been socialized and understands the warning signals that other horses give before an actual violent reaction.

A group that is used to each other has usually worked things out. But in that process of establishing the pecking order, injuries do occur. Whenever possible, it is best to let horses be horses and exist in groups. Occasionally, however, there are horses that are worth too much money to chance injury or horses that just will not get along, and these horses should be separated if you have the means.

Introduction of new horses into the group should be done gradually. Allow the group to see and smell the new horse first for a few days. This can be done from a stall, a paddock that doesn't share a fence line, or by hand grazing him near the group.

Then, give them contact over a fence, either by hand or turnout. They will probably work out most of their issues there in relative safety. This period should last about a week or until there is little drama over the fence line.

Next, choose a horse from the group that in your experience will be a good ambassador. If your alpha horse is benevolent, he might be a good candidate since the new horse will be least inclined to challenge him. Expect some snorting, squealing, nipping, and chasing when you make the introduction which is normal. But, be ready to pull your horse out if the situation becomes dangerous. He might need to gain a safe distance from this first encounter, and future encounters with the whole group later on, so make sure the paddock you have chosen is large enough—an acre would be fine. After you have introduced him to the group, you might want to separate him with a horse or some horses that he gets along with best.

Typically, horses are less rambunctious and so less destructive to the land and ultimately safer in smaller groups. Depending on your means, it will pay to separate the group into buddy groups of two horses that have grown accustomed to each other.

Types of Shanks and Lead Ropes

There are two basic kinds of leads. The most commonly used is a lead rope. A lead shank is more severe and is used mainly for problem horses or when you might need a little extra control, such as when you are loading your horse onto a trailer.

Lead Rope

A standard lead rope is six feet long with a clip on the end. The lead rope is attached onto the ring on the bottom of the noseband of the halter. This method of leading a horse will suffice for one that is generally well behaved. Nylon leads should be avoided because they will not break in a dangerous situation like cotton or leather leads would.

Lead Shank

A lead shank is a cotton rope or leather strap with a two-foot length of chain and a clip on the end. It might be used like a lead rope, but the chain must be shortened so that your hand nearest the horse's chin is holding rope or leather and not chain. In order to do this, feed the chain through the lower ring on his halter, then wrap the chain around itself several times before clipping it to the ring where the leather meets the chain.

ALERT!

Turning out a horse can be the most dangerous handling situation you will face. Correct procedure is important as well as paying attention to the horse you are leading and other horses on the farm.

A lead shank might be longer than six feet, considering the various ways in which a lead is used. The shank might be fed through the left side ring on the noseband of a halter, wrapped over the nose, fed through the far side ring of the noseband, and then clipped onto the ring of the far side cheek piece. A horse's nose is extremely sensitive, so this is a way to exert extra control over a misbehaving horse and should be practiced with care. Downward pressure on the shank used in this way will be more effective than a lead rope simply clipped to the halter. When removing the shank, it must be fed back through the rings and not just pulled through. This might hurt the horse and will certainly scare him, turning a potential training experience into one of fear and negativity.

Types of Halters

A halter is a harness that is fitted over the head of a horse. It is used when you wish to lead, handle, or tie a horse. There are four basic types of halters that come in five basic sizes. "Over size" will fit a draft horse or large warm blood. "Full size" is the next size down and will fit most medium-sized horses, like quarter horses and thoroughbreds. "Cob" is for a small horse, an Arabian for instance, or large pony like an Icelandic. "Pony" speaks for itself. There are smaller, farm animal halters that can be used for foals.

Like lead ropes and shanks, halters can get caught on or in objects around a farm. They should therefore break away, so a horse doesn't hurt himself trying to get free.

Leather Halters

Leather halters are common, safe, and generally the most aesthetically pleasing. However, they are costly and require cleaning and conditioning in order to stay strong and comfortably supple for the horse. Leather halters will also retain moisture from sweat or rain and could develop mold or rot, which is unhealthy and uncomfortable for the horse.

Nylon Halters

Nylon halters are less expensive, but they will not break if a horse catches it on something, and so are not recommended. However, a nylon halter with a leather breakaway headstall is safe and inexpensive.

A grooming halter has no throat latch, which makes it easily maneuvered while grooming your horse's face. These halters are not designed for leading or turnout and should not be used for any purpose other than grooming.

How to Fit a Halter to a Horse

Correctly fitting a halter to a horse is important for the effectiveness of the halter and your horse's comfort. The noseband should lie about two inches below the bottom of his cheekbone. You should be able to fit two fingers comfortably between his nose and the band, signifying that it is tight enough to be effectual, and not easily snagged on something, while loose enough to allow free movement of his mouth. A well fitting halter shouldn't cause rubs or marks.

The throatlatch must also be loose enough not to inhibit his windpipe and choke his throat, but snug enough so that the halter won't slip off. This space should be about four fingers wide.

Halters On or Off During Turnout

It is generally believed that halters should be removed for turnout. A halter can get snagged on something in the paddock. A horse that wears his halter while turned out is more likely to get rubs and sores on his face. Damage could be caused to the halter by horses playfully chewing on each other's halters which, along with rain and mud, will wear them out faster.

However, there are many reasons why you might leave halters on during turnout. If the paddock fencing is unsound and a horse might end up on the wrong side of it, you will find catching him a less daunting task if he is wearing a halter. You might want to leave the halter on a sick horse which might require emergency handling in the field. Likewise, a horse being introduced to a paddock or a group of horses for the first time might require a halter. He might jump or go through a fence, might cause trouble, or be bullied by the others, and need to be identified, singled out, and caught in a hurry. Keeping the halter on will also save time and handling.

You should remove the halter while a horse is in his stall for all the same reasons you might want to remove a halter during turnout. However, you might consider keeping a horse haltered in his stall if he is sick or if he is prone to "casting" himself; in both situations, the horse might require special handling. Casting will be discussed in Chapter 22, Troubleshooting.

Chapter 16

Staying Healthy with Exercise

Exercising your horse is an important aspect of his physical and mental well-being. A routine of exercise will help to curb bad behavior under saddle as well as on the ground, in the stall, and during turnout. Regular exercise stimulates tissue repair, the bowels, and the expulsion of lactic acid from muscles. Exercise will keep your horse fit and develop his coordination and agility, while enforcing an attitude toward discipline and work.

Lunging

There are many different ways and reasons for exercising. Lunging is an unmounted form of schooling and is a great way to give your horse the attention he needs. The two main types of lunging are free lunging and lunging with a surcingle, side reins, and a bridle or lunging cavesson. Each type has its own virtues and limitations, and in some ways, lunging can be a more effective exercise and training technique than riding.

Free Lunging

Free lunging allows a horse total freedom of movement while being in a controlled environment. It can be used as a training technique or just to burn off extra energy before a ride. You will require a round pen or a riding ring that is divided, perhaps by tape or jump standards, to be about the size of a round pen. A lunge whip or any long whip will encourage his forward movement. Begin by letting him have a few minutes to himself. Let him check out the space and stretch out, which might include walking, rolling, bucking, and general horsing around. All training programs should allow an aspect of play, which is one of a horse's primary inclinations.

ESSENTIAL

A happy horse is one that is allowed to play. This is a primal instinct and should be encouraged. Even a disciplined workout, whether on the ground or under saddle, can be considered by your horse as a play date. Letting your horse have his playtime, or even playing with him, will deepen your bond with him.

After a few minutes of play, you should pick up the whip and, from your position in the center of the circle, step firmly toward your horse asking for a trot. Entering his space, stepping confidently toward him, and giving the voice command to "trot" will tell your horse that it's time to get down to business. The trot should be forward but not frenzied. With your whip, encourage him to keep a steady forward pace and to stay to the outside of the ring or circle.

After ten minutes or so, slow him to a walk in preparation for a change of direction. Use the opposite body language and voice command, which is to step backward, lower the whip, and ask him quietly to "walk." Praise him as you walk to him and ask him or help him to change directions. Horses are very quick to pick up your voice commands during lunging and quickly recognize and remember the drill the next time. After trotting in the other direction for about ten minutes, let him cool down at the walk. Give him ample time to stretch out after his workout. He will probably stretch his nose down toward the ground. This is a good thing, showing you that he is relaxed and calm.

ALERT!

A horse should respect but never fear the whip. The whip is a training aid used to create energy and forward movement. It can be used to remind him that you are in charge, but you shouldn't use the whip to instill fear in your horse. Often, the mere presence of a whip, or crop, will suffice to keep a well-trained horse on his best behavior.

Finally, call him or let him into your space in the center of the ring and praise him if he has done his job. Positive re-enforcement will go a long way to make your horse want to please you.

Lunging with a Surcingle, Side Reins, and a Bridle

Not only is lunging an excellent way to exercise your horse, but you can teach him new things without the burden of the weight of a rider. It also affords you a good opportunity to observe your horse's movement from the ground and watch out for any subtle lameness that might be harder to detect while riding him.

Equipment you will need:

- A cotton lunge line
- Surcingle, with side reins
- Lunging cavesson, or a bridle with a snaffle bit and bit stoppers in place

- A long whip
- Bell boots
- Gloves

Mastering the technique of lunging will take time. Coordinating the lunge, excess line, and long whip can prove challenging at first. Work in the walking gait until you feel comfortable with the equipment. To prepare for lunging, the horse should be tacked up and side reins adjusted. Side reins act similar to the reins you hold while riding. They help to stabilize your horse, thus helping him to flex at the pole, so you have more control and he has better balance. The side reins are attached to the lower ring on the surcingle and connected with the bit. The reins of the bridle should be removed or kept out of the way by twisting them a few times and then securing them through the chin strap. If a saddle is used instead of the surcingle, the stirrups should be "run up," so they're not flopping against the horse's sides.

To attach the lunge line, feed it through the near side of the snaffle bit, run it over his head just behind his ears, then clip it onto the far side of the bit. This pressure on the back of his head and the outside of his mouth will encourage him to flex at the pole and stay to the outside of the circle.

Holding your horse close by the lunge line, enter your lunging space and stop with your horse in the center. From here, ask him to walk out away from you in a circle, giving him a little more slack with each revolution, so that the circle gets increasingly larger. A standard lunge line will be about thirty feet. Use the whole thing to prevent injury to your horse from a circle that's too tight, which puts undue strain on the horse's inside leg or "lead." A horse that is reluctant to leave your side can be encouraged by pointing the whip at his shoulder while giving some slack in the line. As soon as he is out on the perimeter of your circle, about thirty feet or so, point the whip at his hindquarters and ask him to trot. As in free lunging, the horse should have a forward swinging trot, which will encourage him to stretch down and seek the bit. This will, in turn, incline him to flex at the pole and be better balanced.

Keep him moving forward with clucks, voice commands, and the whip for about ten minutes. When you're ready to give a walk or halt command, your voice should be your primary aid. Steady pressure should be applied to the lunge until your horse responds. During downward transitions, as from a trot to a walk, the whip should be pointed down toward the ground.

ALERT!

Whether on the ground or under saddle, always exercise your horse equally in each direction. Muscle must be promoted equally on both sides of his body. A "one sided" horse will favor a particular direction and "lead" over the other, which is a bad habit and might lead to lameness from uneven use of that lead leg.

What Gaits to Work on the Lunge

The lunge can be used to work a horse in walk, trot, and canter. However, consider your horse's agility, fitness, level of training, and balance before you let him canter in such a tight circle. Injuries can occur in this seemingly benign situation. Without a rider on his back, a horse might not know when he is strained. Or encouraged by your commands, he might not think he is allowed to stop and so keep going on a new injury that is somewhat masked by his adrenalin. Also, if he is not used to lunging, he might get carried away in a canter and break the circle, trailing the lunge line with him. You or he could get tangled in the line and could suffer potential injury.

Exercise at the Walk (Under Saddle)

Some professionals will say that the walk is the hardest gait to ride correctly. Like a toddler getting his legs for the first time who runs awkwardly rather than walks, a horse is a big, rangy quadruped that often finds it easier to balance and collect himself in a more "forward" gate such as the trot or canter.

Benefits of the Walk

Because of the relatively slow rate of speed at the walk, your horse's attention will be concentrated more on you and your commands than if you were in a faster, more complicated gait. You and your horse will really have an opportunity to think about the commands you give and to work them toward perfect execution.

Walking up hills is good exercise for a horse. Walking works more muscles than any other gait up hill, particularly in the horse's hind end, because there isn't the advantage of propulsion from forward momentum as in the trot or canter.

When to Walk

It is standard practice to walk a horse for about ten minutes before a ride and about ten minutes after. A "warm up" will help to loosen and stretch his muscles before a workout. A "cool down" after exercise helps do the same. When you are cooling down your horse after a ride, he will probably stretch his neck down to the ground. Give him the reins to let him do this post-ride stretch. By gradually bringing him down from strenuous activity, you help to prevent sore muscles and possible "tying up."

Warming him up is also important for his mental well-being. It will help to establish control and calmness, which will set the tone and mood of your ride. Cooling him down after the ride also calms him down and inhibits the bad habit of his getting excited and "strong" on the way home, which is a common vice of horses.

QUESTION?

Don't horses get enough exercise running around outside on their own?

Although some horses will exercise themselves to some extent, especially pasture-kept horses, muscles and tendons atrophy when a horse is not routinely exercised. This could lead to injuries and ailments if the horse is suddenly forced back to work or becomes rambunctious during turnout. These injuries include pulled muscles, bowed tendons, and azoturia (also called tying up).

Benefits for the Young Horse

The walk is the best gait for early mounted work. Walking over flat or uneven terrain will help a young horse develop coordination and balance with a rider on his back. The slow pace of a walk will allow for a gradual learning process. The young horse might need a little extra time to respond to your commands if he is green and isn't sure what you're asking him to do.

Mistakes at the Walk

All too often the walk is considered by the rider to be an unserious gait, the gait that you don't have to pay attention to while you talk to your riding partner or think about other things. If you aren't paying attention, then your horse probably isn't either. He might meander rather than walk in a straight line or be lazy about using his rear end. An unfamiliar obstacle on the trail or a deer that suddenly pops out of the woods could startle him if he's not alert. If you aren't paying attention either, you could fall off. So ride the walk with discipline and purpose.

The Trot

A trot is the best gait for building muscle and stamina. It is thought of as the "conditioning" gait, because it consistently works all the muscle groups at a pace that your horse can endure for a long period of time, as opposed to a canter or gallop that tires him quickly.

FACT

Contrary to the once-popular notion that thoroughbreds lack prowess in the trot because they are bred for the gallop only, their typically long, springy trot proves an excellent gait for Dressage competition.

Rhythm

The trot develops rhythm. Although some types of horses are naturally more coordinated than others, coordination depends on rhythm. Coordinating four legs in four or five different gaits is not as easy as your horse makes it look. His sense of rhythm, which can be enhanced or confused by a rider, is his most important asset to this coordination. Alacrity in his gaits and then in the even more complicated activities we ask of him, such as jumping, is a function of his rhythm.

Other Benefits

The swinging motion of the trot helps a horse to "open" or loosen his shoulder and so lengthen his stride. It is a long and low gait, ideal to teach a horse to stretch and "seek the bit." By pushing him from behind with your leg in this gait, he will be inclined to drop his head and neck and, therefore, arch his spine, thus stretching and "lengthening" the spine. Not only will this incline him to seek the bit, but it will produce a more comfortable and correct ride instead of when his head is up in the air, which would make his back "hollow" and hard to sit.

The Canter or Lope

The lope is a Western term for the canter, and it is usually ridden slowly. The canter is an excellent gait for a horse to practice his balance and collection. It is most often an enjoyable gait for the horse and can be sustained for long periods of time. The canter, like the trot, is also a good rhythm-developing gait. You can hear him keeping his rhythm with his breath, exhaling when the front feet hit the ground and inhaling with his upward motion. The canter can be enjoyable for the rider because it is more comfortable and easier to follow rhythmically than the trot. The canter is an excellent preparation for jumping.

The Gallop

The gallop is a non-restrictive gait, meaning that besides exerting control over the speed of the gallop, there is very little training you can accomplish. You are basically just along for the ride. Good terrain is necessary for your safety and his in this gait, which is the most potentially dangerous.

Benefits

The gallop can benefit a horse in certain ways. It can stretch and lengthen a horse's stride like no other gait and help to wake up a lazy horse. Horses were born to run, so most healthy horses like to gallop. Letting him gallop can be a physical and mental reward. Some horses should never be galloped, however.

When and What Horses Not to Gallop

Some horses should never be galloped. Obviously, a lame horse, or one that is even slightly "off," though he might want to gallop, will risk further injury to himself. One misstep at the gallop can send you and your horse tumbling. This also holds true for a horse returning to work from an injury. His muscles and tendons might have atrophied during his lay up, putting them at risk to strains, pulls, or tears. Don't gallop a green horse or one you're not familiar with. A galloping horse could stop thinking, reverting to more wild and instinctual behavior and disregarding anything he has been taught. Know your horse before you gallop him. A horse that gets carried away in this gait might refuse to stop and could become a "runaway." This would most likely go down in your book as the scariest horse situation you could find yourself in. Once he gets a few steps into the gallop, there is not much you can do to stop him. He can get going too fast for his level of fitness and agility and trip, fall, or otherwise hurt himself—and you!

Ponying

Ponying is when you ride one horse and lead the other alongside you with a lead line and halter or bridle with the reins removed. The lead horse should be experienced, since the horse in hand will require a good deal of the rider's attention. The lead horse should be steady and responsive, remaining calm if the ponied horse becomes fractious. These two horses must be willing to work together. If one horse is dominant over the other, this should be the one you ride while leading the other. The horse in hand is taught to travel at the shoulder of the lead horse, but should also be taught to move behind or in front depending on trail conditions.

This is an excellent way to exercise two horses at once and a way to save yourself the hassle of extra riding in foul weather or when your time is limited. Although you are somewhat limited as to the work you can accomplish with the horse in hand, he will learn much from the lead horse. If similar in type and size to the horse being ridden, he will most likely mimic his rhythm and gaits. In this way, ponying can educate a young or green horse, which will also gain confidence and sense of purpose from the horse in front. Ponying could also be a good way to bring a horse back to work that had been sidelined with an injury and could do without the extra weight of a rider on his back.

ALERT!

Shoulder injuries are common among novice riders who practice ponying. You must know the horses that you are working with and be able to anticipate their reactions. Follow the golden rule of leading: Never wrap the lead line around your hand or any other part of your body, and don't get caught in the slack of the line if it suddenly becomes taut.

Using a Hot Walker

A hot walker is a method of exercising a horse that requires no effort on your part other than to hook up the horse to the machine and keep an eye on him. It offers nothing in the way of training and the absolute minimum of exercise.

A hot walker is often used for thoroughbred racing stallions, where turnout is a problem because of potential difficulties with other horses, both stallions and mares. A hot walker is also common where yearlings are sold. The walker puts a level of fitness and attractive muscle on young horses that are too young to be ridden into condition. A hot walker can be a handy thing to have around in foul weather, or if you cannot, for whatever reason, exercise or have someone else exercise your horse. It is not a substitute for training.

Chapter 17

(E) **Locomotion and Gaits**

People who love horses have fallen not only for their physical beauty while inactive, but also the animal's incredible beauty while in motion. The horse is an extremely powerful animal; yet in motion, his movements are light and free, much like a dancer's. Locomotion translates as the power behind the motion. Gait is the term we commonly use when we refer to the way a horse travels.

Which Gaits to Use

The most common gaits you will learn to sit are the walk, trot, and canter. As a rider you need to train your eye to recognize correct movement in a horse in order to evaluate the horse's quality and health. You also need to train your body to follow the movement of the horse to not interfere with his balance. All gaits are ridden when training a horse. Different gaits develop different muscles and are typically ridden at different speeds. The beauty of an individual gait is determined by conformation, type of horse, training, and the horse's balance. If you view a horse going through his paces while in the field, at most times it will look effortless. This same effortless look takes time to develop under saddle. Some horses are more naturally balanced than others.

Figure 17.1:
Hoof Patterns in the Most Common Gaits

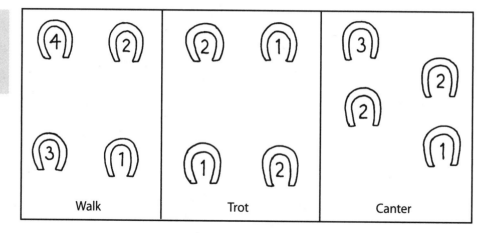

Walk   Trot   Canter

Some words used to describe a horse's way of moving are:

- **Daisy cutter:** This describes a good moving horse that moves well from the shoulder.
- **Rhythm:** Rhythm refers to the sound the rider hears when the horse's hooves contact the ground. A consistent rhythm is very important and an indication of a well-balanced horse.
- **Stride:** The distance traveled in one movement of a gait is the horse's stride. For example, the average canter stride is twelve feet.

- **Scope:** The ability to jump various heights and spread fences is called the scope.

When a horse is evaluated for a particular riding discipline, her way of moving, or gait, will be very important. A healthy, well-rounded horse should be worked in all gaits, no matter what your riding discipline. However, some horses might be weak or uncomfortable to ride in one particular gait.

FACT

The power that a horse generates while performing in any gait is generated from the hind end. The goal of every rider is to engage the hind end to create energy for forward movement.

Consider your riding discipline before buying a horse whose poor gait is the one you will be using the most. For example, the horse whose job will be to fox hunt will need to have a good canter stride. An eventing horse will need, among other things, a strong and agile gallop as opposed to a Dressage horse that will never need to gallop in competition. A trail horse will need to have smooth comfortable gaits, which are less fatiguing on the rider, in particular a good trot. Different breeds of horses are known for certain characteristics of gait. You should look around and see what horses other riders who ride within your discipline are mounted on and decide for yourself which gaits will work best for you.

The Walk

The walk is the slowest of the horse's gaits, covering approximately four miles per hour. Four distinct beats can be heard when riding the walk as follows: left hind, right fore, right hind, and left fore. The horse should carry himself in a relaxed frame during walk with the neck stretched and low. You should maintain light contact with the bit. The walk should be far reaching. Ideally the hind legs contact the ground four to eight inches in advance of the front hoof prints, but in the front prints are sufficient. The front legs swing forward from the shoulder, while the hind legs step well under the body.

The walk is a tempting gait for both you and your horse to be lazy in. For many reasons, it is important to ride this gait with as much attention and diligence as the other gaits. If you let your horse be bored or lazy at the walk and he is not paying attention, the slightest object or variation on the trail or around the ring might spook him. If you are not paying attention either, you could fall off.

The walk is an excellent gait for training both horse and rider. This can be a hard gait for your horse to be collected in without the propulsion achieved in the other gaits. Without collection, he will probably not be using his hind end correctly. That is to say, he will rely too much on his front end for propulsion for you to have a balanced and comfortable ride. If you start your ride off in a strong, straight collected walk, it will be easier to keep him like this in his other gaits.

You should generally begin your rides with walk to loosen your horse's muscles and make him supple before demanding more forward movement. It is also the gait you should end your ride with, relaxing the muscles of the horse, letting him stretch his neck to the ground, and allowing his heart rate to return to normal.

ALERT!

Beginning and ending your ride in the walk is just as important for a horse's mental well-being as his physical well-being. A horse that begins a ride nervously or anxiously might not calm down for the duration of your ride. Likewise, a horse that ends a ride in a fast gait might become a perpetually nervous or high horse. Horses appreciate gradual transition.

Any rider can ride a horse in walk. To ride a "good" walk is as demanding as riding any of the other gaits correctly. All too often, novice riders treat the walk as a non-serious gait, letting the horse meander or fall out of discipline. Don't let this be you.

When to Ride the Walk

The walk is your most cautious gait. When your horse is scared of something on a trail, or a trail is muddy, rocky, or otherwise unstable or unsafe, you should walk. This will not only allow your horse to get a good look at the situation so he will see there is nothing to be afraid of for the next time, but it might prevent him from getting hurt from a more reckless, more concussive, and less controlled passage through poor footing in a faster gait. It is also the "resting gait," employed to let your horse catch his wind or normalize his heart rate after momentary or prolonged exercise. The walk might also serve to "bring him down" or calm him after more excitable activity.

The Trot

The trot is a two-beat diagonal gait. The diagonal pair of legs extend forward then back as the opposite pair extend forward. For example, left hind and right front move forward together, then there is a moment of suspension before the opposite pair extend. In the working trot, the horse should carry himself long, with a low neck, and slight flexion at the poll.

The Feel of Trot

Whatever speed the rider is working in trot, the rhythm should be consistent, and the rider should feel the horse's back relaxed. It is this relaxation that makes the trot comfortable to sit. A tense horse tends to be difficult to sit and might jar the rider out of the saddle. The trot can be quite beautiful to watch, with the horse appearing to float above the ground. This look of floating comes from the moment of suspension in trot.

ESSENTIAL

On a straight trail there is no correct lead, but the horse will often pick up the lead that is easiest for him. However, you should remember to work both canter leads when riding out to build equal muscle on both sides of the horse. This will promote balance and reduce stress on the leg the horse prefers to lead with.

Individuals in the early stages of learning to ride will spend a good deal of time in trot. This is the gait the student practices to follow the horse's motion. Relaxation is the key to becoming comfortable and confident in the more forward gaits. With a relaxed posture, the horse takes you along while you remain at the center of his balance. The rider also learns to rise to the trot, or "post," which relieves the horse's back and also keeps the rider from becoming fatigued.

When to Ride the Trot

The average speed of the trotting gait is about eight miles per hour, although the trot can and should be ridden at different speeds. This is why it is known as the "conditioning gait," allowing you options for various terrain or topology in the field or different modes of exercise in the ring. A fit and healthy horse can trot for long periods of time. It is an appropriate gait for bringing a horse into fitness that has been out of exercise or laid up, while walking will do very little to build his stamina or muscle.

ALERT!

For the green or unpredictable horse, a canter might be unnecessarily dangerous, especially in wide open spaces. In the horse's mind, canter is only one gear below gallop, which is the gait where you will have the least control over your horse. It is easy for him to make that transition into gallop from canter, after which you might not be able to stop him.

The Canter

Three beats are heard when listening to the canter. An example of a canter stride is as follows: The first beat strikes off with the right hind leg, second beat diagonal pairs left hind and right fore, third beat is the leading left fore. When the horse is in canter, he is said to be on either the left or right canter lead. In left lead canter, the right hind strikes off first; the left front strikes the ground before the right front. When working in a ring, the horse should lead with his inside leg in canter. If he leads with the outside leg, he is said to be on the wrong lead and will cause unnecessary stress to his inside leg and an uncomfortable ride. Most horses working in a ring will naturally pick up the correct lead when on a circle.

The canter is usually ridden at a faster pace than the trot, on average about twelve miles per hour. However, like the trot, the canter too can and should be ridden at different speeds. It is also a good conditioning gait, but cannot be sustained over long stretches of time and space like the trot.

When to Ride the Canter

The canter will obviously cover more distance in a period of time. For the field rider, it will allow you, simply, more field for your time. In wide open fields or basically straight trails with consistently good footing, the canter can be fun for you and your horse. It is also a good gait in which to ride to a jump. The extra speed and power of a canter over a trot will help a horse feel confident to jump. The canter should be practiced along with the other gaits for a well-rounded horse and rider.

The Gallop

When the canter is urged more forward, the footfalls become four beated and the gallop is engaged. Most riders spend little time in gallop. It is most common to track racing, fox hunting, eventing, and Western competition riding. It is an excellent gait to increase condition and is often good for the horse's mind. As the saying goes, horses were born to run. A gallop can reach speeds of up to forty mph, making the modern horse one of the fastest animals on the planet. Little training and technique can be accomplished in this gait. On most horses, it is a technically easy gait to ride.

ESSENTIAL

In all gaits, proper balance is the key to the gait's visual beauty and the comfort enjoyed by the rider. Watching the horse go through his paces loose in the field is a good way to observe the horse working on balance. This observation will give the rider a clear picture of the effort a horse will extend when he includes the weight of a rider on his back.

When to Ride the Gallop

Choose your space and your horse carefully for this gait. An open field or trail that you are familiar with that is void of deep mud, varmint holes, and unapparent obstructions hidden by tall grass, woods, or various ground cover is ideal. One slip or trip at this speed can be devastating to you and your horse. Gallop will work and stretch your horse's back and muscles in a way that no other gait can, but not all horses should be galloped. Very young horses that are still growing need time for muscles, bones, and tendons to develop. Very old or unfit horses might have the heart but not the agility to sustain this gait in a way that is safe for them and you.

ALERT!

Cantering or galloping past horses in a paddock might incite those horses into galloping as well, which might not be safe for them for many reasons. Therefore, this is bad etiquette. Similarly, cantering or galloping up to or around other riders on the trail might incite those horses to do the same, which might also be unsafe for the riders.

A Word of Caution

Not all horses have an instinct toward self-preservation and even fewer of them have an instinct toward preservation of their rider. A galloping horse probably won't slow down if left to his own devices when he comes upon unsuitable footing. He might not slow down either if he comes to a bend in the trail for which he is going too fast to negotiate. A galloping horse might even run himself to death, as will happen on the race track, by exploding his heart, lack of oxygen to the lungs, or trying to run on a broken leg.

The Gaited Horse

The walk, trot, and canter are considered the three natural gaits. Most horse breeds possess these three gaits. There are several breeds of horses that have additional gaits, such as a smooth ridden gait that puts them in the category of "gaited horse." Some gaited horses are the American saddle bred, the Paso Fino, the Tennessee Walker, and the Icelandic. Some of these horses have acquired their gaits naturally by adapting to terrain conditions in the wild. Others were developed by horsemen or plantation owners looking for a smooth and comfortable gait that was not fatiguing to sit and that the horse could maintain for long stretches of space and time. Regardless of the origins of the individual gaited breeds, they remain popular choices for many horsemen. One characteristic of most gaited horses is the high stepping that is often seen when watching these horses perform. Higher steps are desirable in some gaited horses while others look for swinging movement from the shoulder and little knee action.

The Paso Fino

The Paso Fino is of Spanish origin and is known for the smooth gaits known as the Fino, Paso Corto, and the Paso Largo. All these gaits have the same four-beat rhythms, but are ridden at different speeds and collection. The Fino should be very slow with rapid footfall. It is difficult to perform since it requires a great deal of collection. The Paso Corto is a ground covering four-beat gait in which the horse travels at the approximate speed of a trot, eight miles per hour. It is an ideal gait for trail riding. Lastly, the Paso Largo is a four-beat rhythm, but is very fast; the horse could travel up to twenty miles per hour. Regardless of the speed, this horse's gaits are very smooth and are comfortable to sit. The gaits of the Paso Fino are not taught but are natural.

FACT

"Brio," meaning "controlled spirit," is a desirable quality in a Paso Fino. A horse with brio appears to be full of spirit and energy while under saddle, but is utterly under the rider's control. The quality of brio is judged in this horse's competition.

The Peruvian Paso

The Peruvian Paso was developed in Peru in the nineteenth century from the blood of the Andalusian, Arab, and thoroughbred horses. Her gaits, the Paso llano, the Sobreandando, and the Huachano, were all developed to cover the vast mountainous regions of Peru at a pace that is comfortable for the rider and sustainable for the horse. Like the Icelandic, they are small, measuring from 14.1 to 15.1 hands, and are known for being able to carry a large man comfortably.

The Tennessee Walking Horse

The Tennessee walker is a breed developed in Tennessee from the blood of the thoroughbred, standardbred, Morgan, and saddlebred horses. They vary in size, temperament, and refinement, but the horse has the smooth gaits known as the flat walk and the faster running walk. This breed also has canter and gallop. The flat walk is a four-beat gait in which each foot strikes the ground separately. If the gait is correct, there is a characteristic head nod along with the rhythm of the walk. It is a long reaching gait and can be as slow as four miles per hour and as fast as the canter when the running walk is performed.

FACT

The second largest population of Icelandic horses is in Germany. In the early 1950s, famine overtook Iceland. In a successful effort to help the struggling Iceland economy and preserve the unique Icelandic horse from annihilation through slaughter for food, Germany bought shiploads of Icelandics. The bloodlines of these German Icelandics remain pure.

The Icelandic Horse

The Icelandic horse's origins can be traced back to Germanic and Celtic breeds that are now extinct. It was brought to Iceland in the ninth century and remains one of the most homogeneous breeds of horse in the world. Although they almost never grow past 14 hands, they are not considered ponies but rather are a horse breed able to carry a large man across their rugged landscape. It was, in fact, the horse that Viking warriors used for battle.

The Icelandic has five distinct gaits. In addition to a clear walk, trot, and canter, the Icelandic horse has a fourth gait known as the tolt and a fifth gait known as the flying pace. This horse is known for its smooth gaits, stamina, and speed. The tolt is a four-beat lateral gait, with one foot always maintaining contact with the ground. There is no moment of suspension, making the gait smooth and comfortable at all speeds. Said to be similar to the Paso Corto and the running walk of the Tennessee walker, the flying pace is a two-beat lateral gait, meaning the front and hind leg on the same side work together to extend. The pace can be very fast, with speeds up to thirty miles per hour. The tolt and pace are natural gaits.

Chapter 18

Keeping Your Horse Safe and Happy Indoors

Most of the potential problems or accidents that can occur at home with your horse can be ameliorated or prevented by a well-planned barn. Barn design is variable depending on what region of the country you are living in. If you are building a stable from scratch, then it's a good idea to have several professionals give you advice after you have talked with a barn builder. Because there is so much to consider for your and your horse's safety and convenience, each professional will most likely have something different to say.

Stall Construction

A stall must be constructed with a horse's general destructive nature and proclivity toward injury in mind. The stalls must hold up to kicking, rubbing, pawing, and corrosion from urine and manure. Protruding corners should be rounded, edges should be beveled, and any sharp hardware should be recessed. Metal or iron strips should run the length of any wooden edges that the horse can reach to chew. Metal bars can be used in the stall, above 4 feet, but the space between them must be no more than two inches, because the horses can get their mouth caught. Doors that slide laterally into a pocket in the wall are expensive, but are better than doors that open out into the aisle or into the stall. The shortcomings of both of these designs will be immediately apparent but they are more than sufficient.

ESSENTIAL

If you're starting with horses at an existing barn or boarding your horse somewhere that might not be designed according to your ideal specifications, it's particularly important to know the rules that govern the safety and happiness of your horse so that you can anticipate potential accidents or compensate for the shortcomings of the facility.

Size

A stall must be large enough to permit a horse to move around, which is essential for his circulation and digestion. An adequate stall is anywhere from 8' × 10' to 14' × 14', depending on what you can afford to have, or build, and maintain. A roomier stall might incline him but not ensure that he will choose one spot to urinate in and another one for manure. This will of course make for a more sanitary stall environment, saving you labor in mucking and cost in bedding. A clean stall might also give him the option of lying down to sleep, which he will appreciate.

Surfaces

Rubber mats offer the best advantages over other kinds of stall surfaces in terms of time you will save mucking, cleaning, and bedding conservation. They can be laid over dirt, clay, stone dust, sand, wood, or cement; the latter being perhaps the best combination. Rubber is a great cushion and insulation from cold and dampness that comes up from the ground. Unlike clay or dirt, it is hygienic, odor free, and easy to disinfect. This might be done either in the stall or the mats can be dragged out and hosed off. Textured mats that are made specifically for stalls provide adequate traction. They will prevent urine and pawing holes that would otherwise require maintenance and the mixing with bedding as well as with hay and dropped grain that will occur with most organic surfaces. Concrete alone has few advantages over rubber, except that it is a little cheaper, provides better traction, and is permanent, whereas rubber lasts only about twelve years. Sand should be avoided altogether unless covered by rubber. Although it is cheap, soft, and a good insulator, the grains can work their way into the hoof wall of a horse. It can also mix with hay and grain that falls to the ground, be eaten, and cause colic.

FACT

Horses possess the ability to lock their stifle joints, which is equivalent to the human knee. This allows them to remain in a ready position while sleeping in case of a threat from a predator. Although they can sleep lying down, they will expend more energy this way. Either way affords them the rest they need.

Aisle Safety

Much of the handling of your horse will probably not be done in the stall but in the aisle of your barn, so it should be safe and accommodating to you and your horse. Loose or sharp objects and equipment shouldn't clutter the aisle. Neither should pointed objects protrude from the walls, such as hooks or uncollapsible saddle racks. Blacktop or smooth concrete might need to be covered with a rubber mat for better footing.

An aisle must be at least six feet wide to allow a horse to make a 180 degree turn and for two horses to be able to pass by each other comfortably. A ten- to twelve-foot-wide aisle allows room for tack trunks, horse vacuums, and other conveniences.

What to Have in a Stall

A stall is generally the place where your horse will get into the least trouble, provided it is an environment that is comfortable, safe, and healthy. This means that it must be sanitary, roomy, and ventilated.

There are three basic requirements for a stall. A stall must have places for:

- Fresh water
- Hay
- Grain

The nutritional value of these requirements is discussed in Chapter 4, Feeding and Nutrition.

Water

Standard water buckets hold five gallons and are long and deep rather than wide and shallow. This design prevents the mess and waste of spillage, while being a manageable size for you to handle on a daily basis for cleaning. There should be two water buckets per stall spaced about a foot apart to avoid spillage from one being knocked into the other. They can be attached in several different ways, but a double end snap clipped onto the bucket and then onto an eyehook in the wall is simple and safe. The buckets should be about four feet high, low enough that you can handle them if full, but high enough so that your horse cannot get a foot into one of them and also high enough to prevent the collection of debris.

Since clean water is so important to a horse, the water buckets should be closest to the stall opening where you can easily access them and check their water levels and cleanliness. They will stay cleaner if they are placed on an opposite wall from the feed bucket. Also, remember not to place them directly underneath a hay drop from the loft.

Automatic waterers are a big time and labor saver. They can be expensive but should be considered with new construction or if you have physical limitations. They must be cleaned and checked every day to see if they are working properly. Their major drawback is that you cannot keep track of how much a horse drinks while in his stall without the further expense of monitoring equipment.

Hay

A hayrack mounted high in the stall can be a clean, efficient way to feed hay. It can prevent the wastage of feeding it on the stall floor because a horse could trample and defecate on his hay. A hayrack is not nearly as cumbersome as a hay net. However, once the hayrack is empty, it becomes an obstacle in the stall and could be dangerous. Also, because of the hayrack's position high on the wall (so the horse cannot get a foot through it), particulate matter from the hay can end up in a horse's eyes, causing irritation and other problems.

Feeding hay on the floor of a well-kept stall is perfectly adequate for most horses. It will save time and labor, and the horse will be eating from a position that is natural for him. Besides, hay served from a hayrack or net will end up on the floor of the stall anyway.

Grain

A grain bucket should not have hard corners on the inside where grain can get trapped and spoil or attract flies. It can be wider and shallower than a standard water bucket. Because horses get excited about their grain, eating habits can be somewhat violent. Therefore, grain buckets should have a lip around the top to keep flying food in the bucket. Grain that ends up on the stall floor will mix with bedding and could, over time, attract rats. A grain bucket is usually best situated in the corner of a stall where it can be stabilized by the two walls.

Bedding

Your bedding choice might depend on what is most readily available in your neck of the woods and your farm's capacity for storage. Bedding should be absorbent, soft, and free of dust, mold, or sharp objects.

Sawdust

Sawdust is adequate bedding. It's inexpensive, usually delivered by the truckload. It requires a dry space and must be double handled, as opposed to bagged shavings that can usually be dropped into the stall from the loft. Sawdust is very absorbent, which prevents urine from seeping into an organic stall floor. However, its high absorbency might mean that by morning the horse is standing in a sopping wet mix of manure, urine, and sawdust. Also, the wheelbarrow load that you remove while mucking will be very heavy. Sawdust can be just that, dust, which should be measured against the cost savings.

Ammonia, a by-product of urine, is a noxious gas that can be harmful to a horse's eyes and respiratory system. Hydrated lime can be sprinkled over wet spots of an organic stall surface. The lime will absorb excess moisture and alleviate acidity and the smell of ammonia.

You can obtain other sawmill waste products by the truckload, but they can be rough textured and you must make sure that the chips or shavings are from softwoods. Avoid hardwoods because they are not very absorbent, and some, particularly black walnut, can cause founder when in contact with a horse's feet, and death if ingested.

Straw

Straw is a very clean, non-dusty bedding option. It is ideal for a horse with a wound that must be kept clean or for use on a breeding farm. Shavings and most other bedding will adhere to a newborn, possibly interfering with his mucus membranes and respiratory system. Horses might tend to eat oat straw, so wheat straw is a better choice. However, some horses will eat either, and they should not have their stalls bedded with straw.

Straw comes in bales, like hay, and tends to be about the same price. Like hay, it must be properly stored and can be heavy and cumbersome to handle.

Pine Shavings, Kiln Dried and Bagged

Depending on what area of the country you live in, this material might be the most expensive type of bedding. It tends to be convenient, requiring the least amount of handling and is easily transportable. It is generally considered to be the most aesthetic, and if kept replenished, the most pleasantly smelling. It is easy to muck and can aid in the breakdown of a manure compost pile. It is soft, absorbent, and comfortable, which makes it ideal bedding for most horses. Pine shavings shouldn't be used for horses with dry foot problems or for a foaling stall.

How to Muck a Stall

A stall must be cleaned of manure and urine for sanitary purposes. Mucking the stall is basically like cleaning out a giant cat litter box. First, remove visible manure piles and urine wet spots. The tines of a mucking fork are spaced so that manure balls of a full-grown horse will remain on the fork while most bedding material will fall through. Turn over the middle of the stall, picking out the rest of the manure and wet bedding. The perimeter of a stall should be banked. Bedding mixed with manure can be tossed against the wall. The manure should roll down the banked shavings against the wall, making it easier to separate and remove. The hay corner and under the feed tub should be swept clean so hay chaff and spilled grain won't be ingested with bedding.

Ventilation

Bedding and hay generate dust, urine generates ammonia, and horses expel vast amounts of carbon dioxide into the air (about two gallons per horse per day). Warmer air can hold this moisture, while a discrepancy between outside temperature and inside temperature will create condensation. Either situation will create a breeding ground for mold, fungus, and a host of bacteria. Therefore, your barn must be properly ventilated. The health of a horse's respiratory system depends on it (discussed further in Chapter 3, Systems of the Horse's Body).

If your facility is not conducive to natural airflow and sunlight—a natural disinfectant and dehumidifier—fans should be utilized, especially in warmer climates or warmer months. Individual fans can be used in addition to a system of ventilation fans, where one impels fresh air into the barn and another on an opposite wall expels air. This is especially important in a hayloft, where heat generated from horses and the sun will rise and create a potentially hazardous situation.

ALERT!

Wet, moldy, or uncured hay can spontaneously heat up and combust under the right conditions, which can cause barn fires. Smaller hay deliveries can help prevent the chances of a bad bale going unnoticed. Also, keeping the loft clean of loose hay might inhibit the progress of a barn fire when time is of the essence.

High ceilings and a wide aisle will promote air circulation. Windows and doors however are most essential for adequate ventilation and should be situated to accept the natural breeze. Louvered windows in the loft or at either end of a barn will allow air flow but not a draft, and prevent birds from setting up a home in your barn. Other places that can be vented are soffits, the roof in the form of a ridge vent, and a cupola, which can also be mechanized for a greater effect.

Even in cold and inclement weather, a barn should never be entirely closed up. That is why louvers and vents are handy. It is also why sliding doors and windows that can be opened or closed easily are ideal and used to whatever degree necessary in order to encourage airflow and prevent drafts.

Tying the Horse

You will need to tie your horse to restrict his movement for performing such duties as shoeing, grooming, tacking up, medical exams, and other occasions for general care. There are different ways of tying your horse according to your purpose and situation. When tying him, keep in mind that you are taking away his ability to protect himself; mainly you are depriving him of his natural ability to flee in the face of what he considers danger. Take care to make sure not only that the horse is safe, but also that he feels safe and comfortable. This would mean a place free of obstacles and variables he's not used to, like out of place farm equipment or farm implements such as rakes and shovels that he could knock over and startle himself.

In the event that you need to tie your horse in the woods, pick a tree with a low hanging, supple branch about head height that will give a little but exert enough stability to incline him to stay put. This is risky and not a good idea for a hot or nervous horse.

The horse should have adequate protection from flies and predators, including aggressive dogs or even other horses that might harass him. If he is comfortable, he will most likely stand for being tied. If something scares him in this vulnerable situation, he will most likely try to escape the tie, pulling backward from it and panicking when he meets with resistance from the rope. He'll have no regard for your safety or his own. Obviously, this is when accidents happen.

Common Mistakes and Consequences

If your horse has decided, for whatever reason, that he wants to break free from his tie, you want him to be able to, for your safety and for his. This is why when you tie a horse, the knots or clips used must slip or break away. The full force of a horse is awesome. A horse trying to free himself of a situation where he instinctively feels that his life is in danger will probably, if not tied in a breakaway manner, break whatever he is tied to. Whether it is a fence, a wall, or a post not meant for tying, the horse will break free, trailing it as he gallops off, which, needless to say, will probably injure him. If the horse cannot break off from whatever he is tied to, he might break his own neck trying to.

Cross Tying

Cross tying is the safest, most convenient, and most common way to attend a horse. All shoeing, medical exams such as x-rays, and grooming will probably be done on cross ties. Cross ties are lines with breakaway clips on the end, which are attached to each wall of the aisle of a barn, or to well-set posts. The horse is then brought to the center of the aisle or between the two posts, and clipped onto each line. Each line should have about a foot of slack in it, which gives him a comfort zone of about a step or two of lateral and back and forth movement, but secures him from getting carried away with too much momentum.

ALERT!

Never get your hand, arm, or leg in the slack of a tied rope. If your horse pulls backward, the rope could tighten on you with incredible force. A quick release knot or breakaway clip will not help you because the tension will be on you, not the knot or clip.

Besides having breakaway snaps at one end of a tie, you can ensure a safe break away by attaching the far end of the tie to the aisle wall with a piece of bailing twine, or something of the like. Your horse will quickly understand that his job on cross ties is to stand for the tasks that will be performed on him.

Single Tie Slipknot

The single tie slipknot can be used instead of cross ties, but is mostly used when cross ties are not available and you need to tie your horse to whatever is convenient. You might use this tie in the field, in a stall, or when several horses must be tied at once. The knot is designed to exert enough pressure to keep him put under normal conditions, but to come undone if he is panicking. Therefore, almost any solid structure can be utilized. The tie should be 2 feet to 3 feet in length, and tied high enough on a structure that the slack in the rope never falls below his chest. This ensures that he won't get his leg over it. He will scare himself and probably escape if this happens. In a worst-case scenario, he could get tangled in the line and flip himself.

Figure 18.1:
A Quick-Release
Knot

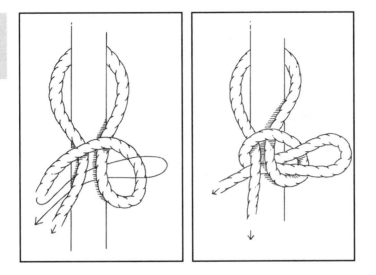

Hobbles

Hobbles are used as a way of semi restricting a horse without the limitation and confinement of tying her. They bind the two front or two back ankles together with enough line so that a horse can walk, but not trot or canter. They are usually made of cotton with a safety snap in between. Breeding farms will sometimes hobble a nurse mare until she accepts the orphaned foal. They might also hobble a brood mare during mating to prevent her from kicking the stallion. Horses can also be hobbled and then set out to graze on unfenced pasture. This could be a great way to get some extra nutrition into your horse, while giving him a special treat.

You might think twice about hobbling a hot or nervous horse. This unnatural restriction might be met with severe protest. A horse could easily trip and fall. A hobbled horse is helpless against a predator, among other things, and so no horse should be left completely unattended when hobbled.

Management in Extreme Temperatures

Horses have adapted to being able to adjust to extreme temperatures. As a caretaker, you can aid your horse's transition from one type of climate to another, or from hot weather to cold, and help him to stay comfortable and healthy in extreme temperatures.

Care for Horses in Extreme Heat

Horses have specific needs in very hot temperatures. Protection from the sun and from flies can be accomplished by a run-in shed during turn-out and with fans while in the stall. If night turnout is an option, then horses will probably appreciate spending their days in the stall and the cool nights out. The drawbacks of night turnout are that it often leaves them out at the two peak mosquito hours of dusk and dawn. Also, you are less likely to be around or awake at night when they are turned out and most apt to get into trouble. Clipping can ease your horse's burden of heat, as well as hosing your horse down with cold water.

A horse can be tested for dehydration by pinching the skin on his neck. If it does not return to its normal flat position within two seconds, he might be dehydrated. Capillary refill is another way to tell if your horse might be dehydrated. Press your fingers to his gums, then release. Within two seconds, the white spot where your finger was should be replaced by the normal pink color. If it does not, or if his gums aren't pink to begin with, then he might be sick.

Horses' nutritional needs change as well in extreme heat. They will drink more water than usual and require a higher salt intake. Refresh their water often in the paddock and in the stall so it stays cool and clean. Salt blocks in the stall or in the paddock will help. Electrolytes are a supplement that will incline a horse to drink more water. They can be added to grain or water during the summer and winter months, when horses are more likely to dehydrate.

Cold Weather Management

The best thing you can do for your horse in very cold temperatures is to encourage a thick, clean, oil-rich coat. His natural hair is as good protection from the cold as any blanket. Half a cup of flaxseed or corn oil added to their daily grain will promote a healthy, thick coat.

Contraction of pilorector muscles straighten the long hairs on a horse's body, trapping warm air. This insulating measure is drastically reduced by the wind. So if he is turned out, make sure he has protection from the wind. If you blanket him, you are also hampering his natural defense against the cold; you should make sure his blanket is dry and warm.

FACT

A horse with a thick coat of hair might be hiding a winter weight loss problem. If you can feel his ribs protruding from under a thick winter coat, then he is too skinny. If anything, your horse should carry a little extra weight in winter.

To stay warm, horses expend energy; therefore, they will need extra calories and protein. Horses on pasture might need supplemental hay. Horses on hay and grain might need an increase of hay consumption at more regular intervals, and possibly a decrease in grain. Digestion of grain is more taxing on a horse's digestive system, and so requires more energy. A longer and harder digestion process concentrates his blood around the digestive system, taking it from his muscles where he needs it to stay warm.

A cold horse will use precious energy to stay warm, which will cause weight loss. Shivering will also cause weight loss, burning fat and muscle that he desperately needs to stay warm.

Finally, make sure your horse has plenty of water in cold temperatures. Outside water tubs and natural water sources freeze and must be checked daily. If horses are forced to eat snow, their body will use precious energy to process it, not to mention that they could never take in enough snow to keep themselves properly hydrated.

For the Barn

The greatest problem with cold weather management of a barn is frozen water. If the water system of your barn is a series of pipes that lead from a source to a water spigot in each stall, then the system should be drained to the source and then bled. Turning off the water at its source, and then opening each water outlet to let excess air and water out, usually does this. This should be done whenever the water is not being used, and especially at night. The source should itself be designed to drain below the frost line, which is anywhere between one and four feet deep, depending on what region of the country you live in. Insulation and/or heat tape on each individual pipe, as well as on the source, will help. Never use an open flame, such as a blowtorch, or an unsupervised space heater to thaw frozen lines or prevent them from freezing.

Prevention of drafts on a frigid night in the barn is important. Horses can easily catch a chill. This does not mean that fresh air shouldn't be allowed to enter the barn and circulate. Find a balance that seems to suit your horses.

Water buckets come with heating elements built in, which will ensure that your horse's water won't freeze over a cold night. Heating elements are available for use in outdoor water tubs as well, and should be utilized throughout the winter. Horses tend not to drink water that is too warm, but water heated to about 40 degrees will require less energy for consumption than water at just above freezing temperatures.

Chapter 19

Keeping Your Horse Safe and Happy Outdoors

A well-managed and well thought-out turnout situation will go a long way to keeping your horse safe and happy, and your property healthy. The fences you choose, along with the footing and grasses of your turnout, will be major factors in the look and feel of your farm, as well as the degree of maintenance necessary. You will find that working according to sound environmental considerations will save you money, time, and horse illnesses.

The Paddock

The paddock should be a safe and healthy environment for your horse. It is a confined space, so it must be designed, built, and maintained with the horse's safety, your convenience, and the health of the land in mind.

Size

A paddock should be spacious enough to allow a horse to move comfortably in his first three gaits: walk, trot, and canter. A space becomes dangerous if it is too small or overcrowded with horses, especially a rambunctious group or a group whose order is being constantly upset. A half an acre per horse, or for two horses that get along, will suffice and is a big enough space to incline your horse to move around. The larger the turnout the easier it will be to maintain your paddock.

Footing

Grass is the most ideal footing for a paddock but very tough to maintain where space is limited. Horses will quickly eat or trample a grass turnout. It must be maintained and kept on a rotation schedule with other paddocks if you don't want it to turn to dirt and mud. Fast and deep rooting grasses such as rye and timothy, as well as cool season grasses like brome and orchard grass, can establish a good, strong pasture. Clovers are also good because their root system is a network and harder for a horse to completely dig up.

Dirt is an adequate footing, and if your space and money is limited, often your only choice. It can turn hard without the natural aerating of grass, which can be bad for their feet. Dirt can also become dusty in dry and hot weather, which is bad for their respiratory system. In rainy areas or seasons, dirt will turn to mud, which can be very slippery, not to mention messy, and ultimately drying to their hooves. In deep mud, the lower legs must be checked every day for cuts and scratches. Sand is inexpensive but can cause colic, and so is not recommended.

Wood chips are also an adequate footing. Depending on where you live, wood chips can be free from tree companies, who will be happy to have a place to dump them. Otherwise, the need to constantly replenish them would become costly. A wood chip paddock cannot be dragged like grass or dirt, but must be picked instead, which is labor intensive and time consuming. In low or soggy areas of the paddock, the wood chips might become too thick or wet, which can make it very poor, deceiving footing. As with stall bedding, you must be careful that certain woods are not present, which can cause founder, or be appetizing to horses.

Management

Paddocks must be managed in order to keep them safe, clean, and dry. A buildup of manure will not only make your farm smell, but will eventually cause mud. Picking your paddocks once a week is a good idea. This will decrease the amount of parasite infestation that occurs. A pronged chain drag can be used to break up remaining manure, so that it can be more easily absorbed into the ground. A drag will also aerate the paddock and promote the growth of grass. This can be pulled by a truck or tractor, but an all terrain vehicle (ATV), is more maneuverable and less abusive to grass.

During heavy rains and in emergency situations, a shovel and a pick ax will do the trick to give drainage to a field. Follow the natural path that the water is trying to take. Sometimes, it only takes a little encouragement to get the water to flow.

Areas around gates, water tubs, and automatic waterers will need extra maintenance. Horses will congregate there, often toward feeding time when they are most excited, causing a muddy and generally poor footing environment.

Drainage can be an expensive proposition but worthwhile. Acreage that might not ordinarily need drainage may once horses are introduced. An extremely wet area might require professional advice. For normal areas, a tractor with a backhoe attachment can be rented, and a curtain drain cut, for a reasonable price.

Dig a trench 3 feet deep and 2 feet wide. Then line the bottom of the trench with a layer of drainage stones on top of which you lay a drainage pipe. Now fill in the rest of the trench with stone. A curtain drain should run slightly diagonally to the natural slope of land so that water is caught and directed downward and off the paddock.

Run-in Shed

A run-in shed in the paddock can give protection year-round from wind and precipitation in colder months and from the sun and flies in summer. It should be big enough to give each horse the same space he would otherwise have in a 12' × 12' stall. It is a three-sided structure, with its opening about 12 to 14 feet high, sloping down to no less than 10 feet at the rear. This design promotes ventilation, hospitality, and a wide berth and easy escape for horses that might not get along.

Figure 19.1:
A Run-in Shed

Although wind patterns are variable according to region and the topography of your land, a southerly facing run-in shed is generally the direction that gives the horses the best protection from winter winds and the longest access to the winter sun. In very cold climates, a shed that faces southeast will give horses direct morning sun, which they will appreciate after a cold night.

Run-in sheds must be surfaced and bedded so they stay dry, sanitary, and level. All the surface and bedding options for a stall apply to a run-in shed, although peat moss, not previously mentioned, might be the ideal bedding.

It is an excellent insulator and very comfortable. For a stall, however, it has disadvantages and would be prohibitively expensive. It is too absorbent, which can create a wet and toxic mush and cause thrush among other problems. It can be dusty as well. But horses, if given the option, will usually stay outside, and so a run-in shed is much less used than a stall. Furthermore, its open design promotes the ventilation that is necessary for this dusty product.

Fencing

There are many different kinds of fencing, and as many different opinions on which kind is the best. A helpful perspective is to remember that any kind of fence is an unnatural barrier and obstacle for a horse, and is potentially dangerous to her. Your fencing choice might be determined by cost, aesthetics, what type of horses you will be keeping, size of the area you wish to fence, material that is available in your area, or what kind of terrain you are dealing with. Whatever materials you use, your fence must be strong, visible, four to five feet high, and whenever possible rounded at the corners so that a horse never feels cornered and compelled to go through or over when threatened. Whatever the drawbacks of the fence you choose, any fence can be enhanced with electricity, which will save you many headaches. Here are descriptions of the more popular kinds of fences.

Wooden Post-and-Board

This is a strong, safe, and highly visible fence. It is perhaps the most ideal all-around fencing available, but relatively expensive to buy and install. The expense can be offset by the aesthetic and monetary value it will add to your property.

Post-and-board fencing can be three or four boards, which are nailed on the inside of the post unless fitted into the post itself. Four-rail is recommended if you have or might have foals on the property to keep out wolves and coyotes and so that your horse can't get her head or foot through. This fence is only as good as the wood that it is made of, which should be a hardwood, usually oak, and kiln dried to prevent shrinkage.

When laying out your fencing plan, keep in mind that single trees or groups of trees should be fenced around as well. Trees spaced closely together could pose a threat to running horses. Horses will also kill trees by chewing the bark off of them.

The wood of the fence should be treated with a preservative to prevent horses from chewing it and from rot, mold, and termites. Any number of horse-safe oil products can be used. Creosote is the ideal substance to protect fencing, but might be illegal to buy in certain states. It is an excellent protector against ground rot, insects, and fungi, and it also deters chewing, but you must take care when handling it. Wear protective clothing and gloves, and if it comes in contact with your skin you will have to wash it off immediately to avoid a nasty burn.

This fence should be inspected at least once a week for protruding nails, broken boards, and rotten posts, which can compromise the integrity of the fence and cause safety hazards. It is wise to have a supply of pre-treated boards and posts readily available.

Posts should be sunk three feet into the ground and never set in cement, which will cause rotting. The standard boards for this kind of fence are eight feet long, two inches wide, and eight inches deep. A well-maintained post-and-board fence could last about twenty to twenty-five years.

Post-and-Rail

Many of the same qualities and faults of post-and-board fences are also true of the post-and-rail fence. A post-and-rail fence has three or four round or angular shaped rails that are tapered on the ends. They slide into the posts and overlap with the rails of the next section. Because of the thick, dense rail, each section can be ten feet long. However, the rails of this fence tend to shrink and after a few years often need to be nailed in place, which is contrary to the design. The new rails are often difficult to replace because they must be fitted into the stationary posts from both sides. The increased surface area of rails versus boards also causes them to catch and hold precipitation over time, which increases their susceptibility to rot.

ESSENTIAL

The benefits of perimeter fencing should be considered if you live near a major road or in a residential area. A perimeter fence closes in your entire property. If your horses get loose or escape their paddock fencing, as they will from time to time, there will usually be enough grass or curiosities on the property to keep them busy and prevent them from trying to break the perimeter fence. If nothing else, perimeter fencing will help you sleep at night.

Polyethylene-Coated Wood

This kind of fence is a more technologically advanced version of post-and-board fencing. It is more expensive but probably worth it in the long run. It enhances all the good qualities of traditional post-and-board while improving on some of the faults such as excessive maintenance, the need for nails, and splintering of boards. In addition, horses won't chew it.

PVC Fencing or Polyvinylchloride

Like polyethylene-coated wood fencing, PVC is expensive and can give an artificial appearance to your farm that might take some getting used to. It can be unsubstantial for particularly rambunctious horses and is subject to cracking in ground frost and very cold weather. But with PVC it is easy to replace rails, it won't be chewed, and there are no nails to come loose or protrude. The high degree of elasticity of PVC could prevent accidents that might occur with other types of fencing.

Buck Fencing

A buck fence is adequate to keep horses in pastures where they are generally happy and nourished and where they don't have a reason to try to leave. It isn't very substantial, but it is inexpensive, easy to maintain, and easy to install since it requires no post hole digging. These reasons make buck fencing a popular fence for areas where the ground is hard or for vast spaces.

Wire and Metal Fencing

There are any number of wire and metal fencing materials. High tensile wire, woven wire, pipe fencing, and polymer-coated wire, which is an easily electrified nylon tape, are just a few. They are usually much cheaper than wood fencing and each could be used to its ideal purpose. When fencing in large tracts of land, these types of fencing materials, particularly high-tensile wire, can be strong, durable, relatively cheap, and fast to install. This kind of fence is less visible, less giving, and therefore less safe. It should also be considered that wire and metal fencing materials, and even wooden fences amended with wire mesh, will attract lightening.

ALERT!

Barbed wire is never an option for horse fencing. It is hard to see and horses that get tangled in barbed wire will struggle, resulting in severe or fatal injuries.

Gates

Like fencing, there are many different types of gates. It will not ruin the look of your wood fence to use metal, wire, or aluminum gates. These gates are lighter and therefore easier to handle, and they will not sag if installed properly. Since a great deal of the handling of horses takes place at the gate, it is safer to have a gate that is easily handled.

Proper installation of a gate means that it opens all the way and to the inside of the paddock, or if you prefer, freely in each direction. There should be no sharp edges, bolts, or protrusions. A four foot opening is the minimum for a handler and one horse to pass through. However, if you will need to handle more than one horse at a time, the gate should be at least eight feet wide. You will also need a gate into each paddock that is twelve to fourteen feet wide so that farm equipment can pass through for maintenance of paddocks or pastures.

Pasture Life

Although horses turned out to pasture in winter months will benefit from hay, and working horses might need the extra nutrients of grain, a healthy pasture provides horses with all the nutrition they need to survive. They enjoy pasture life. It provides them with the freedom and social life they appreciate. Not only that, pasturing horses is cheaper and involves much less labor than if the horses are stall kept. Horses in pasture are usually self-exercising and therefore stay more fit, and they are less prone to leg injuries than a stalled horse. They rarely develop the vices and sicknesses such as cribbing, pawing, and weaving, respiratory illness, and thrush associated with stall life. A pasture-kept horse will tend to be more agile and instinctively smarter in the field about such things as prairie dog holes and unstable footing, which can be a huge benefit when you are riding the horse on trails.

The pasture-kept horse must have adequate shelter from the wind, whether it's natural, like trees, rock ledges, or arroyos, or a man-made run-in shed. A water source can be natural as well, but must be checked often, if not every day, for quality, quantity, and freezing.

Of course, horses will play and fight more in a twenty-four-hour turnout situation than in a regimented barn environment, so injuries will occur. When horses are in pastures, it might be more difficult to assess their overall health and to check for cuts and puncture wounds on a daily basis. Horses turned out for too long might revert to a wilder state, and therefore your horses should be brought in periodically and handled.

It is best to confer with your state or local agricultural department on proper management of your pasture. A soil test every few years will determine what nutrient might be deficient in the soil and what will need to be added as fertilizer to sustain the grasses and your intended uses. The agricultural agent will also suggest a suitable pasture mix of grasses that would thrive best in your region.

A healthy pasture of grass will control the weeds. Strategically timed mowing will also help with weed control. Pre-emergents and other herbicides could help with weed control or could harm if used improperly. The best defense against overgrazing is to rotate the horses out of one pasture and into another. If the horses are allowed to overgraze an area, they will eat all the grass and paw out the roots, preventing regeneration. Only the weeds will grow, go to seed, and eventually take over.

Environmental Considerations

Environmentally sound farming practices are not only healthier for you, your horses, and your property, but will also keep your neighbors happy. It is very important that you protect your horses from environmental hazards, while at the same time protecting the environment from the potential damage caused by your horses. Keep in mind that while the outdoors might be a horse's natural habitat, it is vulnerable to destruction from these large, active animals and could also be dangerous for them.

Protecting Natural Water Sources

A watering station in your pasture has a double function. It will keep your horses from drinking water out of streams and rivers that might have gotten contaminated upstream, while also encouraging them to stay out of the water, which they would otherwise pollute themselves with parasite-carrying urine and manure.

Fencing off natural water might also be necessary to deter horses from polluting it. Fencing should keep them twenty-five to fifty feet from water or wetlands and should allow for a grass or sand filter strip of at least twenty-five feet, depending on the grade between the pasture fence and the water.

A manure compost heap should also have a grass or sand filter strip, depending on the type of soil around it and the grade of the land. Because of the smell and contaminants, the manure heap should be strategically located away from your property line, water, the barn, and any residences. The heap should also be stored on top of impervious stone or concrete to prevent leaching into the ground.

FACT

Horses compact the ground more than most other farm animals, so pastures should be aerated every few years. This will encourage healthy grass and pasture regeneration.

Pastures that are wet should be used only in dry seasons or when the ground is frozen. Horses will trample a wet field much more quickly, turning it to mud. Pasture rotation will encourage healthy, nutritious grasses, while discouraging weeds and pasture burnout. Grow your grass to about eight inches tall, then let horses graze it down to about four inches.

Poisonous Plants

Horses instinctively know when a plant or weed might be poisonous to them. Even if poisonous plants are available in a paddock or pasture, they probably will stay away from them, unless they are malnurished or starving. Here are some of the most common poisonous plants, weeds, and trees that occur naturally in the United States:

- Laburnum
- Hemlock
- Rhododendron
- Milkweed
- Laurel
- Larkspur
- Acorns
- Yew
- Black Walnut

A spring walk in your pastures and paddocks to identify poisonous plants is insufficient to prevent poisoning your horses. Poisonous plants will continue blooming into October. Check out which poisonous plants grow in your area and when.

Manure Management

A horse can generate fifty pounds of manure a day, which must be dealt with responsibly. Depending on where you live, there are laws governing the removal of horse manure from your property. To limit bacteria and parasite infestation and for the look and smell of your barn, regular removal is necessary.

A stall should be cleaned every day. If space is limited at your stable, the easiest and most sanitary option is to muck into a Dumpster and have it hauled away periodically. This can be expensive and unsightly, but necessary.

If you have the acreage, you might want to spread the manure. Your agricultural extension office will advise you according to how many horses you have and how much land you need to spread manure. It is nitrogen rich, which will encourage healthy grass. Some spreaders are small enough to fit in the aisle of your barn, so you can muck right into it and spread every day or two. Spreading on fields that are in use with horses is not sanitary. For proper decomposition, fast drying, and ease, a spreader should be used rather then a shovel. If you choose to spread, you might want to use a finer bedding material, like sawdust or wood shavings. Wood chips or straw bedding will be difficult to spread cleanly and will take a long time to decompose in a field without the heat generated from compost.

ESSENTIAL

Horse manure is valuable potential fertilizer and can be matured into various fertilizers. A manure hauling company or a garbage company in your area that specializes in manure hauling should charge you about half of what it costs to haul garbage.

Composting manure is a cost-effective and environmentally friendly plan. After a few months, composted manure is dry, light, and not smelly. It has undergone a fermentation process that concentrates its nutrients, kills parasites and their eggs, and frees it of some of its nitrogen, which makes it useable as fertilizer for plants and gardens.

Chapter 20

Boarding Your Horse

A big part of your and your horse's health and well-being depends on the environment where he boards and you ride. If you choose to entrust your horse into the care of someone else's stable, then you should know some of the telltale signs that he is being properly cared for. You and your horse might also benefit from being in a barn situation with other horses and riders of the same riding discipline and with trainers to suit your and your horse's requirements.

Is Your Horse Well Cared For?

If your horse is stabled off your property, you might only see him a couple of times a week or just once in a while. If you know what to look for, you can sometimes tell at a glance whether your horse is being well cared for.

Over Blanketing

Excessive blanketing is not uncommon. Horses have natural mechanisms to keep themselves warm that blankets interfere with, especially sweat-soaked blankets. If your horse is not clipped and has a natural coat, he should not need a blanket above freezing temperature, and often not below freezing either. Exceptions could be made for very young or very old horses, or horses that don't grow a good winter coat, like some thoroughbreds and Arabians. In most parts of the country, blankets should be stripped off for the day or at least during turnout for the horse's skin and coat to breathe and synthesize the vitamins it receives from the sun. The sun is also a natural sanitizer against bacteria and fungus that could accumulate on the skin and coat of a horse. However, blankets are often heavy, smelly, and time consuming to handle. They also keep a horse clean during turnout, reducing the time it takes to groom her. In large part, this is why blankets are often kept on 24/7 during the winter, regardless of the temperature change from night to day.

You can check to see if your horse is warm enough by feeling his chest, behind his ears, or his armpits. He should feel warm to the touch. If he isn't, then you might want to consider additional blanket options.

Other Daily Needs

Horses with absentee owners often don't get the love and sense of purpose that many horses appreciate. Even if you can't always ride, your horse would love for you to visit with some carrots a few times a week. Other important things to consider are:

- Does she have fresh water in her stall and in turnout?
- Are her feet picked before and after she is ridden?
- Is she properly cooled out after exercise before she is returned to her stall or is she "ridden hard and put away wet"?
- Is your horse getting adequate turnout? If she is uncharacteristically full of energy under saddle, she might not be getting enough exercise.

Is Your Horse Being Ridden by Others?

It is common that trainers will use your horse while you are not using him. This might benefit you and your horse or might be harmful. Regardless, your horse should never be used without your knowing who else is riding him and how they are riding him. Anyone riding your horse should be at least as good a rider as you are or should probably be a better rider. You might allow your trainer to teach lessons on him to riders who are more advanced than you. This can give him the exercise and training he requires. Stay away from allowing him to be used as a school horse for beginners. He could become ring sour, hard mouthed, and learn bad habits among other things.

FACT

It is not uncommon if you are the absentee owner of a good natured, sound, quiet horse for him to be used as a school horse. If your horse is digressing, this might be the case. Pop into the barn some afternoon after school lets out and young riders are taking lessons. Find out whether your horse is being used as a school horse without your knowledge.

When your horse is being ridden hard or recklessly, especially outside and especially by an inexperienced rider, his likelihood of injury increases. Unless you have an agreement with the caretaker of your horse, any expense or time out from an injury will be your problem. On the other hand, other riders can complement the kind of riding and training you do. A Dressage rider can round out your horse's experience if you are primarily a jumper and vice versa. A ring rider can give the horse the disciplined training and consistency that might be difficult to accomplish if you are mostly in the field with your horse. A field rider can give your horse the freedom, fun, and variation he might appreciate if you are primarily in the ring where horses can get bored or "ring sour." However, if your horse is uncharacteristically lethargic or unhappy about being tacked up and ridden, this might be a sign that he has already been out that day and is being ridden by others without your knowledge.

Finding a Like-Minded Barn

If you ride in a specific discipline, you and your horse might be happier and better off boarding with the trainers, other riders, and horses of the same discipline. Training methods and facilities for the several different disciplines of riding can be very specific. If you are in a stable situation that is primarily Dressage, for instance, the trainers and other riders there might know very little and even have a disdain for jumpers or field riding. It might be, in effect, a whole other world as far as they are concerned.

ALERT!

Your ability to get along with the barn owner or manager might be more important than you think. These are notoriously rigid and difficult people with a typical attitude of "my way or the highway." Take your time and find a friendly stable.

On the other hand, a stable that specializes in your discipline will give you more in-house options as you and your horse progress. A particular jumper trainer, for instance, might only be able to teach you safely over four-foot jumps, beyond which you might have to switch trainers. In a jumper stable, you wouldn't have to switch stables, only trainers.

Horses Must be Trained in Their Disciplines

You cannot expect your horse to perform in his particular discipline if he is not being trained in it. Field riders are often guilty of this fault. A field horse must be worked primarily in the field and should be professionally ridden in the field as aggressively, if not more aggressively, as you plan to ride him.

If the stable where you board is more of a show barn, chances are that your horse is mostly ridden in a riding ring. All the ring work in the world might not make your horse confident and competent on the trails. Likewise, competent field training will not prepare your horse for the show ring. Such a stable might not even have a trainer who specializes in field training. Believe it or not, there are many good professionals who have gotten so used to the invariability and order of a riding ring that they become afraid to aggressively ride and train a horse in the field.

FACT

Novice riders who find themselves in a stable that is not oriented to the discipline they have in mind often become discouraged in their discipline and are converted to the prevailing one, which they will often abide by but without their initial enthusiasm.

The Right Facility

A stable that doesn't specialize in your chosen discipline might not have the proper facilities to suit you and your horse. A Dressage ring is set up much differently from a jumping ring. Though stadium jumps are portable, they are heavy and cumbersome and cannot be brought into the ring and later removed every time you want to ride. If you are an Eventer, then the stable you choose to board at should have event style field and stadium jumps and an adequately sized field such as you would find at competition. If you have to sacrifice a riding ring for the right field situation, then so be it. However, a riding ring is an invaluable training situation to have. Find one close by that you can borrow from time to time.

If you are a field rider, then your stable should be situated on a trail system. You and your horse will quickly get tired of trailering to every riding destination. You might also get tired of hacking twenty or thirty minutes to the good part of a trail system. As attractive as a stable might be, keep what's important in mind and find a situation right on a trail system.

ALERT!

Be wary of a stable owner who won't allow you to train with anyone but herself. A trainer with such a policy will often be a very rigid person, with a one-dimensional style of teaching. There are many ways of riding and training, and you can learn different things from different trainers.

Are You Being Held Back?

It is not uncommon for a trainer to retard your progress. This might be out of concern for your safety or to keep you in a long-term program that would generate money for the stable. Take lessons at another barn with another trainer and another horse. This might help you gain perspective on your riding ability and progress past your trainer.

Some Tricks of the Trade

Like in any business, not all trainers and stable owners are good, honest people. There are some very common ways in which novice horse owners are taken advantage of. Learning these tricks of the trade can give you a great advantage on the road to having a positive experience in the horse world.

Some of the most attractive things about horses, their mystery and sometime inscrutability, are what makes it possible for people in the know to pull the wool over the eyes of amateurs, even ones that have been riding their whole lives. Horses are esoteric. In a sport where confidence and ability do not always go hand and hand and the stakes are high, namely your safety, it becomes easy for trainers, while otherwise honest people, to manipulate their clients. The trainers don't always shoot straight.

Over-Mounting

If you are over-mounted, you are mounted on a horse that is too much horse for your ability and experience and beyond your skill to ride well. You might have bought the horse without appreciating his size, strength, temperament, or greenness, or he might have behaved in a riding ring where you tried him out but won't behave in the field. He might have behaved under one trainer or work regime, but not under another. However you ended up in the situation of being over-mounted, it might work to your trainer's best interest to have you in this position.

Over-mounting is more often than not due to the owner's stubborn refusal to give up on a horse. This is often for sentimental reasons or because the rider doesn't like to think of herself as a quitter. There is no shame in changing horses to one that suits you better and that will keep you safe.

Over-mounting is generally much more beneficial for your trainer than for you. Over-mounting will generate money for the trainer in the way of extra training for your horse and extra lessons for you. You will be all too happy to pay for the extras to hasten the great potential your horse seems to have from time to time, especially when you are in a lesson or when your trainer rides him for you.

Your confidence and ability will diminish as you continually have bad experiences on your out-of-control horse and embarrass yourself. Even though you will from time to time, especially in a lesson with your trainer, ride him well and feel the thrill of coming out on top of a challenge, ultimately, such a horse in such an environment will destroy your confidence.

Your confidence in and dependency on your trainer will increase in converse proportion to your own waning confidence and ability. You might be susceptible to this because of your pride, the embarrassment of being over-mounted, or that you simply don't have the experience to know that you are being fooled.

Under-Mounting

If you are under-mounted, your skill, talent, or job you have in mind for your horse surpass the talent, level of training, or ability of your horse. A common scenario that occurs between trainer and client is that your trainer will encourage you to buy such a horse so that in a year's time you will be looking to trade up. The next horse will most certainly be a more expensive horse, which means another commission for your trainer on the sale of your old horse and on the purchase of your new one, as well as a more rigorous training schedule for you and your new, more demanding horse.

Your Horse Is Always Lame

Another common scenario is that your trainer tells you your horse is lame and that you can't ride him. It is not uncommon for this to continue, off and on, for years, and you spend more time at the barn feeding carrots to your horse than riding him. This, of course, is an easier horse for your trainer to keep while still getting paid for the stall.

FACT

Some stables are full of these perpetually lame horses. If such a horse cannot be managed to be useful, then you should consider a twenty-four-hour turnout situation, which is better for the horse and usually much cheaper than stabling in an active riding stable.

The horse might be lame, but the degree to which he is lame might or might not prevent you from riding him. There are plenty of good horses that are not 100 percent sound but rather "serviceably sound." This means that with medicine or special care their health can be managed to the point where they are perfectly useful and happy horses.

Exercise Riders

If you are paying extra for your horse to be exercised or trained, make sure that the people doing the riding or training are professionally trained. If you are paying a head trainer or barn owner for this service, then she should be paying the riders who work for her. If they are riding for free, then chances are they are not professional quality riders and might be doing more harm than good to your horse. Ask to ride along some time with the rider who exercises your horse and assess her riding ability. You have the right to do this. The professional riders should at least be better riders than you are.

Tipping the Barn Staff

If you tip your groom for the extra care and attentiveness he shows to your horse, make sure you tip him directly and not as an add-on to your monthly board check. The barn owner or manager might choose to disperse your tip to all the help or might choose instead to keep the specified tip for herself. Keep track of where your money goes. Likewise, if you are paying for extra training, grooming, turnout, or whatever, take care to make sure that the person providing the service is the one getting the tip.

Barn Etiquette

For all the possible ways in which trainers and barn owners can give you trouble, there are equally as many ways that clients can drive the professionals crazy. With some experience, a little common sense, consideration, and respect for their professionalism, you can be a pleasure for your trainer or stable manager to have around the barn.

Don't Come to the Barn Unannounced

A barn manager must know exactly what goes on at her farm at all times. Unannounced clients or ones that show up when the barn is closed can disrupt an orderly system at a working stable. A client who takes charge of her own horse when no professional is around might cause harm.

If you come to ride unannounced or on a day when the stable is closed, you might, unknown to your trainer or barn manager, ride your horse just before or after he is fed or medicated. You might feed your horse when he is sick or when he has already been fed. You might ride a horse that is freshly lame, but his lameness is undetectable by you. You might turn your horse out into the wrong situation, either with an unfamiliar horse or alone when he needs a buddy. These could be very detrimental or even fatal errors of miscommunication between you and your barn manager.

I like to give the horses a little hay when I visit. Where's the harm in that?
It is a natural impulse for people stopping by a barn to give all the horses a flake of hay. Keep in mind that the cost of this practice, done by just a few people on a regular basis, adds up and could cost the stable owner hundreds or thousands of dollars a year.

Be on Time

A lot of professional preparation goes into your riding your horse. When you show up late to ride, your horse probably would have been standing on cross ties for the whole time or tacked up in his stall waiting for you. If you don't call to say you're going to be late at least a half hour in advance, then your horse will probably have been ready and waiting, and then have to be untacked and tacked up again later. Horses hate that and it is likely to affect the quality of your ride. Horses, like humans, get bored, frustrated, and impatient. Place yourself in your horse's shoes when you ask him to do something for you. Be considerate to him as you would to another person.

Pay for the Needs of Your Horse

Your horse has nutritional, mental, and training or exercise requirements. Don't try to save money by skimping on what he needs. Unless you have reason not to, trust your trainer to tell you what your horse needs in these departments and follow her advice. When you go against the advice of your professional, then you cannot expect your horse to be sound or perform well, and you have no one to blame but yourself.

ESSENTIAL

A common problem arises when clients don't understand, or take for granted, the need for a horse to be ridden at least several times a week in order to stay fit and well behaved on the ground and under saddle. This costs money and is a matter of safety for you and your horse, so don't skimp on the cost of having your horse exercised and trained.

Bringing Your Friends to Ride

If your horse is in training, then you, your trainer, and whoever you decide to let ride your horse should be the only ones to ride him. Bringing your inexperienced friends to ride your horse can be detrimental to your horse's training, among many other things. Don't blame your trainer if your horse gets away with murder with your inexperienced friend, and then tries the same games with you. In general, too many riders aren't good for a horse's state of mind.

Chapter 21

Traveling with Your Horse

Traveling with your horse can be a fun and exciting way to add new dimensions and possibilities to your experience of the sport of riding. For most people, transporting your horse will be a learn-as-you-go process. If you obtain the right tow vehicle and horse trailer according to your and your horse's needs and follow certain basic procedures for driving, loading, and unloading your horse from the trailer, you will avoid common problems and pitfalls of the novice horse transporter.

Different Types of Trailers

You will probably see as many styles of horse trailers at a horse event as there are kinds of horses. This might be daunting when you are trying to decide which kind to buy for your specific needs or for future needs. All trailers are really just variations on a handful of basic designs. The kind you choose might be determined by your requirements, your finances, or might just be a matter of preference.

QUESTION?

What sort of trailer should I buy?
An adequate used trailer could be purchased for about $4,000 to $7,000 and might be the way to go if you are just getting into the sport of riding. Over time, enthusiasm for traveling off your property might dwindle. Or else your enthusiasm might grow along with the number or type of horses you want to transport. Then, another kind or size of trailer might be needed.

Bumper Pull

A bumper pull trailer is pulled behind a truck or other suitable vehicle from a tow ball attached to its bumper and or sub-frame. Most two-horse trailers are pulled in this way. Virtually all trucks and most full-size SUVs come with this kind of tow package, which might need to be re-enforced for pulling a three-horse trailer. If you will be pulling a three-horse or anything bigger, you would be better off with a gooseneck trailer.

Gooseneck

A gooseneck trailer is pulled by a pickup truck from a ball that is bracketed to the frame of the vehicle and centered in the middle of the pickup bed. With this design, the weight of the trailer and its load is balanced better and more easily carried because the point of the load is situated over the rear axle where the truck is being powered from rather than from the bumper. A gooseneck will give you a more stable feeling of carrying a load, rather than pulling it, while causing less stress on your tow vehicle.

FACT

Today's gooseneck setups for trucks can mount under the bed, making it possible to remove the tow ball from the bed, and cap the hole that remains, transforming your truck back to its full utility potential.

Of course, you cannot use an SUV with this style of trailer, and you will need to outfit your pickup truck specifically for pulling it, which will limit the space in the bed of the truck while the trailer is hooked up and might limit the uses of the bed even when it is free of the trailer. If you have a gooseneck trailer, it might also be more difficult to find a tow vehicle to borrow in a pinch than if you had a bumper pull.

Straight Truck

A straight truck is a truck and trailer all in one. It is ideal as a four- to six-horse vehicle. Not only does it save you the hassle of hooking up a trailer to a truck, which can be very difficult and time consuming if you are by yourself, but it tends to be more substantial than a trailer. Among other benefits, this arrangement might incline a horse that has difficulty loading to feel safer and enter in the trailer more easily.

Straight trucks have their drawbacks. Unlike a truck and trailer that are two separate vehicles with different life expectancies, a straight truck's entire life is over once one part of it ages past the possibility of repair.

If you have several horses and you plan to travel long distances on a regular basis with them, then a straight truck might be the better vehicle. Its greater substance makes for an easier journey for your horse than in a lighter trailer.

Depending on the laws of your land, you might need a commercial driver's license in order to operate a straight truck over a certain unloaded weight. If you are not comfortable driving a big truck, you might find it easier to drive a pickup truck that pulls a gooseneck trailer, which can have the same carrying capacity. A straight truck is usually higher off the ground than a trailer of the same carrying capacity, requiring a relatively steep, high, and narrow side ramp. Although horses sometimes prefer the extra size and space of the straight truck, a loading accident off this ramp could have much worse consequences than an accident from a trailer.

Loading Systems

Along with the capacity, convenience, and drivability of a trailer, you will want to consider the way the horses are loaded, tied, and unloaded off a trailer. There are variations on three basic styles.

Ramp Loading or Step Up

Some horses prefer to walk up a ramp, rather than stepping up into a trailer. Some that refuse to walk up a ramp, however, will step up. It is simply a matter of preference for you and your horse. A ramp might be safer in case a horse decides to back off the trailer; the horse wouldn't have the one foot to one-and-a-half foot drop off from a step up. Ramps can usually be added to any trailer if you decide at a later date that you prefer it. Ramps can also be convenient when you are using your trailer for other purposes besides hauling horses, such as hauling motorcycles, hay, or furniture.

FACT

Most of the larger capacity trailers have a back opening into the trailer as well as a side opening. This is an opportunity to have a ramp on one side and a step up on the other to accommodate a picky horse.

Straight Stall Trailers

A standard late model trailer is seven-and-a-half feet tall and six feet and nine inches wide. There are smaller trailers, specifically for ponies or polo horses and larger sizes for warmbloods and driving horses. A straight stall trailer is divided into standard straight stalls about three feet wide and seven feet deep. Securing horses in these stalls makes for orderly loading and unloading. Also, they provide the horse with her own space and stability while on the road, and with the help of cross ties and a chest bar keep her from moving freely about the trailer. A horse that has her freedom in a trailer can become rambunctious, possibly resulting in injury and sudden and dangerous shifts in your trailer load, which could cause you to lose control of the vehicle you are driving.

ESSENTIAL

Horses can become testy on a journey. Sometimes, even horses that otherwise get along well can become hostile to each other. A filled hay net between two horses or shortening the outside cross tie chain by pulling it through the outside halter ring and clipping it back on itself could prevent two horses from fighting.

Stock Trailer

A stock trailer is the alternative to a stalled trailer. It is one or sometimes two unpartitioned spaces. Once loaded into the trailer, horses are tied with a slipknot or breakaway trailer tie to the wall. A stock trailer is usually more affordable and will accommodate more horses than a stalled trailer of the same size. Its open space is also more convenient if you use your trailer for other things besides horses, although the partitions in most stalled trailers can usually be dismantled. However, the absence of any partitions means that a stock trailer provides no stability and much less safety for your horse from another horse or horses on the trailer that might kick, bite, or inadvertently step on each other's feet while trying to keep their balance. Therefore, stock trailers are not ideal for larger, less agile breeds of horse, or for hot temperament horses, which would tend to get nervous or excited and not travel harmoniously in such an environment. This activity could create a dangerous situation while you are driving by shifting the load and during loading and unloading as well.

Tow Vehicles

Choosing a tow vehicle is a big and expensive decision. It is a common misconception that a vehicle that has the engine power to pull your trailer is automatically sufficient. Just as important as the power to pull is the capability to stop your load, which is not only determined by a sufficient braking system. The towing capacity specs of any truck will be in your owner's manual, but if you are buying new, you can get a good education by talking to someone knowledgeable about trucks at your dealership.

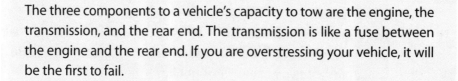

ALERT!

The three components to a vehicle's capacity to tow are the engine, the transmission, and the rear end. The transmission is like a fuse between the engine and the rear end. If you are overstressing your vehicle, it will be the first to fail.

Towing Capacity

The following information on the towing capacities of vehicles according to different size trailers is based on GMC specs for Chevrolet vehicles. There are so many variations of engine sizes, transmissions, suspensions, and rear ends or "axle ratios" that can be combined in any one truck to give it different towing capacity that these specs are approximations. Also, trailers vary significantly in weight, depending on their construction and the size of the horses you are towing. Fifth wheel or gooseneck towing for three- to eight-horse trailers, as well as automatic transmissions and four-wheel drive, are all presumed in the following information. They raise a vehicle's towing capacity from bumper pull, manual transmissions, and rear wheel drive respectively. The diesel option on 2500 and 3500 trucks also can increase your towing capacity, as will a dual wheel rear end or "dually" as they are referred to.

If your intended trailer load is nearing the limit for the vehicle you intend to purchase, you should consider the next truck size up. The difference is usually just $2,000 or $3,000, and the truck will probably more than pay for itself in less wear and tear.

Ford and Dodge have equally competent corresponding vehicles. However, GM has exclusive rights to quadra-steer technology, which enhances truck and trailer maneuverability.

The gross combined weight rating (GCWR) is the maximum weight a vehicle can safely pull plus the weight of the vehicle itself and its load, including passengers. As the weight of the trailer and the amount for the horses you're pulling increase, the GCWR of the vehicle must increase.

The Chevy 1500

The 1500 is a half-ton truck. Its GCWR is typically about 12,000 pounds, which gives it a maximum trailer weight of about 7,000 pounds. It will pull most two-horse trailers. The price is about $25,000 to $30,000.

The Chevy 2500

The 2500 is a three-quarter-ton truck. Its GCWR is about 20,000 pounds, which gives it a maximum trailer weight of about 14,000 pounds. It will adequately pull a three-horse trailer. Its price is about $32,000 to $40,000. If your three-horse trailer is extra heavy or your horses are extra large, you might want to upgrade to a diesel 2500 or a 3500.

The Chevy 3500

This is a one-ton truck. Its GCWR is about 22,000 pounds, which gives it a maximum trailer weight of about 15,000 pounds. It will adequately pull a four-horse trailer.

The Chevy 3500 Dual Rear Wheel

This is also a one-ton truck with four wheels on the rear axle. This increases the GCWR and the truck's stability while trailering significantly. This truck will pull a six- to eight-horse trailer. The diesel option on the three-quarter and one-ton trucks adds about 1,000 pounds to your towing capacity, and about $6,000 to your purchase price. Today's diesel engines are relatively quiet, smooth running, and efficient. Torque is the force that drives the power of a vehicle or its power potential. Torque is usually lower in the power band of a diesel truck, which is better for towing. If you are buying a truck that you will be using mostly for towing and especially for towing long distances, a diesel is the way to go.

FACT

Manual transmissions are no longer recommended for tow vehicles as they were in the not too distant past. Transmission technology has made automatic transmissions far superior, with better cooling and torque converters, which convert power from the engine to the transmission in a smooth and efficient manner.

General Rules of Loading

Perhaps more than any other horse-related activity, safe transportation of your horse depends on thinking ahead and using your knowledge of how a horse acts and reacts together with your common sense. Asking a horse to walk into a horse trailer is one of those things that goes completely against his nature. This is when he needs you to give him confidence. Although most experienced horses will walk right on if you lead them in the right way, it is important to consider a horse's apprehension so you can reassure him that it's okay. Horses that have never loaded might need to be coaxed. Others who have been on a trailer and stubbornly refuse to load could also be encouraged. Accidents to horses and handlers are common while loading. Safe and effective loading practices could drastically reduce the risk to you and your horse.

Prepare the Trailer

Before you load the horse onto the trailer, make sure that it is ready to receive him. The stall or space where the horse will stand must be free of obstacles such as hay bales or buckets that you might be taking with you on your journey. Tail bars or chest bars must be down or up, depending on what kind of trailer system you have. The space is tight, so it will be difficult to do any of this or maneuver your horse once he is in the trailer.

Don't ever find yourself in the straight stall of a trailer with your horse, no matter how gentle she is. The stall is so narrow that there is simply no space to get out of the way or to push her away if she squeezes you against the bar or wall of the stall.

The Approach

Give your horse about five steps or about fifteen feet as an approach. Walk at a brisk, deliberate pace in front of him, insisting that he follow likewise. Look straight ahead. Don't turn around and make eye contact with him as you approach or climb the ramp, or step up into the trailer. He might take that as an intimidation, a sign that you don't intend to go forward, or communication that you want him to do something other than what he is doing.

Common Accidents While Loading

When a horse is following you up a ramp, never let him veer off to the side and try to climb up the side of the ramp. If he veers off, stop, take him back in a circle, and make your approach straight. Another person standing on the ground to the outside of the ramp might help deter a crooked approach.

A horse that "runs out" the back of the trailer before you have secured him or when he is unloading could do major damage to himself, and anyone who might be behind him. Take care to load and unload knowledgeably and expeditiously, and always try to have a helper, who can steady the horse from behind.

Tricks for Loading a Difficult Horse

There are ways to encourage a horse onto a trailer when he won't walk on of his own volition. It should first be noted that such a horse should be worked with by a professional, who will build your horse's confidence and show him that it's okay to walk onto the trailer. A horse that is forced or scared onto a trailer every time will never be a good loader and will probably cause injury to you or himself eventually.

Horses are encouraged toward forward movement from behind, more than from in front. A long dressage crop could help you if you're alone. The presence of a broom behind him will often encourage him forward onto the trailer. For a little extra encouragement, your helper can touch it to his rump. For a horse that needs a little more support, two people can lock arms just behind his rump and push him forward while he is simultaneously led from the front.

ALERT!

If your horse rushes out the back of the trailer, he will probably hit the back of his head on the way out. This accident can be fatal, so make sure he backs up slowly and easily, and most of all have a partner behind him as he backs up, giving him assurance with a hand on his rump.

Never pull him from in front. He will only pull away from you. You will never win a tug of war with a horse.

You might win your horse's trust by bringing him to or even on the ramp, and then backing him off a few times. He would have paid attention and obeyed your commands a few times, and then might be inclined to walk on when you ask him to.

Sometimes with a ramp but more so with a step up, pulling one of your horse's feet up onto the ramp or trailer might encourage him to take the next few steps on his own.

Safety Check Before Hitting the Road

It is of utmost importance to do a safety check on your loaded trailer before you hit the road. Forgetting any of the steps crucial to a safe ride for you, your vehicle, and your horses could result in a dangerous situation.

- Check that the truck and trailer are successfully coupled.
- Make sure that safety chains from the trailer are connected to your tow vehicle.
- Have another person help you to see if the electrical hookup from the tow vehicle to the trailer is sound. Check the running, brake, and blinker lights.
- Make sure the emergency brake on your trailer is not engaged and that the wheel or stabilizing leg of your trailer, if it has one, is cranked up.
- Check to see that all trailer doors, latches, bars, and chains are secured.
- Make sure the windows are open according to the temperature outside. Even on a cold day, horses would prefer some fresh air. On a day above seventy degrees, all windows should be fully open.

Using the Different Types of Trailers

How you load the horse onto the trailer and tie her will depend on what kind of trailer you have. The three most common systems are an open stock trailer, a rear-load, two-horse straight stall trailer, and a slant load, three-horse trailer.

Stock Trailer

Walk up the ramp or step up onto the trailer with the horse to your right side and about a step or two behind you, or if you prefer right at your side. Lead her all the way up to the front of the trailer and tie her with a slipknot onto the side of the wall or clip her onto an existing trailer tie. The next horse that goes on should stand right beside her, facing in the same direction, leaving you an unobstructed exit route out the back. Some stock trailers are equipped with partitions to separate difficult horses that might be inclined to kick or misbehave. If your stock trailer is completely open in the interior, some good thought needs to go into which horse will be tied next to which.

FACT

Many later model trailers are made of aluminum rather than steel. Although they are more expensive, aluminum is rustproof and much lighter than steel, which will save you money in gas, as well as wear and tear on your vehicle.

Rear-Load, Straight Stall, Two-Horse Trailer

This is a little trickier. You will need a partner to load safely onto this trailer. The horse should be at a safe enough distance behind you (about four feet) as you lead him up the ramp. This is because you cannot remain at his side, but must be directly in front of him as he loads, and he might be inclined to jump onto the trailer. Lead him through his straight stall. Your partner should follow behind the horse, giving him encouragement and re-assurance with a hand on his rump.

Once he is all the way on, your partner must close the tail bar, thus preventing the horse from backing out. Clip his halter to a trailer tie, which should be located on the outside post. A hay net or other hay dispensing device could be tied head high either to his out side, or between him and another horse that you might load to keep them occupied and from fighting with each other.

ESSENTIAL

If you will be transporting a single horse, it is recommended that he be loaded on the left side. This puts the weight of the horse behind the driver, which will allow for a better sense of the uneven load when driving. All stalled trailers will have a side door, which should be opened from the outside before you load, so you can exit. Never try to squeeze between a horse and the stall bar to exit out the back.

Some trailer companies will allow you to design the inside of your trailer to suit your own needs. One design that will maximize space and give you more options is a rear-load, straight stall trailer, with occupancy for two horses, and a side entry ramp into a box stall in front, which should be at least six feet by six feet. This space can accommodate a mare and foal, a single horse that won't load into a straight stall, or two horses tied to the wall in the fashion of a stock trailer. One entry can be a step up, and the other a ramp for a choosey horse.

Slant Load, Three-Horse

Loading a slant load is much the same as loading a rear-load, straight stall, two-horse trailer. Horses are loaded diagonally, while a telescoping partition is moved into place and secured after each horse. This kind of three-horse trailer maximizes the space best and leaves room as well for a dressing room. This system can be a little more confusing than the others. Also, it can be inconvenient if you need to access a horse that is not situated in the last stall, because you would have to take off whichever horse or horses that are between you and him.

Unloading

A horse can be unloaded from a stock trailer by backing him up and letting him step off the back and out. Or, he can be turned around inside the trailer and led out head first.

Unloading from a stalled trailer is necessarily a two-person job, although if you know your horse well, the rules could be bent. Standing by his head, unclip him from the trailer tie and clip on a lead rope. From outside the trailer, your partner should then drop the tail bar and stand to the outside, so the horse doesn't step off the side of the ramp. While you encourage him backward, your partner should keep a hand on the horse's rump or grab his tail. Your partner will encourage the horse to slowly back out of the trailer while you follow him out, holding him close without slack in the rope.

Things to Bring with You

When you start to do some traveling with your horse, you will quickly miss the comforts and conveniences of riding out of your barn. A properly stocked and equipped trailer will make things easier. Some of the things you bring with you in the trailer might seldom if ever get used, but nevertheless are essential when you need them. Keep extra tack clean and supple and medications up to date. Some important things to bring are:

- Water for your horse to drink. An unused five-gallon gas container is better for the road than an open bucket, but bring a water bucket also to pour the water from the gas tank into it.
- Water for cleaning and cooling your horse before and after a ride. A separate bucket from his drinking bucket should be used, along with a sponge.
- Hay to keep him occupied and happy if he must stand around before or after you ride.
- A hay net to keep hay within his reach.
- A mucking fork and muck bucket to keep his small stall clean and sanitary.
- A small grooming kit, including hard and soft brushes, towel, and hoof pick.
- A small first aid kit, including banamine, duck tape, hoof wrap, bandages, betadine, electrolyte paste, and a horse shoe puller.
- A hole puncher.
- An extra bridle and reins.

You also want to remember to bring protective gear to make the ride safe and comfortable for your horse. It is easy to go overboard purchasing what your horse might need in the way of protective wear. Therefore, it is wise to see how he does in a trailer on a short trip before making a purchase of items that won't be used.

Many horse owners feel their horses need to wear shipping bandages, and there are many varieties. Shipping wraps will cover from just below the knee to the coronet band. There is benefit to wrapping your horse. Traveling by trailer can be tiring. Often your horse will be balancing and shifting his weight. Giving him some extra support, with the addition of protecting his legs from injury, make shipping wraps something to carefully consider. Many people either make their own wraps or buy quilts and bandages, but shipping wraps come ready made in all sizes and usually have Velcro fasteners. These wraps are easy to use and tend to be time savers.

Whatever protective wear you choose for your horse when traveling should fit well and be in good condition, since anything that might come loose could cause a bigger problem in the confinements of a trailer than at other times.

Bell boots are boots made of rubber or soft foam material and are also commonly used for shipping. A horse can step on himself in the trailer and cut his heel or even pull a shoe. For a horse that tends to carry his head high in a trailer or is tall and very close to the roof, protective gear called a "head bumper" can be purchased. These look something like a small helmet and are attached through the halter. You might want to wrap your horse's tail for travel, especially if you're using a two-horse bumper pull type trailer. A wrap will protect the tail from being rubbed when the horse leans against the back door.

Driving and Maintaining Your Trailer

When driving a vehicle with a trailer in tow, there is more to consider and certain rules to practice. You not only are responsible for the safety of your horses and your truck and trailer, but for other motorists who could be affected by the quality of your driving. It will also behoove you to learn how to maneuver your trailer. Often enough, you will be in a position where you will be forced to get yourself in or out of a tough parking situation. A little practice and confidence will make you an expert.

Driving a Loaded Trailer

The golden rule when driving horses is that you must always be conscious that you have horses in tow and drive accordingly. Driving accordingly means that you must take extra care not to upset your load around turns and corners. Generally, this means that you should drive slower than you normally would. Avoid sudden braking or acceleration as well. You might practice defensive driving to avoid situations where you might have to suddenly brake or accelerate. Not only would you be risking injury to your horse, but it could be dangerous. Your vehicle could not respond to a demanding handling or stopping situation the way it would if it were not laden with the extra weight and cumbersome burden of a trailer. Other drivers on the road usually don't understand this and will not account for the limitations of your rig, so don't expect them to. This is the golden rule for commercial truck drivers.

You must also remember that your trailer will not take a turn or corner at the same radius that your vehicle takes it. Therefore, it is necessary that you take any turn, especially a 90-degree turn, extra wide. Again, don't expect that other motorists or pedestrians on the road will assume that you must make extra wide turns.

Backing Up Your Trailer

There is a simple rule to backing up with your trailer which is that the trailer will go in the opposite direction from the direction that you turn the wheel of your vehicle. Even with this rule in mind, expert maneuvering will take time and practice, which, for the sake of your horse, should be practiced without him in the trailer.

ALERT!

Keep in mind that as you are looking backward or in your rear view mirror while trying to maneuver the trailer backward, the nose of your vehicle is moving in the opposite direction of your trailer. Not paying attention to this is a common cause of fender benders.

Trailer Maintenance

Your horses are only as safe as your trailer. A trailer, like any vehicle, must be maintained. The fact that they usually remain unused most of the time means that they will require special maintenance. Mechanical or moving parts could seize or become stiff, which could lead to failure. Tires could also sustain damage from sitting for long periods of time between uses and from use. You should pay particular attention to the following:

- **Coupling device.** This is where the trailer and the tow vehicle become joined. This area, along with the stabilizing wheel on a bumper pull, must be kept greased. Grease nipples will protrude from the coupling device and from other areas that require greasing.
- **Tire maintenance.** Dry rot is a common problem with trailer tires because of limited use. Dry rot will make a tire unsound, which could cause a blowout on the road. Replace any tires with signs of dry rot or excessive wear. Wheels also need to be greased, either through grease nipples or "repacking," which is a job for your local mechanic.
- **Trailer floor.** Some older trailer floors are made of wood, while newer ones are metal. Either way, the rubber mats should be removed once a year to check the soundness of the floor for rot or rust. Clean the trailer from the corrosive effects of urine.
- **Registration.** Because your trailer will probably be in limited use, it's easy to forget that the registration must be kept up to date. Remember to check it.

In the interest of ultimate safety and peace of mind, it would behoove you to have your trailer checked out by a professional once a year, the same as you would your personal vehicle. Brake and electrical problems could be hard to determine on your own. If you bought the trailer new from a dealer, they can do this for you, or your car mechanic can give your trailer a yearly checkup.

(E) Chapter 22
Troubleshooting

This final chapter provides you with the know-how to deal with some common problems you and your horse might face, such as falling from your horse, socialization with other horses, and changes in your horse's behavior. It is important to always be aware of your surroundings and vigilant in monitoring your horse's moods and reactions. Keep in mind that in all situations, both you and your horse will benefit from your remaining calm and knowing where to go for help when you need it.

If You Fall from Your Horse

If you take a fall from a horse, you should remain still for a few moments. A fall could be physically and mentally traumatic and could disorient you. Taking a few minutes will give you a chance to get your bearings and to feel for pain. If you feel any sharp pain, numbness, light-headedness, or disorientation, you should wait for help to arrive (a cell phone can be a life saver in some situations). In cooler weather, keep an injured rider warm with your coat if necessary until help arrives. If you're just a little shaken up but confident that you are not injured, by all means get back in the saddle. This will be the best thing for your confidence and your horse's training.

The buddy system is crucial to safe trail riding. Even a minor fall in the woods could become catastrophic if no one is around to help you, or get help for you, or catch your horse so you can ride out of the woods. Also, your horse is more likely to stick around after he is loose if there is another horse and rider present.

If Your Riding Partner Falls from a Horse

Your first concern is always with the rider and not catching the horse. That being said, a loose horse, especially around roads, can be a very dangerous element. She might cause damage to others and herself. More often than not, a loose horse will hang around another horse or horses. Sometimes they will head off in the direction of home, scared and insecure from what has taken place. The stirrups smacking against her sides will encourage her to keep moving as well.

What to Do Next

Once a horse has decided to leave the scene of the crime, you can do one of two things. First, you could hope that he changes his mind and stops not too far away. Then you can wait for him to walk back, or if he doesn't, you can approach him slowly on horseback, preferably getting ahead of him first. This is the most common strategy.

Your other option is to chase him with the horse you are on. If, however, the loose horse has more than a few steps on you, this will be difficult and dangerous. Use your judgment and knowledge of the loose horse and your own mount to gauge the possible success of this method.

Cast Horse

This is a term to describe a horse that has gotten down, usually in a stall or on a fence line, and cannot right himself. His legs will be up against the wall or perhaps under the fence, and he will be agitated. Casting is most common with older horses, or horses put into an environment that is unfamiliar to them. This happens in cases where a horse that has always lived outside has suddenly been put in a stall, or when a horse that is used to one kind of pasture or paddock fence is presented with another kind that has room between the ground and the bottom rail.

Be Careful

Helping a horse that is cast, whether in a stall or outside, is extremely dangerous. She might be agitated and scared, flailing, and scrambling while trying to get on her feet. Remember, she will instinctually feel life threateningly vulnerable in this position. After a few hours on her side, lack of blood flow might have induced paralysis or semi paralysis to the down side, so if she did get up, she could stumble and fall back down immediately. Take care to be cautious, while bracing her and helping her to steady herself as she regains her strength and mobility.

What to Do

First, go for help if it is near by or make a phone call. It is possible for one strong person to get the job done on a normal-sized horse, but two or three people is ideal. Before entering the stall, make a game plan. You want to pull his front end away from the wall, since it is his front end that he utilizes initially to right himself. Put a thick rope or lead line around his neck, positioned down toward his chest and withers. A helper can grab his mane and help you pull his front end from the wall or obstruction. If he cannot be pulled, you can try pulling him over onto his other side by tying his feet together and pulling him with a rope or by hand. This is a very dangerous proposition and should be attempted only if the horse is agreeable to having his feet tied or if he is too tired to protest.

ALERT!

Hopefully, you know the people in your neighborhood who might be experienced in these kinds of difficult situations. Local farm or livestock owners have usually seen just about everything and will probably have the knowledge and equipment to help you in such dire situations.

In Extreme Cases

Depending on how long the horse has been down, he might be too exhausted to right himself once he is moved from his cast position. He might need help with his head to get from a laying position to a sitting position so that blood can start circulating again on the prone side of his body. You can help him by pushing his head up as he tries to do the same. A rope can be tied to the horse's neck, just under his head, and the horse pulled to a sitting position. Hay and water should be offered if he remains in a sitting position for a few minutes. If he is too weak to right himself from a sitting position, then a harness can be fashioned for him, and he can be lifted to his feet with a system of pulleys rigged to the ceiling of the barn. If he is outside, a heavy tractor or backhoe can perform this task.

Changes in Manure

You should take note of the fresh manure your horse leaves in her stall or favorite spot in the paddock. Her manure will indicate whether she is properly hydrated, has worms, and is chewing and digesting her food properly.

Normal manure are moist fecal balls that stay heaped together; this texture indicates that your horse is healthy. Loose manure indicates that her manure passed through her system too quickly to form consistent fecal balls. This can be from a change in diet, usually with a change to a richer grass or alfalfa hay. It can be from nervousness, drinking a lot of water, or a bacterial or mechanical problem in her gut. Dry manure means that the horse could be dehydrated.

Grain Spillage During Eating

If you notice grain spilling out of your horse's mouth when he eats, grain on the floor of the stall, or chewed clumps of hay on the stall floor or feed manger or caught in the side of his cheek, then he might have a problem in his mouth. A horse dentist should be called out to see your horse and to evaluate the condition of his mouth. About one visit a year from a dentist should suffice for your horse until he becomes a senior, when he might need to be seen twice a year.

Allergic Reactions

Horses respond to common allergens with itching and skin eruptions, varying from mild to severe. Symptoms will exhibit as bumps, hives, or scaly patches. Many times, the exact nature of the allergen will remain unknown even after you have relieved its effects. Possible allergens could be reaction to pasture weeds, a product in a grain ration, or an insect bite. Stress can also predispose a horse to hives. Occasionally, a horse could suffer an allergic reaction to medication, but this is rare. Medications to relieve symptoms of an allergic reaction could be an antihistamine or any number of anti-itch topical preparations.

Changes in Behavior

Changes in behavior are important to note. They might be an early indication that something is wrong with your horse. His health could be failing because of an unbalanced diet or he might have developed an allergic reaction. He might have a lameness issue that is hard to detect or brought on by certain stimuli; for instance, your saddle might be pressing on a sore spot on his back. Your mare's ovaries, located just behind where you would sit on her, might be sore, which could indicate a variety of problems. Careful attention to how and when your horse is acting poorly will help you and your vet figure out the problem and correct it. Be careful not to discipline your horse for acting badly before you know if he is suffering from an underlying problem or has just a behavior problem.

Socialization with Other Horses

Not all horses get along. Some have a hard time fitting into a herd or making friends in general, while others take to almost any other horse and are liked by other horses just the same. If you always see your horse alone in a corner of the paddock full of other horses, then he might prefer to be alone or he might have been ostracized. Give him a few days' trial with a smaller group of gentle horses or with just one turnout buddy who is older or not overly aggressive. Generally speaking, horses are social animals and prefer to be with other horses; usually there is a place in the herd for everyone, but there are exceptions to the rule. So, if you've tried a few combinations and for whatever reason they don't work, let your loner horse be alone.

If you have two horses that you would like to get along or need for them to get along and they don't, try putting them in an unfamiliar situation together. For instance, if one or both of them is not used to night turnout, then let them spend the night together outside, where they will rely on each other for comfort and safety. In the morning, they might be the best of friends.

Appendices

Appendix A
Glossary

Appendix B
Further Reading

Appendix C
Additional Resources

Glossary

Abscess: A localized area of infection. It can occur almost anywhere, but it most often affects the foot of a horse. This can be very painful to the horse, and will cause lameness.

Action: The way a horse moves at various gaits.

Aged: A horse that's over nine years old.

Azoturia: Prolonged cramping of a horse's muscles during exercise. The condition often appears in healthy horses that are exercised after a long period of rest. Also called "tying up."

Bale: A measurement of hay.

Bedding: Materials used to line the floor of a stall, such as wood shavings or straw.

Bit: Metal bar on a bridle that goes in the horse's mouth and is used to control the horse while riding.

Bowed hocks: A conformational fault in which the hocks on the hind legs are turned too far outwards. Also called "cow hocks."

Bowed tendon: A permanently swollen tendon resulting in weakening of the tendon but not lameness.

Breeder: A person who breeds purebred horses for a living.

Bridle: The entire headpiece, including the bit, chinstrap, reins, and headstall.

Buck: When a horse jumps and arches his back. This behavior is sometimes only playful and is not always intended to unseat the rider.

Cannon: A bone located between the knee and the fetlock and the hock and the fetlock.

Canter: One of a horse's four basic gaits; a three-beat gait.

Cavesson: Headgear with attachments for side reins and a lunge line that is worn by the horse during lunging.

Cob: A small, strong horse descended from draft horses; about 15 hands high.

Coffin bone: A bone located between the second phalanx and the horny sole.

Cold blood: Term used to refer to heavy European breeds of horse, such as draft horses.

Colic: General term for abdominal pain in the horse that can be fatal. There are two kinds of colic, gas colic and an impaction. A veterinarian should always be consulted in case of suspected colic.

Colt: A male horse under four years old that has not been castrated.

Conformation: The overall build of a horse. A horse with good conformation will look proportional. Each breed has its own standards of conformation, but what is considered acceptable conformation depends on what the horse is used for.

Coronet band: The coronet band encircles the horse's hoof, and produces new hoof wall. Injuries to the coronet band can bleed a lot, and may also show up as marks on the outside of the hoof wall as the hoof grows.

Cow hocks: A conformational fault in which the hocks on the hind legs are turned inward toward each other.

Cribbing: A vice in which a horse will arch his neck, stretch his esophagus, grab hold of a surface with his teeth (such as a fence railing), suck in air, and swallow it.

Cross ties: A method of restraining a horse so he can be worked on. The horse is secured using two ropes or ties, one on each side, connected to a solid post or wall.

Currycomb: A plastic or rubber comb with several rows of short flexible bristles. Used for removing loose hair and dirt from the horse's coat.

Dam: A horse's mother.

Dressage: A method of horse training including basic turns and the three basic gaits along with more elaborate exercises meant to give a horse self-confidence, balance, poise, and discipline. For riders, Dressage is considered to be the ultimate test of horsemanship and skill.

Easy keeper: A horse that easily maintains a proper weight. Also known as a thrifty horse.

Eventing: Equestrian competition held over one or three days and including events in Dressage, cross country, and show jumping.

Farrier: A professional blacksmith who puts shoes on horses.

Fetlock: The joint formed by the pastern, cannon, and sesamoid bones. Also known as the ankle joint.

Filly: A female horse under three or four years old.

Flake: One-tenth of a bale of hay.

Foal: A male or female horse under one year old and still unweaned.

Founder: The condition that develops as a result of laminitis in the foot of a horse. It is a separation of the sensitive laminae from the hoof wall. Founder causes extreme lameness.

Frog: A triangular structure located in the middle of the horse's sole. It acts as a pump to re-circulate blood back up the horse's leg.

Gait: Term describing the different ways a horse can move. The four basic natural gaits are walk, trot, canter, and gallop. There are also additional gaits that horses can be bred or trained for, such as the tolt or the flying pace.

Gallop: One of a horse's four basic gaits. A three-beat gait that is usually the fastest gait that a horse can run.

Gastric ulcer: Gastric ulcers in a horse are usually caused by stress and/or diet. They can be difficult to diagnose and will cause pain.

Gelding: A castrated male horse.

Girth: The strap that goes under the horse's belly to secure the saddle in place.

Green: Term used to describe a horse that has been ridden but is still in the early stages of training. Can also be used to describe a beginning rider.

Grooming: Maintenance of a horse's coat, including clipping, brushing, washing, and trimming the mane and tail.

Groundwork: Lead rope and lunge-line training.

Gut sounds: The noises that emanate from a horse's stomach.

Halter: A harness of leather or rope that fits over a horse's head. Similar to a bridle but without the bit or reins, a halter is used for leading a horse.

Hand: Equal to 4 inches, a hand is the standard way to measure horses. Horses are measured from their withers to the ground. An average horse is 15 hands, or 5 feet tall.

Hard keeper: A horse that struggles to maintain a proper weight.

Haynet: A way to keep hay off the ground or within reach in a stall or during transportation.

Height: Measured in hands from the highest part of the withers to the ground.

Herd health: Term used to describe the method that horsepeople use to protect their farm's population of horses. New horses are vaccinated and wormed before joining an established herd, after which they are wormed and vaccinated on the same rotation as the existing animals.

Hock: The joint between the gaskin and the cannon bone in the hind leg of the horse. The hock is similar to the human ankle.

Hoof: The horny outer covering of the foot.

Hoof pick: A metal or strong plastic tool with a pointed end for picking debris out of the underside of hooves.

Horn: The surface of the hoof.

Hot blood: Term used to refer to Arabian or thoroughbred horses.

Lame: Caused by illness or injury, lameness is a condition that prevents a horse from carrying weight equally on all four legs.

Laminae: Membranes lining the hoof that attach the hoof to the bones.

Laminitis: Painful condition causing inflammation of the laminae. Severe conditions can lead to founder.

Laryngeal hemiplegia: Partial paralysis of the larynx causing a characteristic roaring noise when the horse breathes.

Lope: Western term for canter.

Lunge: The method of training a horse by working him through various paces in a circle using a long lunge rein attached to the cavesson.

Mare: A female horse over four years old.

Martingale: A leather strap that goes from the girth to the bridle. Used to control the position of a horse's head.

Navicular disease: A disease of the navicular bone caused by improper shoeing and excess stress on the hooves, which leads to lameness.

Neurectomy: A treatment for navicular disease where the nerves supplying sensation to the foot are cut.

Nicker: A vocalization thought to communicate a greeting.

Paddock: Outdoor enclosure where horses are turned out for grazing.

Pastern: Part of the leg between the hoof and fetlock.

Pony: Certain breeds of small horses that are under 14.2 hands when fully grown.

Purebred: A horse that is the result of generations of unmixed breeding. Bred to have and produce perfect breed conformation.

Rearing: A vice in which the horse stands on his hind legs, usually intended to unseat a rider or cast off unwelcome tack.

Sesamoid bones: Small bones attached to the cannon and pastern by ligaments. Located behind the fetlock joint.

Sire: A horse's father.

Snaffle bit: A simple bit used most often in English riding styles, it consists of one or two bars joined in the middle, with rings at each end to attach to the reins.

Sound: Term used to describe a healthy horse.

Spavin: A bone enlargement of the hock affecting the hind legs that results in lameness.

Splint bones: Bones found on either side of the cannon bone.

Stallion: A male horse over four years old that has not been castrated.

Stifle: Joint between the femur and tibia, similar to a human knee.

Tack: All gear and equipment that can be worn by a horse, including the bridle, saddle, bit, and halter.

Thoroughbred: Breed of horse averaging 16 hands used as a racehorse. Thoroughbreds also make excellent hunter/jumpers.

Thrifty: A horse that easily maintains a proper weight on an adequate diet.

Tie down: A Western term for a martingale.

Trot: One of the four basic gaits, it is a two-beat gait.

Turnout: To set a horse loose in a paddock or pasture for all or part of the day, either alone or with other horses.

Unsound: A horse with health problems or lameness.

Unthrifty: A horse that does not gain or maintain weight, despite having an adequate diet and no known illnesses

Walk: One of the four basic gaits; a four-beat gait in which each leg moves independently and each hoof strikes the ground separately.

Warm blood: Term referring to a horse type that resulted from a cross between heavier draft horses (cold bloods) and lighter thoroughbreds or Arabians (hot bloods).

Weanling: A horse under one year old that has been weaned.

Wind puff: Any diffuse swelling located below the knees in the front legs, and below the hock in the hind legs. They are usually a warning sign of stress or overwork, but not usually associated with lameness.

Withers: The slight ridge on a horse's upper back from which height is measured.

Yearling: A horse that is no more than one year old.

Appendix B

Further Reading

Bird, Jo. *Keeping a Horse the Natural Way*. Dorking, UK: Interpet Publishing, 2002.

Chamberlin, Harry P. *Training Hunters, Jumpers & Hacks*. New York: Arco Publishing Co., 1978.

Equine Research Publications. *The Illustrated Veterinary Encyclopedia for Horsemen*. Grapevine, TX, 1975.

Equine Research Publications. *Veterinary Treatments & Medications for Horsemen*. Grapevine, TX, 1977.

Goody, Peter. *Horse Anatomy: A Pictorial Approach to Equine Structure*. London: J. A. Allen & Co., 1983.

Hayes, M. Horace. *Veterinary Notes for Horse Owners*. Rev. ed. New York: Simon & Schuster, 2002.

Hill, Cherry. *Horse Keeping on a Small Acreage*. 1990.

Hill, Cherry. *Horse Health Care*. 1997.

Imus, Brenda. *Gaits of Gold*. 1998.

Jacobson, Patricia, and Marcia Hayes. *A Horse Around the House*. New York: Crown Publishing Co., 1978.

Schulte, Briggite, and Heinz Baumann. *Leading with Feeling, a Little Bit More*. Germany: Herm. Sprenger GmbH., 2002.

Snow, Amy, Marie Soderberg, and Nancy A. Zidonis. *Equine Acupressure: A Working Manual*. Larkspur, CO: Tallgrass Publishers, LLC, 1999.

Swift, Sally. *Centered Riding*. New York: St. Martin's Press, 1985.

Additional Resources

Web Sites

Acreage Equines
www.acreageequines.com

AlphaHorse
www.alphahorse.com

American Riding Instructors Association (ARIA)
www.riding-instructor.com

BitsAndBridles.com
www.bitsandbridles.com

Carter Performance Horses
www.carterperfor-mancehorses.com

Cashel Company
www.cashelcompany.com

Equestrian Books and Videos
www.equestrianbooks andvideos.com

Equine Promotions Classifieds
www.equinepromotions.com

EquiSearch
www.equisearch.com

First Horse
www.firsthorse.com

FL Horses
www.flhorses.com

Front Range Frenzy
www.FrontRangeFrenzy.com

Holistic Horsekeeping
www.holistichorsekeeping.com

Horse Books and Videos.com
www.horsebooksandvideos.com

HorseCity.com
www.horsecity.com

Horsekeeping.com
www.horsekeeping.com

Horsetalk
www.horsetalk.co.nz

International Farrier Services
www.tjhorseshoeing.com

Prostepps Grooming Products
www.prostepps.com

StableWise
www.stablewise.com

The Complete Pet.com
www.thecompletepet.com/ horse_care_articles.cfm

The Horse Show Online Radio
www.thehorseshow.com

The Horse
www.thehorse.com

Sources for Horse Care Products and Equipment

AG-CO Products

P.O. Box 126
St. Johns, MI 48879
(800) 522-2426

Allied Precision Industries

705 E. North Street
Elburn, IL 60119
(800) 627-6179
www.alliedprecision.com

Alternate Solutions

103 S. Walters
Poteau, OK 74953
(800) 451-4660
www.buytack.com

American MasterCraft Steel Buildings

1739 East Carson
Street, Suite 160
Pittsburgh, PA 15203
(800) 679-1113

American Steel Buildings

4700 NW Boca Raton
Boulevard, Suite 104
Boca Raton, FL 33431
(800) 715-6482
www.amsteel.com

American Tank Co., Inc.

P.O. Box 340
Windsor, CA 95492
(877) 655-1100;
(707) 535-1400
www.watertanks.com

Armour Gates

1101 E. 25th Street
Sanford, FL 32771
(800) 876-7706
www.armourgates.com

Ashland Barns

990-J Butler Creek Road
Ashland, OR 97520
(541) 488-1541
www.ashlandbarns.com

Bar Bar A Equipment Co.

230 East 1700 South
Farmington, UT 84025
(800) 451-2230
www.synergyplastics.net

Barnmaster

2501 East I-20
Midland, TX 79701
(800) 500-BARN (2276)
www.barnmaster.com

BarnPlans, Inc.

41-049 Ehukai Street
Waimanalo, HI 96795
(877) 259-7028
www.barnplans.com

Bayco Fencing and Kroy Building Products

2060 East Indiana Avenue
Southern Pines, NC 28387
(800) 822-5426
www.kroybp.com

Behlen Manufacturing Co.

P.O. Box 569
4025 E. 23rd Street
Columbus, NE 68601
(402) 564-3111
www.behlenmfg.com

Best Friend Equine Supply, Inc.

3515 Lakeshore Drive
Saint Joseph, MI 49085
(269) 983-3971
www.bestfriendequine.com

Brower Equipment

P.O. Box 2000
Houghton, IA 52631
(319) 469-4141
www.browerequip.com

C&P Engineering & Manufacturing Co., Inc.

5650 Industrial Avenue South
Connersville, IN
47331-7715
(800) 783-4283;
(765) 825-4293
www.aceofgates.com

Caple-Shaw Industries, Inc.

1112 NE 29th Street
Fort Worth, TX 76106
(800) 969-3234
www.capleshaw.com

Centaur HTP Fencing System, Spur Fence

2802 East Avalon Avenue
Muscle Shoals, AL 35661
(800) 348-7787
www.centaurcentral.com

Classic Equine Equipment

100 Wulfert Drive
Fredericktown, MO 63645
(800) 444-7430
www.classic-equine.com

Co-Line Welding, Inc.

1232 100th Street
Sulley, IA 50251
(800) 373-7761
www.colinemfg.com

Comfortstall Stable Supply Company

3388 Regional Parkway, Suite A
Santa Rosa, CA 95403
(888) 307-0855
www.comfortstall.com

Controlled Energy Corp.

340 Mad River Park
Waitsfield, VT 05673
(802) 496-4357
www.controlledenergy.com

Country Estate Fence

P.O. Box 45
Cozad, NE 69130
(800) 445-2887
www.countryestate.com

Country Manufacturing

P.O. Box 104
333 Salem Avenue
Fredericktown, OH 43019
(800) 335-1880
www.countrymfg.com

Cover-All Buildings

3815 Wanuskewin Road
Saskatoon, SK
Canada S7P 1A4
(800) 268-3768
www.coverall.net

Double L Group

2020 Beltline Road
P.O. Box 324
Dyersville, IA 52040
(800) 553-4102
www.doublel.com

ElectroBraid Fence Ltd.

Water Street, P.O. Box 19
Yarmouth, NS
Canada B5A 4P8
(888) 430-3330
www.electrobraid.com

Equi-Master International

P.O. Box 1280
Sundre, AB
Canada T0M-1X0
(800) 570-3848
www.equi-master.com

Equine Comfort

493 Route 22, Suite A
Pawling, NY 12564
(800) 628-8464

Equi-Tee Farm and Fence

10984 Meadows Road
White City, OR 97503
(888) 253-6245
www.fencingsolutions.com

Equustall

1801A Willis Road
Richmond, VA 23237
(800) 788-6223
www.equustall.com

Farnam Companies, Inc.

301 W. Osborn
Phoenix, AZ 85013
(800) 234-2269
www.farnamhorse.com

Fast Trac Buildings

65 Inverness Drive E
Englewood, CO 80112
(800) 379-3754
www.fasttracbuildings.com

Field Controls

2630 Airport Road
Kinston, NC 28504
(252) 522-3031
www.fieldcontrols.com

Franklin Equipment

P.O. Box 271
Monticello, IA 52310
(319) 465-3561
www.franklinwaterers.com

Groundmaster Products

15101 Algoma Avenue NE
Cedar Springs, MI 49319
(800) 411-2530
www.groundmaster-stallflooring.com

Group Summit

P.O. Box 21
Ashland, OR 97520
(800) 782-5628
www.summitflex.com

Hagie Manufacturing

P.O. Box 273
Clarion, IA 50525
(800) 247-4885
www.hagie.com

Handi-Klasp

911 Waterford Street
Wakarusa, IN 46573
(800) 332-7990
www.handi-klasp.com

Hardware for Horse Barns

P.O. Box 140
Livermore, CO 80536
www.horsekeeping.com

Harrison Banks, Architecture for the Horse Industry

790 Boylston Street,
Suite 23-F
Boston, MA 02199
(617) 236-1876
www.harrisonbanks.com

Heritage Building Systems

P.O. Box 470
North Little Rock,
AR 72114
(800) 643-5555
www.heritagebuildings.com

High Country Plastics, Inc.

1502 Aviation Way
Caldwell, ID 83605
(800) 388-3617
www.highcountry-plastics.com

HiQual Mfg. Ltd.

3139 Creek Drive
Rapid City, SD 57703
(605) 343-1234
www.hiqualmfg.com

Homestead Design, Inc.

P.O. Box 2010
Port Townsend, WA 9836
(360) 385-9983
www.homesteaddesign.com

Horse Fence Direct

7268 Commerce Circle East, Suite B
Fridley, MN 55432
(800) 478-0099
www.horsefencedirect.com

HorseGuard Fence

2283 Cornell Avenue
Montgomery, IL 60538
(888) 773-3623
www.horseguardfence.com

Humane Manufacturing Co.

805 Moore Street
Baraboo, WI 53913-2796
(800) 369-6263
www.humanemfg.com

Innovative Equine Systems

7975 Cameron Drive,
Building 900
Windsor, CA 95492
(800) 888-9921
www.equinesystems.com

J. W. Hall Enterprises

P.O. Box 68
Sante Fe, TX 77517
(800) 475-8158
www.jwhall.com

Keystone Steel and Wire Co.

7000 SW Adams Street
Peoria, IL 61641
(800) 447-6444
www.redbrand.com

Ky Steel Truss Buildings

P.O. Box 4092
Winchester, KY 40392
(800) 955-2765
www.kstbuild.com

Lester/Butler Building Systems

1111 2nd Avenue South
Lester Prairie, MN 55354
(800) 826-4439
www.lesterbuildings.com

Linear Rubber Products, Inc.

5525 19th Avenue
Kenosha, WI 53140
(800) 558-4040
www.rubbermats.com

Loddon Livestock Equipment

5280 S. University Boulevard
Greenwood Village,
CO 80121
(800) 779-0285
www.loddon.ca

Lucas Equine Equipment

P.O. Box 158
Cynthiana, KY 41031
(888) 551-6920
www.lucasequine.com

Mac Mountain Tack Repair

61 Falmouth Road
Windham, ME 04062
(207) 892-0161
www.protectavest.com

MD Barns

1720 E. Locust Street
Ontario, CA 91761
(800) 343-2276
www.mdbarns.com

Metro Gate and Manufacturing Co., Inc.

Quicksilver Products
P.O. Box 619
Paris, TX 75461
(800) 657-1906
www.quicksilverarenas.com

Morton Buildings

252 West Adams Street
Morton, IL 61550
(800) 447-7436
www.mortonbuildings.com

National Horse Stalls

P.O. Box 153
Raphine, VA 24472
(800) 903-8908
www.nationalhorsestalls.com

National Well Owners Association

601 Dempsey Road
Westerville, OH 43081
(800) 551-7379
www.wellowner.org

Nelson Manufacturing Co.

3049 12th Street SW
Cedar Rapids, IA 52404
(888) 844-6606
www.nelsonmfg.com

Northern Light Stalls

1438 County Road G
New Richmond, WI 54017
(800) 246-3190
www.nlstalls.com

North West Rubber Mats, Ltd.

33850 Industrial Avenue
Abbotsford, BC
Canada V2S 7T9
(800) 663-8724
www.northwestrubber.com

OK Water, Inc.

1037 Oceanwave Drive
Lake City, CO 81235
(800) 750-2837
www.okwater.com

PortAStall Corp.

P.O. Box 4126
Mesa, AZ 85211-4126
(800) 717-7027
www.portastall.com

Premier Fence Systems

2031 300th Street.
Washington, IA 52353
(800) 282-6631
www.premier1supplies.com

Priefert Manufacturing Co.

P.O. Box 1540
Mt. Pleasant, TX
75456-1540
(800) 527-8616
www.priefert.com

Promat Ltd.

40 Birch Street
Seaforth, ON
Canada N0K 1W0
(888) 337-6265
www.promatltd.com

RAMMfence

515 South Union Street
Bryan, OH 43506
(800) 443-5972
www.rammfence.com

Ranch Life Plastics, Inc.

P.O. Box 503
5260 S. Clinton Trail
Eaton Rapids, MI
48827-0503
(800) 551-4348
www.ranchlifeplastics.com

RB Rubber Products, Inc.

904 E. 10th Avenue
McMinnville, OR 97128
(800) 525-5530
www.rbrubber.com

Ritchie Industries, Inc.

P.O. Box 730
Conrad, IA 50621
(800) 747-0222
www.ritchiefount.com

Rockin' J Horse Stalls

P.O. Box 869
Mannford, OK 74044
(800) 765-7229
www.rockinjhorsestalls.com

Rocking W Round Pens

Rt. 5, Box 173A
Enid, OK 73701
(580) 234-8705
www.rockingwmfg.com

Rohn Agri Products

P.O. Box 2000
Peoria, IL 61656
(800) 447-2264
www.radiancorp.com

Rubbermaid Specialty Products, Inc.

1147 Akron Road
Wooster, OH 44691-6000
(800) 895-2110
www.rcpworksmarter.com

Shelter-Kit Incorporated

22 West Mill St.
Tilton, NH 03276
(603) 286-7611
www.shelterkit.com

Silk Tree Manufacturing

Route 1, Box 3430
Dillwyn, VA 23936-8730
(804) 983-1941
www.silktree.com

System Fencing Stalls and Equipment

11233 2nd Line, RR #1
Campbellville, ON
Canada L0P 1BO
(800) 461-3362
www.systemhorse.com

Tensar Polytechnologies

1210 Citizens Parkway
Morrow, GA 30260
(800) 845-4453
www.tensar-tpi.com

Triple Crown Fence

P.O. Box 2000
Milford, IN 46542-2000
(800) 365-3625
*www.royalcrownltd.com/
products/tc_fence/*

UltraGuard Fence

3773 State Road
Cuyahoga Falls, OH 44223
(800) 457-4342
*www.ultraguardvi-
nylfence.com*

VaFaC

212 Freedom Court
Fredericksburg, VA 22408
(540) 898-5425
www.horsestallsusa.com

Walters Buildings

6600 Midland Court
Allenton, WI 53002
(800) 558-7800
www.waltersbuildings.com

Westwood Co.

50 Westwood Lane
Trout Creek, MT 59874
(406) 827-4675

Woodstar Products, Inc.

1824 Hobbs Drive
Delavan, WI 53115
(800) 648-3415
www.wdstar.com

Woody Pet Acres

16691 16th Avenue
Surrey, BC
Canada V3S 9X7
(888) 535-9816
www.woodypet.com

Alternative Health Care Contacts

American Veterinary Chiropractic Association

(309) 658-2920

www.amimalchiropractic.org/default.htm

International Veterinary Acupuncture Society

(970) 266-0666

www.ivas.org/vet.html

Academy of Veterinary Homeopathy

(305) 652-1590

www.acadvethom.org

International Alliance for Animal Therapy and Healing

(914) 378-5292

www.laath.com

Index

THE EVERYTHING SERIES!

BUSINESS & PERSONAL FINANCE

Everything® Budgeting Book
Everything® Business Planning Book
Everything® Coaching and Mentoring Book
Everything® Fundraising Book
Everything® Get Out of Debt Book
Everything® Grant Writing Book
Everything® Home-Based Business Book, 2nd Ed.
Everything® Homebuying Book, 2nd Ed.
Everything® Homeselling Book, 2nd Ed.
Everything® Investing Book, 2nd Ed.
Everything® Landlording Book
Everything® Leadership Book
Everything® Managing People Book
Everything® Negotiating Book
Everything® Online Business Book
Everything® Personal Finance Book
Everything® Personal Finance in Your 20s and 30s Book
Everything® Project Management Book
Everything® Real Estate Investing Book
Everything® Robert's Rules Book, $7.95
Everything® Selling Book
Everything® Start Your Own Business Book
Everything® Wills & Estate Planning Book

COMPUTERS

Everything® Online Auctions Book
Everything® Blogging Book

COOKING

Everything® Barbecue Cookbook
Everything® Bartender's Book, $9.95
Everything® Chinese Cookbook
Everything® Cocktail Parties and Drinks Book
Everything® College Cookbook
Everything® Cookbook
Everything® Cooking for Two Cookbook
Everything® Diabetes Cookbook
Everything® Easy Gourmet Cookbook
Everything® Fondue Cookbook
Everything® Gluten-Free Cookbook
Everything® Glycemic Index Cookbook
Everything® Grilling Cookbook

Everything® Healthy Meals in Minutes Cookbook
Everything® Holiday Cookbook
Everything® Indian Cookbook
Everything® Italian Cookbook
Everything® Low-Carb Cookbook
Everything® Low-Fat High-Flavor Cookbook
Everything® Low-Salt Cookbook
Everything® Meals for a Month Cookbook
Everything® Mediterranean Cookbook
Everything® Mexican Cookbook
Everything® One-Pot Cookbook
Everything® Pasta Cookbook
Everything® Quick Meals Cookbook
Everything® Slow Cooker Cookbook
Everything® Slow Cooking for a Crowd Cookbook
Everything® Soup Cookbook
Everything® Tex-Mex Cookbook
Everything® Thai Cookbook
Everything® Vegetarian Cookbook
Everything® Wild Game Cookbook
Everything® Wine Book, 2nd Ed.

CRAFT SERIES

Everything® Crafts—Baby Scrapbooking
Everything® Crafts—Bead Your Own Jewelry
Everything® Crafts—Create Your Own Greeting Cards
Everything® Crafts—Easy Projects
Everything® Crafts—Polymer Clay for Beginners
Everything® Crafts—Rubber Stamping Made Easy
Everything® Crafts—Wedding Decorations and Keepsakes

HEALTH

Everything® Alzheimer's Book
Everything® Diabetes Book
Everything® Health Guide to Adult Bipolar Disorder
Everything® Health Guide to Controlling Anxiety
Everything® Health Guide to Fibromyalgia
Everything® Hypnosis Book

Everything® Low Cholesterol Book
Everything® Massage Book
Everything® Menopause Book
Everything® Nutrition Book
Everything® Reflexology Book
Everything® Stress Management Book

HISTORY

Everything® American Government Book
Everything® American History Book
Everything® Civil War Book
Everything® Irish History & Heritage Book
Everything® Middle East Book

GAMES

Everything® 15-Minute Sudoku Book, $9.95
Everything® 30-Minute Sudoku Book, $9.95
Everything® Blackjack Strategy Book
Everything® Brain Strain Book, $9.95
Everything® Bridge Book
Everything® Card Games Book
Everything® Card Tricks Book, $9.95
Everything® Casino Gambling Book, 2nd Ed.
Everything® Chess Basics Book
Everything® Craps Strategy Book
Everything® Crossword and Puzzle Book
Everything® Crossword Challenge Book
Everything® Cryptograms Book, $9.95
Everything® Easy Crosswords Book
Everything® Easy Kakuro Book, $9.95
Everything® Games Book, 2nd Ed.
Everything® Giant Sudoku Book, $9.95
Everything® Kakuro Challenge Book, $9.95
Everything® Large-Print Crosswords Book
Everything® Lateral Thinking Puzzles Book, $9.95
Everything® Pencil Puzzles Book, $9.95
Everything® Poker Strategy Book
Everything® Pool & Billiards Book
Everything® Test Your IQ Book, $9.95
Everything® Texas Hold 'Em Book, $9.95
Everything® Travel Crosswords Book, $9.95
Everything® Word Games Challenge Book
Everything® Word Search Book

Bolded titles are new additions to the series.
All Everything® books are priced at $12.95 or $14.95, unless otherwise stated. Prices subject to change without notice.

HOBBIES

Everything® Candlemaking Book
Everything® Cartooning Book
Everything® Drawing Book
Everything® Family Tree Book, 2nd Ed.
Everything® Knitting Book
Everything® Knots Book
Everything® Photography Book
Everything® Quilting Book
Everything® Scrapbooking Book
Everything® Sewing Book
Everything® Woodworking Book

HOME IMPROVEMENT

Everything® Feng Shui Book
Everything® Feng Shui Decluttering Book, $9.95
Everything® Fix-It Book
Everything® Home Decorating Book
Everything® Homebuilding Book
Everything® Lawn Care Book
Everything® Organize Your Home Book

KIDS' BOOKS

All titles are $7.95
Everything® Kids' Animal Puzzle &
    Activity Book
Everything® Kids' Baseball Book, 4th Ed.
Everything® Kids' Bible Trivia Book
Everything® Kids' Bugs Book
Everything® Kids' Christmas Puzzle
    & Activity Book
Everything® Kids' Cookbook
Everything® Kids' Crazy Puzzles Book
Everything® Kids' Dinosaurs Book
**Everything® Kids' Gross Hidden Pictures
    Book**
Everything® Kids' Gross Jokes Book
Everything® Kids' Gross Mazes Book
Everything® Kids' Gross Puzzle and
    Activity Book
Everything® Kids' Halloween Puzzle
    & Activity Book
Everything® Kids' Hidden Pictures Book
Everything® Kids' Horses Book
Everything® Kids' Joke Book
Everything® Kids' Knock Knock Book
Everything® Kids' Math Puzzles Book
Everything® Kids' Mazes Book
Everything® Kids' Money Book
Everything® Kids' Nature Book

**Everything® Kids' Pirates Puzzle and
    Activity Book**
Everything® Kids' Puzzle Book
Everything® Kids' Riddles & Brain Teasers Book
Everything® Kids' Science Experiments Book
Everything® Kids' Sharks Book
Everything® Kids' Soccer Book
Everything® Kids' Travel Activity Book

KIDS' STORY BOOKS

Everything® Fairy Tales Book

LANGUAGE

Everything® Conversational Japanese Book
    (with CD), $19.95
Everything® French Grammar Book
Everything® French Phrase Book, $9.95
Everything® French Verb Book, $9.95
**Everything® German Practice Book with
    CD, $19.95**
Everything® Inglés Book
Everything® Learning French Book
Everything® Learning German Book
Everything® Learning Italian Book
Everything® Learning Latin Book
Everything® Learning Spanish Book
Everything® Sign Language Book
Everything® Spanish Grammar Book
Everything® Spanish Phrase Book, $9.95
Everything® Spanish Practice Book
    (with CD), $19.95
Everything® Spanish Verb Book, $9.95

MUSIC

Everything® Drums Book (with CD), $19.95
Everything® Guitar Book
**Everything® Guitar Chords Book with CD,
    $19.95**
Everything® Home Recording Book
Everything® Playing Piano and Keyboards
    Book
Everything® Reading Music Book (with CD),
    $19.95
Everything® Rock & Blues Guitar Book
    (with CD), $19.95
Everything® Songwriting Book

NEW AGE

Everything® Astrology Book, 2nd Ed.
Everything® Dreams Book, 2nd Ed.
Everything® Love Signs Book, $9.95

Everything® Numerology Book
Everything® Paganism Book
Everything® Palmistry Book
Everything® Psychic Book
Everything® Reiki Book
Everything® Tarot Book
Everything® Wicca and Witchcraft Book

PARENTING

Everything® Baby Names Book, 2nd Ed.
Everything® Baby Shower Book
Everything® Baby's First Food Book
Everything® Baby's First Year Book
Everything® Birthing Book
Everything® Breastfeeding Book
Everything® Father-to-Be Book
Everything® Father's First Year Book
Everything® Get Ready for Baby Book
Everything® Get Your Baby to Sleep Book,
    $9.95
Everything® Getting Pregnant Book
Everything® Homeschooling Book
Everything® Mother's First Year Book
Everything® Parent's Guide to Children
    and Divorce
Everything® Parent's Guide to Children
    with ADD/ADHD
Everything® Parent's Guide to Children
    with Asperger's Syndrome
Everything® Parent's Guide to Children
    with Autism
Everything® Parent's Guide to Children with
    Bipolar Disorder
Everything® Parent's Guide to Children
    with Dyslexia
Everything® Parent's Guide to Positive
    Discipline
Everything® Parent's Guide to Raising a
    Successful Child
**Everything® Parent's Guide to Raising
    Boys**
**Everything® Parent's Guide to Raising
    Siblings**
Everything® Parent's Guide to Tantrums
Everything® Parent's Guide to the Overweight
    Child
Everything® Parent's Guide to the Strong-
    Willed Child
Everything® Parenting a Teenager Book
Everything® Potty Training Book, $9.95
Everything® Pregnancy Book, 2nd Ed.

Bolded titles are new additions to the series.
All Everything® books are priced at $12.95 or $14.95, unless otherwise stated. Prices subject to change without notice.

Everything® Pregnancy Fitness Book
Everything® Pregnancy Nutrition Book
Everything® Pregnancy Organizer, $15.00
Everything® Toddler Book
Everything® Toddler Activities Book
Everything® Tween Book
Everything® Twins, Triplets, and More Book

PETS

Everything® Boxer Book
Everything® Cat Book, 2nd Ed.
Everything® Chihuahua Book
Everything® Dachshund Book
Everything® Dog Book
Everything® Dog Health Book
Everything® Dog Training and Tricks Book
Everything® German Shepherd Book
Everything® Golden Retriever Book
Everything® Horse Book
Everything® Horse Care Book
Everything® Horseback Riding Book
Everything® Labrador Retriever Book
Everything® Poodle Book
Everything® Pug Book
Everything® Puppy Book
Everything® Rottweiler Book
Everything® Small Dogs Book
Everything® Tropical Fish Book
Everything® Yorkshire Terrier Book

REFERENCE

Everything® Car Care Book
Everything® Classical Mythology Book
Everything® Computer Book
Everything® Divorce Book
Everything® Einstein Book
Everything® Etiquette Book, 2nd Ed.
Everything® Inventions and Patents Book
Everything® Mafia Book
Everything® Mary Magdalene Book
Everything® Philosophy Book
Everything® Psychology Book
Everything® Shakespeare Book

RELIGION

Everything® Angels Book
Everything® Bible Book
Everything® Buddhism Book
Everything® Catholicism Book

Everything® Christianity Book
Everything® Freemasons Book
Everything® History of the Bible Book
Everything® Jewish History & Heritage Book
Everything® Judaism Book
Everything® Kabbalah Book
Everything® Koran Book
Everything® Prayer Book
Everything® Saints Book
Everything® Torah Book
Everything® Understanding Islam Book
Everything® World's Religions Book
Everything® Zen Book

SCHOOL & CAREERS

Everything® Alternative Careers Book
Everything® College Major Test Book
Everything® College Survival Book, 2nd Ed.
Everything® Cover Letter Book, 2nd Ed.
Everything® Get-a-Job Book
Everything® Guide to Being a Paralegal
Everything® Guide to Being a Real Estate Agent
Everything® Guide to Starting and Running a Restaurant
Everything® Job Interview Book
Everything® New Nurse Book
Everything® New Teacher Book
Everything® Paying for College Book
Everything® Practice Interview Book
Everything® Resume Book, 2nd Ed.
Everything® Study Book
Everything® Teacher's Organizer, $16.95

SELF-HELP

Everything® Dating Book, 2nd Ed.
Everything® Great Sex Book
Everything® Kama Sutra Book
Everything® Self-Esteem Book

SPORTS & FITNESS

Everything® Fishing Book
Everything® Golf Instruction Book
Everything® Pilates Book
Everything® Running Book
Everything® Total Fitness Book
Everything® Weight Training Book
Everything® Yoga Book

TRAVEL

Everything® Family Guide to Hawaii
Everything® Family Guide to Las Vegas, 2nd Ed.
Everything® Family Guide to New York City, 2nd Ed.
Everything® Family Guide to RV Travel & Campgrounds
Everything® Family Guide to the Walt Disney World Resort®, Universal Studios®, and Greater Orlando, 4th Ed.
Everything® Family Guide to Cruise Vacations
Everything® Family Guide to the Caribbean
Everything® Family Guide to Washington D.C., 2nd Ed.
Everything® Guide to New England
Everything® Travel Guide to the Disneyland Resort®, California Adventure®, Universal Studios®, and the Anaheim Area

WEDDINGS

Everything® Bachelorette Party Book, $9.95
Everything® Bridesmaid Book, $9.95
Everything® Elopement Book, $9.95
Everything® Father of the Bride Book, $9.95
Everything® Groom Book, $9.95
Everything® Mother of the Bride Book, $9.95
Everything® Outdoor Wedding Book
Everything® Wedding Book, 3rd Ed.
Everything® Wedding Checklist, $9.95
Everything® Wedding Etiquette Book, $9.95
Everything® Wedding Organizer, $15.00
Everything® Wedding Shower Book, $9.95
Everything® Wedding Vows Book, $9.95
Everything® Weddings on a Budget Book, $9.95

WRITING

Everything® Creative Writing Book
Everything® Get Published Book, 2nd Ed.
Everything® Grammar and Style Book
Everything® Guide to Writing a Book Proposal
Everything® Guide to Writing a Novel
Everything® Guide to Writing Children's Books
Everything® Guide to Writing Research Papers
Everything® Screenwriting Book
Everything® Writing Poetry Book
Everything® Writing Well Book

Available wherever books are sold!
To order, call 800-289-0963, or visit us at *www.everything.com*
Everything® and everything.com® are registered trademarks of F+W Publications, Inc.